تاریخ
ضائع

Muslim astronomers perfected the astrolabe to determine astronomical and timekeeping data, as shown above in an 18th-century Persian model.

LOST HISTORY

*The Enduring Legacy
of Muslim
Scientists, Thinkers, and Artists*

MICHAEL HAMILTON MORGAN

NATIONAL GEOGRAPHIC

WASHINGTON, D.C.

Published by the National Geographic Society
1145 17th St. N.W., Washington, D.C. 20036

First paperback printing, June 2008

ISBN 978-1-4262-0280-3

Founded in 1888, the National Geographic Society is one of the largest nonprofit scientific and
educational organizations in the world. It reaches more than 285 million people worldwide
each month through its official journal, NATIONAL GEOGRAPHIC, and its four other magazines;
the National Geographic Channel; television documentaries; radio programs; films; books;
videos and DVDs; maps; and interactive media. National Geographic has funded more than 8,000 scientific
research projects and supports an education program combating geographic illiteracy.

For more information, please call 1-800-NGS LINE (647-5463) or write to the following address:

NATIONAL GEOGRAPHIC SOCIETY
1145 17th Street N.W.
Washington, DC 20036-4688 U.S.A.

Visit us online at www.nationalgeographic.com/books

Printed in U.S.A.

Cover Design: Jan Glinski
Interior Design: Cameron Zotter
Calligraphy: Sanaa Akkach

Lost History author Michael Hamilton Morgan is the author of *The Twilight War* and co-author with Robert
Ballard of *Collision with History: The Search for John F. Kennedy's PT-109,* and *Graveyards of the Pacific.* A former
diplomat, he created and now heads New Foundations for Peace, which promotes cross-cultural understanding
and leadership among youth. He has appeared on ABC and CBS and as a Washington journalist has covered
foreign policy issues. From 1990 to 2000 he directed the International Pegasus Prize for Literature.

Lost History consultant Amin Tejpar is a science and technology education expert. He is an advocate for the
popularization and public understanding of science, with a passion for promoting cross-cultural dialogue
through the history of ideas. He is a frequent speaker on the global history of science at academic campuses,
public forums, and most recently at the 2nd African Congress for Scientific Research and Technology. Tejpar
is a graduate of Columbia University's Teachers College (Science Education) and the University of Toronto
(Molecular Genetics). He currently lives in Cairo, Egypt, exploring the shared histories of Jewish, Christian,
and Muslim intellectual traditions in the Middle East and North Africa.

CONTENTS

TIME LINE

Bold entries denote dynastic rule

ca A.D. 570 The Prophet Muhammad is born in Mecca.

622 Muhammad and followers emigrate to Medina. Year 1 of Muslim calendar.

630 Muhammad conquers Mecca.

632 Death of Muhammad.

632 Abu Bakr succeeds Muhammad. Muslim armies consolidate their power over Arabia.

634-644 Umar succeeds Abu Bakr. Muslim forces advance through the Persian and Byzantine empires.

636 Battle of Yarmuk. Byzantine emperor Heraclius is defeated by Muslim army in Syria.

637-651 Skirmishes from Arabia lead to expansion into Iraq and Persia.

642 Arabs conquer Byzantine Egypt and expand into North Africa.

644 Uthman succeeds Umar.

656 Muhammad's son-in-law, Ali, succeeds to the leadership of Islam.

661 Ali is assassinated. Islam splits into rival Sunni and Shiite factions.

661-750 Umayyads rule in Damascus.

661 Umayyads shift seat of power to Damascus. Muyawiya I becomes caliph.

711 Tariq with a mixed force of Arabs and Berbers invades Spain.

712 Muslims advance into Sind (modern-day Pakistan) and Central Asia.

715 Umayyad mosque in Damascus is completed.

721-815 Jabir ibn Haiyan, alchemist, pharmacist, philosopher, and mathematician, is known as the "father of chemistry."

725 Muslims occupy Nimes in France.

732 Battle of Tours, France; Charles Martel rebuffs Muslims under the command of Abd al-Rahman al-Ghafiqi.

750 Abbasids overthrow Umayyads. Empire is at its greatest extent reaching from Mongolia to Spain.

750-945 Abbasids rule in Baghdad.

ca 750 Ibrahim al-Fazari constructs first Muslim astrolabe.

754 Al-Mansur becomes second Abbasid caliph, after his brother's death.

756-929 Umayyad emirs rule in Spain.

762 Al-Mansur founds Baghdad.

ca 780-850 Muhammad ibn Musa al-Khwarizmi, mathematician and astronomer adopts Indian numerals; known as father of algebra.

786 Haroun al-Rashid becomes caliph in Baghdad.

786 In Mecca an uprising by the Shiites results in the flight of many Shiites to the Maghreb (Libya) in North Africa.

ca 790 Under Haroun al-Rashid, Baghdad becomes a center of learning where Arab and Persian cultures mingle to produce great philosophical, scientific, and literary works.

792 The first papermaking factory in the Muslim Empire is built in Baghdad, leading to greater use of written records.

801 Berber Kharijites set up an independent Muslim state in North Africa.

802 Haroun al-Rashid sends an elephant, silks, perfume, and other luxury goods to Charlemagne as gifts.

809 Haroun al-Rashid dies.

813-823 After civil war and a battle with his brother, al-Mamun (786-833) reigns in Baghdad, enlarging the Muslim empire with the areas of modern-day Turkmenistan and Afghanistan. He founds the House of Wisdom where scholars translate Greek, Syriac, Sanskrit, and Pahlavi classics into Arabic.

823 Beginning of Muslim conquest of Sicily.

829 Al-Mamun builds observatories in Baghdad, Iraq, and Palmyra, Syria.

ca 830 Hunayn ibn Ishaq (809-873), Nestorian physician in the House of Wisdom, translates Galen, Aristotle, Hippocrates, and other classics from Greek into Syriac; writes important texts on ophthalmology, "Ten Treatises of the Eye;" known in the West as Johannitius.

ca 830 Al-Kindi (801-873), philosopher, pharmacist, alchemist, mathematician, and musician toils in the House of Wisdom. His works *De aspectibus* and *De medicinarium* greatly influenced the West in later years.

833-849 Al-Mutasim reigns in Baghdad; moves capital to Samarra, Iraq; employs Turkic slaves at court.

ca 840 Al-Mutasim encourages the building of factories in Baghdad and Basra for the manufacture of soap and glass.

847-861 Al-Mutawakkil rules from Samarra.

852 Armen Firman jumps off a tower in Cordoba with an attachment of wings and lands as if by parachute.

856 Ibn Kathir al-Farghani writes an important treatise on the astrolabe and supervises the construction of the Nilometer in Cairo.

875 Abbas ibn Firnas, chemist, physicist, and astronomer, constructs the first glider at age 70 and launches himself from a mountain; he lands with injuries, and dies 12 years later.

ca 900 Abu Bakr Muhammad ibn Zakariya al-Razi, or Rhazes, (865-925), chief physician of Baghdad hospital, first accurately describes smallpox and measles and prescribes treatments.

ca 900 Abu Nasr al-Farabi, philosopher and scientist, writes a book on music that is still in use today in Arabic music.

909-1171 Fatimids expand in North Africa.

912-961 Abd al-Rahman III rules as emir, then in 929 pronounces himself Caliph of all Islam in Cordoba.

929-1031 Umayyad caliphate reigns in Spain.

945-1055 Buyids rule in Baghdad.

969 Fatimid Ismailis conquer Egypt and transfer their capital to Cairo in 973.

ca 960 al-Zahrawi (936-1013) of Cordoba, one of the greatest surgeons of his time, develops new treatments ranging from dentistry to childbirth.

976 Al-Azhar university is founded in Cairo.

ca 990 Al-Biruni (973-1048), mathematician, astronomer, and philosopher, advances cartography, astronomy, and devises methods of determining gravity; produces some 120 works.

ca 1000 Abu Ali al-Husayn ibn Abd Allah ibn Sina (980-1037), or Avicenna, physician, philosopher and scientist, is considered by many to be "the father of modern medicine."

ca 1020 Ibn al-Haytham, or Alhazen, mathematician and astronomer, refines theory of optics, refraction of light, and human sight.

1037-1307 Seljuks rule in Central Asia and Anatolia.

1050 Kings of Mali convert to Islam.

1054 East-West Schism, dividing the Christian Church into Roman Catholic and Eastern Orthodox.

1058 Seljuks take Baghdad.

1072-1092 Malik Shah is Seljuk sultan.

1076 Ghana is conquered by Morocco.

1090 Cordoba is sacked by Almoravids.

1096 First Crusade. Christians rule in Jerusalem in 1099.

1100 Mathematician-poet Omar Khayyam composes the *Rubayyat*.

1145-1232 Almohads rule in Spain.

ca 1160 ibn Rushd, or Averroes, (1126-1198), philosopher and physician translates works from Arabic into Hebrew, especially Aristotle's works.

1171 Saladin overthrows the Fatimids in Egypt.

1171-1250 Ayyubid dynasty rules in Egypt and Syria.

1187 Saladin returns Jerusalem to Muslim rule.

1175 First Muslim Indian empire is founded.

ca 1200 Ibn Ismail al-Razzaz al-Jazari invents the crankshaft, some of the first mechanical clocks driven by water and weights, and water pumps. Among his 50 other inventions is the combination lock.

1206-1406 Mongol empire.

1206-1526 Delhi sultanate.

1207-1273 Poet al-Rumi.

1218 Beginning of the Mongol conquests.

ca 1230 ibn al-Nafis (1213-1288), physician from Damascus, works in a hospital in Cairo, describes the pulmonary circulation of blood and makes further contributions to ophthalmology.

1232-1492 Nasrids rule in Spain.

1250-1517 Mamluks seize power in Egypt.

1258 Mongols sack Baghdad.

ca 1270 Nasr al-Din al-Tusi (1201-1274), mathematician and astronomer at Maragheh observatory, devises astronomical tables for calculating the positions of stars and planets; develops trigonometry as a separate mathematical discipline.

1285 Hassan al-Rammah writes about the use of gunpowder in rockets.

1325 Ibn Battuta leaves Tangier to travel the world and keeps a written record.

1336-1405 Tamerlane conquers parts of present-day Afghanistan, Persia, India, Turkey, Syria, and Egypt; makes his capital at Samarkand.

1336-1506 Timurids rule in Central Asia and the Middle East.

1453 Mehmet II conquers Byzantine Constantinople, makes it the capital of the Ottoman Empire.

1492 Christian Reconquest of Spain.

1453-1922 Ottoman Empire.

1526 Mughal dynasty is established in India.

1587-1629 Shah Abbas regains much of the ancient territory of Persia.

1494-1566 Suleiman I guides the Ottoman Empire to its fullest extent, ranging from Morocco to the Caspian Sea and the Persian Gulf and into Europe through the Balkans to Hungary.

1922 End of the Ottoman Empire.

FOREWORD

Although one can easily distinguish between "Christianity" and "Christendom," in Western languages no such distinction generally exists between "Islam" the religion and "Islam" the world civilization. In these sometimes turbulent times it is easy to forget the great intellectual tradition and culture to which Islam gave rise. Throughout its over 1,400-year history Muslims have given the world great summits of art, architecture, poetry, philosophy, and science, all while being nourished spiritually by the teachings of the Qur'an and the ambience of Islamic religious piety. The cultural and intellectual achievements of Islam were not unknown to Europe, and indeed Jewish and Christian philosophers, scientists, poets, musicians, and even theologians actively drew upon the achievements of their Muslim counterparts.

This book, with its aim of telling an often untold story, is a welcome addition to the literature about Islam's cultural and intellectual history as well as its relationship with the West. Too often the achievements of Islamic civilization and its strong link to Western civilization are limited to scholarly works or to academic journals. Moreover, many available works paint too stark a picture of confrontation between civilizations, when the reality was often one of exchange and mutual dependence. It is hoped that this work will contribute to a greater understanding of Islam by Westerners, and will help them to appreciate that just as our pasts have intertwined in constructive ways, so too can our futures.

Abdullah II Ibn Al Hussein

INTRODUCTION

LOSS IS A DEFINING human experience. Nothing in the physical world lasts forever. Memory of what has been lost can be both ennobling and painful.

History teaches us that civilizations flourish, die, and disappear. Sometimes they die swiftly, sometimes in a slow lingering death. And sometimes, as with Rome and others, echoes of that civilization find new life in later cultures.

To lose the conscious memory of an entire civilization is especially tragic and dangerous, because each civilization, no matter how grand or flawed, is a laboratory of human ideas and ideals, of dreams and nightmares. We can learn from all of them.

A few days after the 9/11 attack on the United States, I was asked to write a speech for a famous American business executive. While the original subject was to have focused mostly on her business and industry, the continuing national grief meant it would have been insulting to ignore the major issue of the day. And so she agreed to try and bridge the gulf between Muslims and non-Muslims by remembering the greatness the Muslim world had spawned, and how much it meant to us.

Rather than focus on the grim reality of the present, I decided to have her speak about the fascinating Muslim history that I'd uncovered in my reading and research, a Muslim history that was about invention, creativity, big ideas, tolerance, and coexistence. It is a Muslim history that had been more intellectually accomplished than Christian Europe of the day, and a Muslim past where Christians, Jews, Hindus, and Buddhists had flourished and worked together. It is a culture that had seeded the European Renaissance and enabled many aspects of the modern West and global civilization. It is a history that by the beginning of the 21st century had been forgotten, ignored, misunderstood, suppressed, or even rewritten.

I thought that her speech might get some attention and might draw some criticism here at home. What I hadn't expected was that Muslims overseas would also write to her, wanting to know who were these historical figures she was referring to, and how could they find out more?

It was then I knew that there was a huge gulf of misunderstanding on both sides that needed to be filled. And so I came to think, if a deeper appreciation of Muslim history could be recovered, then maybe the very premises of the emerging "clash of civilizations" could be re-framed.

The result is this book. I know there may be those on the non-Muslim side of the divide who will say that I'm distorting history, by choosing to emphasize the bright side of a very complex civilization. I will respond that I am simply balancing the incomplete and negative slant of most of what we non-Muslims have been given.

To apply the argument of these critics fully and fairly, we would need to include in the history of Western Christian civilization not only the thoughts of Voltaire and St. Thomas Aquinas, we would also need to include the thoughts and deeds of Adolf Hitler and Joseph Stalin.

There may also be those Muslims who will say that I have sought to rehabilitate and glorify heretics and impure Muslims, who deserve to be suppressed and forgotten.

By no coincidence, all of the great thinkers, inventors and artists of Muslim civilization were creative minds. Much like today's scientific researchers, they were trained in their various disciplines to constantly question assumptions in a search for higher truth. Their number included some who followed other religions. While they were all versed in the tenets and philosophy of their faiths, few were rigid, doctrinaire thinkers. And they operated in a very different political context than we see today. The Muslim quest for knowledge often drove even the most devout rulers and religious scholars to support freethinking and empirical scientific inquiry. But fascination with the intellect came under increasing attack, beginning in the ninth century. One dispute was between Muslim "rationalists" who believed in finding divine truth through reason and "literalists" who stuck to the narrowly interpreted, literal statements and acts of the Prophet. It was not unlike the current and longstanding American debate between supporters of Darwinism and advocates of creationism or intelligent design.

By writing *Lost History*, I hope to show not only the contributions of an old and rich civilization. I hope to show, as Caliph al-Mamun concluded, that reason and faith can be the same, that by fully opening the mind and unleashing human creativity, many wonders—including peace—are possible.

THIS BOOK IS NOT ABOUT ISLAM or any other religion. It is not about theology or religious doctrine. It is about a civilization in which Islam had a leading role.

By writing this book now, which is intended for popular rather than academic readers, I am entering a potential minefield. The minefield is now given greater intensity by the current convergence of radical Islamist terrorism, the rise in "literalist" fundamentalist religious models for organizing societies and individual lives, continuing battles between Israel and her neighbors, outbursts of anti-Semitism, the United States' invasions of Afghanistan and Iraq and its "war on terrorism", and political and economic crises in selected Muslim societies.

Most Americans, including American Muslims, and even many Muslims from other parts of the world, know only the dimmest outlines of Muslim history, i.e., "they were great once, they invented arithmetic, but then they fell behind." Most Westerners have been taught that the greatness of the West has its intellectual roots in Greece and Rome, and that after the thousand-year-sleep of the Dark Ages, Europe miraculously reawakened to its Greco-Roman roots. In the conventional telling, this rediscovery of classical Greece—combined with the moral underpinning of the Judeo-Christian faith—led to the Renaissance and the Enlightenment, and the scientific and industrial revolutions. The intellectual contributions of Arabs, Persians, Indians, Chinese, Africans, and others in the Muslim world are relegated to mere footnotes.

Most of us are unaware of the details of Muslim history because of language difficulties, the passage of many centuries, a blur of unfamiliar names, places, and events, a triumphalist Eurocentric narrative of the

Renaissance and later advances, orthodox Muslim excision of unorthodox Muslim thinkers, and the burning of books and destruction of libraries.

A fairly small group of serious academics have looked hard on these issues through often different lenses and have come up with different conclusions.

The first group, which has brought much of the detail of Muslim intellectual history to light, is the "Orientalist" camp. This group holds that the Muslim world had a period of intellectual brilliance, from about A.D. 800-1200, largely enabled by the translation of Greek thinkers, and that this essentially Greek body of knowledge was then passed on by the Muslims to the Europeans. But later, because of a combination of the Mongol attacks and internal inconsistencies that prevented the development of a secular, freethinking society, the Muslim world fell behind.

The second group is the "neo-conservative" camp. This group, despite the fact that Arabs only constitute 17 percent of the global Muslim population, concludes from its focus on the troubled Middle East that there are elements in Muslim civilization that make it deeply antithetical to intellectual freedom, social and scientific progress, and liberal democracy. This neo-conservative group has come to have unprecedented influence over United States foreign policy and media, especially in the wake of the 9/11 attacks. Many non-Muslims around the world are probably most aware of this train of thought.

The third group is the "proto-science" camp now joined by a number of contemporary scholars. This group holds that until the 15th century, Muslim science and technology was far superior to that in Europe and that many of its breakthroughs seeped into medieval Europe, providing the seeds of the coming Renaissance. But then the Muslim world hit a glass ceiling of internal inconsistencies and barriers inherent in the culture, plus economic and climatic crises, so that as with China and India, the Muslims could not make the leap to modern science, which was left to Europe.

The fourth group could be called the "liberal" camp. This camp holds that rather than serving as limits or impediments, the higher values of Islam—such as desire for knowledge and equality of all men before God—promoted many advances in science, technology, and civil society that poured into Europe, and then to the world and are still of importance in the 21st century. These thinkers might hold that European Judeo-Christian civilization should add the word Muslim as well.

The fifth camp could be called the "Muslim partisan" camp, though it has few followers in mainstream academia. This group holds that the Muslims invented almost every aspect of modern science, medicine, technology, and social organization, but that attribution has not been given them, and they have been disenfranchised.

Lost History was written with an awareness of all these views and incorporates some elements from each. As such, it doesn't align with any of them, and it aligns in some ways with all.

But *Lost History* was not written to take a stand in this fairly esoteric academic debate. The purpose of *Lost History* is to fill in the sketchy lines of Muslim history that most of us have been given, to adhere to established fact but bring the most important characters and events to life, to make the obscure and remote and esoteric Muslim past immediate and real, and to show how the events and ideas of a thousand years ago are directly relevant to our lives today. Readers should be aware that the present-day sections introducing each chapter are imaginary, and that in the historical sections, the dramatized scenes, while adhering to facts drawn from often-sketchy historical accounts, are imaginary recreations, especially when presenting dialogue or inner thoughts.

And unlike many histories, which tend to focus on thinkers and inventors in the so-called Arab Golden Age that also included Persia and Spain from A.D. 632 to 1258, ending with the fall of Baghdad, this book rather focuses on the many "golden ages" of Muslim thought, including Central Asia, Ottoman Turkey, and Mughal India, up to the 18th century.

Lost History could never capture the immense detail and complicated nuances of a 1,400-year-old civilization that now incorporates one billion people. *Lost History* could never name every great name, or capture every seminal historical event in the evolution of this huge organism we call the Muslim world. But ideally what will emerge is a shape and a meaning—a face—for an old and ongoing civilization that touches all of us.

What may also emerge is an understanding that all of us, Muslim and non-Muslim, are indebted to these often courageous and sometimes ruthless and sometimes misguided actors of long ago, that Muslim civilization is as much a part of Western civilization as it is not, and that many of the conflicts now filling the newspaper headlines had antecedents and parallels in the debates and conflicts of a thousand years ago.

Finally, by recovering our shared lost history, I hope that non-Muslims can gain greater respect and deeper understanding of their Muslim cousins than current headlines and policies would suggest and that today's Muslims can see how Islam was once applied in a way to support creativity, invention, tolerance, and diversity of thought and behavior in both society and in individual lives.

Then, by recovering the lost history, maybe we can begin to understand the issues of today that will never be solved by force. Because if there is no other lesson to be drawn from *Lost History*, it is that force rarely ever positively resolves issues of the spirit and the soul—whether in individuals or in civilizations.

ROME'S CHILDREN

*The Roman Empire has been defeated in a land close by, but they,
even after this defeat of theirs, will soon be victorious.*

QUR'AN (XXX:2-3)

TOURS, FRANCE, 2006—It is a summer day in a mid-sized French
city in the Loire Valley called Tours.

The sun in all its July glory is pouring down through a blue sky holding
suspended towers of cumulus. From cloud level, the noise of earthly commerce and activity is softened and the movements of men are telescoped
down, become part of a large canvas yielding a pattern in what up close
would be almost chaotic movement. Trucks turning corners, children running to a park, a construction crane suspended over a new commercial
center on the outskirts, women talking over a garden fence: These are all
parts of the movement of the city.

From cloud level, you can see the larger pattern. The network of streets is
not random, but defined by needs and activities of a population in motion,
feeding to the highways going north to Paris, south and west toward the
Mediterranean and the Atlantic. It is the greater face of a city and a landscape, a mosaic composed of thousands of components that individually
and up close would seem to be independent and random statements. But
from above and afar, the whole thing is an organism of soil and stone and
concrete, of field and forest and river. It has a larger, longer life than any of
the pieces that make it up.

A summer day in France can look so much like those pastoral canvases
by Fragonard, Poussin, and Watteau with copses of fully leafed trees, oases

in the broader painterly expanse of fields and hedges and villages. This is one of those days.

On this day, people are in the central park of Tours with soccer balls and iPods. Students recently freed from the school year kick a ball. An old woman talks with a grandchild over by a fountain. A Muslim family of day-trippers, the Ghafiqis, are enjoying a picnic, having driven down from Paris. The wife, in the manner of the town in Morocco where she was born, wears a headscarf at leisure times like these but not on the job, because the French state forbids it. The husband is dressed in a sport coat. The Ghafiqi family has lived in France for decades, and their teenage children are native-born French, more fluent in French than Arabic.

They live respectably in the 10th arrondissement in Paris, an established Arab quarter. They feel quite fortunate, considering the continuing tensions around immigration. While the husband Driss and his wife, Karima, have been in France together for 20 years, one of their friends who had long ago immigrated without his wife has just attempted to bring her in with their two children. The wife and children have been forcibly repatriated to Morocco.

Unlike many immigrants who have had trouble assimilating into the French economy and culture, both husband and wife have good jobs. She is a teacher in the public schools; he is an accountant with Credit Lyonnais. They are not wealthy, but they are not disaffected. Their ties to Morocco have become less intense over time. They think of themselves as French Muslims.

Tours is a city of history, a smaller actor in a larger drama that is sometimes so large and so long in time that the larger pattern is lost to most who live there. The town dates back to Gallic and Roman times 2,000 years ago, when it was known as Turonensis after the tribe from that area, the Turones. It was the final home of a Roman imperial bodyguard who adopted Christianity and became the man Christians know as St. Martin. After leaving the service of the emperor, Martin was named a Catholic bishop in the fourth century at the very edge of the Western Roman Empire. He was known for his humility and generosity. Once, when a beggar complained of the cold, Martin tore his own cloak in two and gave half to the poor man. After Martin died, a shrine was built to him with relics of his life, and then a church on top of that, the Basilica of St. Martin.

This shrine became a place of veneration in the long and dark years after the fall of Rome. Pilgrims came there to make their offerings, and the shrine became a place of great wealth. The Vikings pillaged this city twice, in the ninth and tenth centuries, but left no overt signs of their coming.

Later this ancient Catholic city became a center of Huguenot Protestantism and a booming textile industry. Had their power been allowed to grow, the Huguenots might have made France a Protestant country like England or a mixed religious landscape like Germany. But many Huguenots were driven away or converted after the Edict of Nantes was revoked in 1685. Many took their textile skills to Ireland. France and Tours stayed predominantly Catholic. During the French Revolution and the Napoleonic era of the early 19th century, Tours was touched by greater events. A cedar tree planted by Napoleon still towers over the park where people are enjoying their Sunday. During the Franco-Prussian war and the Prussian siege of Paris, Tours even served as a temporary capital of France.

Today Tours is the capital of Indre-et-Loire province, and the jumping-off point for excursions to the castles of the Loire Valley. The town still has its large and proud cathedral, St. Gatien; it is peaceful and prosperous. This, in summary, would seem to be the totality of Tours. Its history seems well recorded, its identity solid and established.

Yet even though the physical evidence of some of the human past is there, it is actually limited, and it is gradually decaying with time. In these parts, for example, all that remains of Roman times are a few gates and towers. We must take it largely on faith, in the accuracy of assorted moldering chronicles and fifth-hand accounts, that many of the events of those times happened, even though most of the physical evidence of Gaul and of Rome is long gone.

When you think about it, the physical evidence of intervening centuries is also spotty. Did the Dark Ages after the fall of Rome in 476 really happen, or were they just a story? Tours has an old medieval section with half-timbered houses that now mostly shelter bistros and shops, and it is a place where people go to eat and drink; does that constitute evidence? The deep forests of Gallic and Roman times have gone to field and back to forest several times over the millennia. The woods once sheltering elks and wolves and bears have become suburbs and highways and farms and pastures.

You have to be far away to see the larger patterns.

The exact location of certain events occurring more than a thousand years ago, but after the fall of Rome, are not known. For example, eighth century events from the time of Charles Martel, the Hammer, cannot be physically located on a map of Tours. Even though Charles is credited with changing the destiny of an entire country, a continent, a civilization, no one knows exactly where he did it. This momentous event is noted only by mention in guidebooks and a few plaques scattered about the area.

It is without a doubt the most important thing ever to have happened in Tours over its two-thousand-year history—but now time seems not to matter. It does not matter to the people in the park today. They are more attuned to their affairs of the moment, their lives, their needs. It is a beautiful Sunday. A few people attend mass at the Cathedral of St. Gatien and the small Basilica of St. Martin. Young people are reveling in being out of school for the summer. The grandmother is happy she has lived to see her granddaughter born. The Ghafiqi family is glad to be away from home for a day, to see something new.

Unlike in their neighborhood in Paris, a new mosque is in the planning stages in Tours. The inter-ethnic French unrest and the burning of cars in 2005 in Clichy-sous-Bois were distant events here. Fewer Muslims live in Tours. The greater tides and patterns of European movement and immigration and culture-mixing seem to have bypassed Tours.

The Ghafiqi children walk over to a fountain. Their parents enjoy a lunch of cheese and lamb. They are not conspicuous to the others in the park and, from above, looking down on this landscape, they are nearly invisible.

This would seem to be the totality of the story of Tours. Even though some of the history of Tours is lost, it doesn't matter.

While Karima reads a newspaper, Driss is sitting on the blanket, looking out across the panorama. He has a guide brochure they picked up at the tourist office. He glances at it. He looks out at the city beyond the perimeter of the park. He very much likes classical music and auto racing. He wonders if there is a racetrack nearby.

He was expecting more from this day trip. He thought he had heard good things about Tours, but it was just a mishmash of hearsay in his head, and now he can't remember any specifics. Of course he won't tell his wife, but he wonders if they should have gone somewhere else. Maybe to the shore in Brittany, which he enjoys. Maybe to Provence, which he has never seen. But that was too long a drive for a day trip. And they have to be back for a family event tomorrow.

He was expecting more. He doesn't know what, but it isn't here.

Several times he looks over to the city, as though he has missed something. Was there something happening just out of his field of vision? Did he see a glint, a flash? Did someone shout in the distance?

Later, when they walk by the Gothic cathedral of St. Gatien and then the rebuilt Basilica of St. Martin, both these places intrigue him. He is Muslim, though not terribly devout. He allows himself to drink wine and beer. He does not go to mosque often. Not like the more recent immigrants. Too much religion makes him uneasy.

But these cathedrals.... The kids seem uninterested, the wife wants to go see the shops. But he stops, he looks up at the parapets, the pointed arches. While the others go ahead, he stays behind and stands in stained-glass gloom.

These cathedrals remind him of something. Something from far away and long ago. But what could that be? Far away and long ago for him mean Morocco. What do these Christian cathedrals have to do with Muslim Morocco? Is it in the pointed arches, the colonnades, the towers?

Above him, the clouds loom even taller. There might at one point even be rain, and off to the west the horizon is a darker gray tinged with deep blue. He didn't bring an umbrella. He had better catch up with the family. The day may be cut short by rain, and they want to see as much as possible before heading home.

What was the point of Tours? Why had he come? Was there something somebody wasn't telling him, showing him? Was there another Tours somewhere, a better Tours, a more interesting one?

Did he forget something? Did he lose something?

MECCA, ARABIA, A.D. 570—Among many strands in the tapestry of lost history, there is a thread of divine revelation. This revelation is shared in similar though distinct form by three faiths descended from the prophet Abraham. The three religions spring from the same source, worship the same God, hold many of the same values, use many of the same names from the same root language, and revere many of the same saints and prophets.

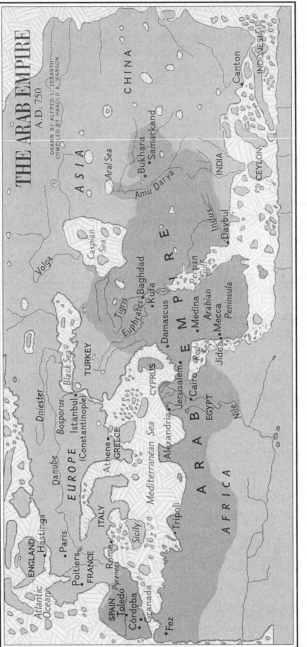

By A.D. 750—a little more than a hundred years after the death of Muhammad—the Muslim Empire had grown to its largest extent.

The third and most recent strand of revelation begins on the outskirts of the ancient Arabian shrine town of Mecca.

The pre-Islamic shrine of Mecca has arisen around a holy place marking a spring said to have been found by Abraham, father of the Jews, Christians, and Muslims, in a visit there in the dim mists of time. The shrine also holds a black rock fallen from the sky—the Kaaba. In the cube-shaped shrine are relics of Judaism and Christianity including a portrait of the Virgin Mary and infant Jesus; symbols of Mithraism, Zoroastrianism, and Manichaeanism; and a few golden calves and artifacts holy to other cults, sects, and beliefs. The clans of Mecca, who depend on religious visitors leaving offerings and spending money on food and lodging, rightly believe that to attract the largest number of pilgrims the maximum number of religions should be represented.

Mecca is a trading city grown out of faith, with believers and nonbelievers of many stripes. An economy based on polytheism would be a simple way of describing it. Christian priests report to the Byzantine Church, or to the Assyrian Church of the East also known as the Nestorian Church; Jewish rabbis teach the Torah; there are fire worshippers, Mithraists and fertility cults; seers and oracles; healers and witch doctors. There are those who pick and choose what to worship—and those who choose nothing.

Life and society here are defined by landscape and climate. Water is in scarce supply. The landscape of Arabia is almost totally given over to deserts of fiery sands, rugged shorelines and beaches washed by clear indigo waters, periodic outcrops of barren hills and knife-sharp mountains, black flats of volcanic stone left from lava flows in ancient times. While a few towns and port cities dot the margins of this vast place, the interior is forbidding and often proves fatal. Life away from the seacoast is given by those few springs and oases that, as if by miracle, appear in the most barren of places. These oases enable farming of wheat and barley and cultivation of date palms; and they afford a bit of shade. Out in the open sun in summer, daytime temperatures can regularly hit 120°F, among the hottest on Earth. At night and in winter, heat escaping into space from the cloudless atmosphere can produce bone-chilling freezes.

Yet such harshness does not mean an absence of life, or even of civilized life, or history. While the lack of water prevents the rise of large cities and societies, it does not prevent Arabia's long and rich history. By the sixth century Arabia has long interacted with ancient civilizations such as Egypt, Phoenicia, Assyria, Persia, Greece, India, Rome, and Byzantium with a trade in precious spices and frankincense and myrrh. Arabia is directly adjacent to the early landscapes recorded in the Jewish Torah and the Christian Bible.

In such a rich and harsh place, the basic unit of law and order is the clan arrayed into tribes. Society is a mosaic of clans, constantly making alliances, doing business, pursuing grievances, and sometimes coming into conflict. While in the sixth century much of the Arab population is nomadic, a similar clan code applies to the towns. It is the clan that ultimately decides everything, and woe be to the individual without a clan, for he or she will as often as not end up as a slave, with no rights at all.

This Arabian political landscape is set against the backdrop of nearby looming empires and lesser vassal states. The superstates are Byzantium and Sassanid Persia; the vassal states are Egypt, Syria, Palestine, and Mesopotamia. Christian Ethiopia is just across the water.

Born into this fiery landscape, about the year 570, is Muhammad, a young man of good lineage but humble circumstances, orphaned at an early age. Though he has neither wealth nor power, he is intelligent and sensitive.

As a young herdsman, he watches the sun, the moon, and the stars as they proceed across the skies. He watches the movement of the caravans and the struggle of animals in nature. He hears the song of many religions; and he feels the harsh reality of poverty.

Muhammad is from a tribe called the Banu Quraysh, part of the Hashemite clan that will one day provide a line of kings in a yet unknown country called Jordan.

He is exceedingly handsome and trustworthy, and when he is of age he tends camels for one of the great caravan clans of Mecca. From there he is promoted to run the caravans and manage the business. And he does very well at it, increasing the wealth of the owners. By the time he is 25, one of the owners is a wealthy widow. Her name is Khadija. She is entrepreneurial and independent and possessed of a strong sense of ethics. But she is also alone. Nonetheless she turns away many rich suitors.

Yet Khadija takes note of this young man who has been working for her. Though she is 15 years older, at some point she sends to him the message that she would be available for a proposal of marriage. And he acknowledges it. And they are married.

The business prospers, and though they lose two sons in infancy, four daughters survive. Because of his marriage and his success, Muhammad now is able to have impact on the community commensurate with his lineage. As is the custom in his time and culture, over the coming decades after Khadija's death, he will marry other women; most of his marriages will be mandated by divine order or will be for religious reasons.

Like most everyone in that time, Muhammad is not formally educated. Traditional sources claim that he cannot read or write. The medium of communication is oral, and the highest art is poetic verse. The greatest and most creative minds of the society express themselves in poetry, and among the community's prize rituals are contests of recitation and storytelling. This young man, though not a poet, is like everyone in Arabia deeply affected by the poetic voice.

The language of the people is classical Arabic, and for those who can write, the script they use is a looping filigree of calligraphy, expressing an entirely different awareness and consciousness from Roman script. The Roman alphabet has letters as solid and regular as the capitals of columns and the logic of Roman law; Arabic calligraphy is more a work of art and spirituality.

And the story might have ended here, with this successful man of Meccan commerce, following his wife into old age and then death, leaving behind a large and prosperous and influential clan.

Except at about age 40, Muhammad begins to receive divine revelations. At first he fears he is going mad. According to biographical accounts, he confides in Khadija, and baffled, she takes him to a Christian monk of the Nestorians. The priest tells him to relax and be thankful, for the visions are messages from the divine.

Muhammad accepts that these revelations are the Word of God. The archangel Gabriel commands him to recite, and through his mind and out of his mouth comes a torrential, voluminous, lyrical recitation that is to continue for another 23 years, committed to memory at first by this new Prophet and then by his followers. And over time, in that word-stream emerge the images and structure of a religious faith that, though descended from and honoring the line of Jewish prophets and Jesus, adds specific new guidance, not only about one's direct relationship to God, but how to relate to many other elements of God's universe, which are all expressions of Him. This body of recitation is known as the Qur'an, which, according to Muslim belief, is the verbatim Word of God revealed to the Prophet by Gabriel. A separate compilation of the Prophet's other sayings is called the *hadith*. A compilation of his actions and sayings is called the *sunnah*.

The five pillars of the new faith are: submission to God and his one Prophet, praying in the direction of Mecca five times a day with certain sacred words, setting aside part of one's resources for the needy, fasting and abstaining from other pleasures from dawn till dusk during the month of Ramadan, and if one is able, making a pilgrimage to Mecca.

Beyond these points, the Qur'an addresses the importance of staying clean and healthy, of conducting one's worldly affairs ethically, and of making society more generous and humane. It supports the need to give women rights, to acquire knowledge, to engage in a personal struggle for righteousness *(jihad),* and to defend Islam.

According to the Qur'an, the name of this faith is Islam, which in Arabic means something akin to "submission" or "surrender to God's will," and is related to the Arabic word for peace, *salaam.*

In its final form, the Qur'an was organized not in the order it was revealed, but corresponding roughly in length from longest to shortest chapters. While committed to memory and written down, it is not collected into a codex until 20 years after Muhammad has died. The task for some of his followers, and the source of future conflict and struggle, will be to agree on God's intent as seen in the words uttered by the Prophet, especially in new situations that unfold over time and that seem to have no direct parallel in the recitation, or that seem to be in contradiction.

Certain statements attributed to the Prophet will help drive the coming intellectual flowering of Muslim civilization and spark a quest for knowledge and discovery. Such statements include:

The ink of the scholar is holier than the blood of the martyr.
Acquire knowledge, because he who acquires it in the way of the Lord performs an act of piety; who speaks of it, praises the Lord; who seeks it, adores God; who dispenses instruction in it, bestows alms; and who imparts it to its fitting objects, performs an act of devotion to God.

Knowledge enables its possessor to distinguish right from wrong; it lights the way to Heaven; it is our friend in the desert, our society in solitude, our companion when bereft of friends; it guides us to happiness; it sustains us in misery; it is our ornament in the company of friends and an armor against enemies.

The broadest cultural and historical impact of those words will come in the future.

As the Prophet also follows the commandment to spread this message to others, he upsets the order of Mecca. His requests to throw away the many idols in the shrine for the one God are rejected as bad for business. His continuing insistence that he is bringing the very Word of God causes longtime friends and allies to turn against him, while others take his message on faith and join him.

Finally, as his recitations begin to tear the consensus of Mecca apart, his enemies are so many and vehement that they plot to kill him. To escape, he leads his followers to an oasis near Medina, and there begins to fortify himself against the establishment of Mecca.

His enemies in Mecca try to attack him several times but fail, and some of his allies turn against him. He wins the final battle and conquers Mecca, and to those who join him he is generous; to those who cease to oppose him he is tolerant. Then he and his followers begin the process of creating a series of alliances with other clans to bring the faith across all Arabia. At the same time he observes his injunction to give special status to the People of the Book, followers of those two other faiths descended from Abraham: the Jews and the Christians.

The Prophet is now in his sixties. He begins to speak of his own mortality, though it is not clear that he is being heard. In what is considered his farewell sermon, he also sets out some visionary and progressive concepts with which men will struggle for a thousand years to come, such as the following on racial and ethnic equality:

All mankind is from Adam and Eve, an Arab has no superiority over a non-Arab nor a non-Arab has any superiority over an Arab; also a white has no superiority over a black, nor a black has any superiority over a white—except by piety and good action.

And not long after that sermon, the Prophet takes ill and dies. Though he has been warning his followers for some time that he is not immortal, when he does die, his followers are bereft and astonished, and they mourn for days. And many of them are uncertain as to who is to lead them.

The issue of succession becomes a point of contention in the young Muslim community. The question remains: Who among them is worthy of taking the Prophet's place and guiding the community into the future?

One group supports Abu Bakr, the father of Muhammad's wife Aishah, citing his leadership, his integrity, his kindness, his wisdom, and his closeness to the Prophet—he was a companion of Muhammad, one of the earliest converts to Islam, whom the Prophet loved and trusted. Had he not while on his deathbed asked Abu Bakr to lead the community in prayer? Then surely, they argue, the Prophet would choose a man like this to lead the community.

Another group vouches for Ali ibn Abi Talib, citing that he is from the very house of the Prophet, whom he loved as his own son, whom he had favored above all men to be the husband of his daughter, Fatima. They claim that the Prophet had once held Ali's arm high in the air in the hot afternoon sun proclaiming him as his successor and leader.

The day of the Prophet's death, a group of men gather in the courtyard of a house to consult and elect a successor. The group chooses Abu Bakr and bestows on him the mantle of leadership. The next day, in front of the community, Abu Bakr stands at the pulpit of the mosque where the Prophet once preached and is invested as the first Caliph of Islam.

But not all are in agreement. There are those who feel Ali has been usurped from his entitlement to the caliphate, that the people who chose another man have dishonored the very wishes of the Prophet. These political tensions around succession create deep rifts in the community, dividing its loyalties and priming it for what later forms the schism in Islam between Sunnis and Shiites.

Abu Bakr says in his first speech:

O Men! Here I have been assigned the job of being a ruler over you while I am not the best among you. If I do well in my job, help me. If I do wrong, redress me. Truthfulness is fidelity, and lying is treason. The weak shall be strong in my eyes until I restore to them their lost rights, and the strong shall be weak in my eye until I have restored the rights of the weak from them.

Though the issue of succession will plant the seeds of the coming split in Islam, it will also spur a rich debate on the issues of leadership and political consultation that will animate coming questions of state and policy. They will include issues such as how a leader should be chosen and by whom; what qualities a leader should have; how important personal appeal and learning would be; and what social, political, and spiritual role such a leader should play in society.

One important idea that plays a role in Muslim political and legal thought is the concept of majority opinion in decision-making. The idea appeared under several names, including *ijma* (consensus), *jumhur* (majority), and *shura* (consultation). Shura was the tradition Muhammad valued, according to which decisions that affect the community are to be made in consultation with members of the community. In fact, one chapter of the Qur'an is named *al-Shura,* referring to a verse that states that those close to God should conduct their affairs by due consultation with others.

In the matter of leadership in the early Muslim community, consultation and majority opinion will become important points of contention. While some Shiites will later insist that not everyone was consulted when Abu Bakr was chosen leader of the community over Ali, many Sunnis will argue that the majority were, indeed, consulted and that they agreed on the leadership of Abu Bakr. Although the idea of majority opinion and its importance to politics, law, and theology will continue to be debated for centuries throughout the Muslim world, in more modern times there will be an effort by some Muslims to dovetail traditional concepts like the shura process with more modern political ideas like representational democracy.

But in those first days of Islam after the death of its founder, the issue is still uncertain new leadership. Though most of Arabia has come into the fold of the Muslims, Arabia is still a poor land, a relatively isolated region removed from the rich cities and power centers of the Mediterranean, Persia, and India. Weaker than neighboring Byzantium and Persia, it seems an unlikely candidate to change the world.

But that is just what happens over the next hundred years. Precisely why this unexpected transformation happens is lost to history.

Conventional narrative written centuries after the event draws the rise of the Arab Muslims as a campaign of conquest driven by the single strand of faith. In this view, the Arab armies led by Abu Bakr, inspired by the injunction to spread the faith and following the example of the Prophet's successful campaign against huge odds, pour forth from Arabia into the surrounding world.

Another view is that while the faith is important, other threads like a sudden taste of wealth, good luck, and two once formidable enemies weakened by fighting each other are just as critical.

In the Prophet's era, the two rivals—Byzantium and Persia—have not only fought each other to stalemate and exhausted each other in the process, they have begun to encroach on the Arabs in the north and east. So the first Muslims, having just founded their new state in Arabia, set out to evict the Byzantine and Persian occupiers to fortify their borders and safeguard their new experiment.

But something strange happens. As the Arabs push forward, their two foreign enemies retreat. Probably expecting a solid line of enemy resistance to form somewhere outside Arabia, the Arabs are astonished to find their enemy constantly receding. And so the Arab attempt at reinforcing borders acquires a whole new, self-fulfilling dynamic. Suddenly, tribute, booty and taxes are flowing into the Arab treasury from the conquered lands. Just as the Byzantines have taxed and occupied Egypt and Syria to support the empire based in Constantinople, now the Arabs get a taste of the same thing.

ONCE-CLOSED DOORS ARE OPENING; unforeseen opportunities are arising. And so it happens that, singing old battle songs and reciting war poems of ancient Arabia, the women and children praise and bless their husbands and fathers and brothers and send them surging out of the Arabian towns and camps, bound for the fabled cities to the north, east, and west. The Arab warriors head for the same places that they have long known from the caravan trade. Accustomed to resisting or harassing or making truce with the more powerful armies of Byzantium and Persia, the Arabs are transformed, infused with a zeal and power disconnected from any great wealth of land or learning, from any great and grandiose history or tradition of conquest and domination. They pour forth in the manner of the Prophet himself, who started with nothing and managed one day to transform all of Arabia.

The results of this accidental and improvised campaign are almost beyond belief. Two years after the Prophet's death, the Arab armies are swiftly absorbing vast parts of Byzantium, including Syria and Palestine. Caliph Abu Bakr is succeeded by Caliph Umar, who leads his forces deeper into the Byzantine and Persian Empires. At the Battle of Yarmuk in Syria in 636, Umar destroys the forces of the Byzantine Emperor Heraclius. By 642 Umar has sent his armies to conquer Byzantine Egypt, and they begin to advance across North Africa. In 644 Caliph Uthman succeeds Umar; his forces annex Persia in 651.

In the Western telling of the history of the Arab Muslim advance, this critical first century of Islam is reduced to a string of dates, battles, and conquests, painted as the forced imposition of a new religious order. Yet while the Arab advance in these early years is, indeed, largely a military campaign, with all the attendant unfortunate effects that happen during wars, some of these accounts lose the history of other more nuanced events happening at ground level.

First, the tapestry of conventional history loses the strand that Islam's rapid spread is caused in part by its economic success, not by conquest and forced conversion. The Arab system of paying soldiers with cash plays an important role in creating the urban, cash-based market economy of the early Islamic world. This means a massive amount of coinage is put into circulation, leading to urbanization and revitalization of commercial life in towns and cities that were beginning to decline economically under the Byzantines and Persians.

Second, this tapestry misses the thread that the religious conversion of conquered peoples is often low on the political agenda of the emerging Muslim Arab empire. Muslims remain a minority in many regions they rule. In some places, Persia for example, Muslims make up less than ten percent of the population in the first century of the Islamic empire.

The Arab rulers have no strong religious injunction—and perhaps a major financial disincentive—to convert the people they colonize. Arab rulers derive major revenue by taxing the People of the Book, so converting Jews and Christians means a loss of revenue. It also means extending social services to the converts, which costs more money.

What conversion does occur in these early days seems more to be the converts' choice so they can lower their taxes, improve their social mobility, and engage more easily in commerce and government. But for some decades, even voluntary conversion does not free them from the religious tax. Those who keep their old faith, can even build their own places of worship, though those cannot be taller than a mosque. But proselytizing and blaspheming the Prophet are forbidden.

This forgotten strand of Muslim tolerance of other faiths is demonstrated in the following account of the Muslim capture and assimilation of Byzantine Alexandria, and how the Muslims deal with the Coptic Christian patriarch Benjamin, as narrated by a forgotten Coptic chronicler:

Then Amr, son of Al-Asi, wrote to the provinces of Egypt a letter, in which he said: 'There is protection and security for the place where Benjamin, the patriarch of the Coptic Christians is, and peace from God; therefore let him come forth secure and tranquil, and administer the affairs of his Church, and the government of his nation.' Therefore when the holy Benjamin heard this, he returned to Alexandria with great joy, clothed with the crown of patience and sore conflict which had befallen the orthodox people through their persecution by the heretics, after having been absent during thirteen years, ten of which were years of Heraclius, the misbelieving Roman, with the three years before the Muslims conquered Alexandria. When Benjamin appeared, the people and the whole city rejoiced, and made his arrival known to Sanutius, the dux who believed in Christ, who had settled with the commander Amr that the patriarch should return, and had received a safe-conduct from Amr for him. Thereupon Sanutius went to the commander and announced that the patriarch had arrived, and Amr gave orders that Benjamin should be brought before him with honour and veneration and love. And Amr, when he saw the patriarch, received him with respect, and said to his companions and private friends: 'Verily in all the lands of which we have taken possession hitherto I have never seen a man of God like this man.' For the Father Benjamin was beautiful of countenance, excellent in speech, discoursing with calmness and dignity.

Then Amr turned, and said to him: 'Resume the government of all your churches and of your people, and administer their affairs. And if you will pray for me, that I may go to the West and to Pentapolis, and take possession of them, as I have of Egypt, and return to you in safety and speedily, I will do for you all that you shall ask of me.' Then the holy Benjamin prayed for Amr, and pronounced an eloquent discourse, which made Amr and those present with him marvel, and which contained words of exhortation and much profit for those that heard him; and he revealed certain matters to Amr, and departed from his presence honoured and revered. And all that the blessed father said to the commander Amr, son of Al-Asi, he found true, and not a letter of it was unfulfilled.

This policy of interfaith tolerance will mark the beginning of a tradition of Muslim coexistence with Christians, Jews, Hindus, and other religions that will endure in many predominantly Muslim places until the 21st century.

As for Islam itself, in 661 a fateful event occurs, one that will forever split its followers. Passed over in 632 when Abu Bakr was chosen as the first caliph, Ali ibn Abi Talib finally becomes caliph in 656. But in 661, Ali is removed and slain, and Muawiya of the Meccan clan descended from Umayya becomes caliph. Some of the followers remain faithful to Ali and openly refuse to accept the new caliph. They become known as Shiites, from Shiat Ali, or "followers of Ali," while the supporters of Muawiya become known as Sunnis, from the word *sunnah,* or "the words and example set by the Prophet," and their dynasty is known as the Umayyads.

In another critical move, though they are from Arabia, the Umayyads choose to leave the religious center at Mecca and put their political and commercial center at the old Byzantine city of Damascus.

Why do these loyal sons of Mecca decide to turn their backs on the holy city, as their empire grows? Most probably because even as the desert Arabs advance, they are relatively few in number. Their ranks begin to fill with more formally educated peoples of Egypt, Syria, Palestine, and Iraq, plus Persians and Byzantines and Turkic speakers from Central Asia. Men who have seen and known the opulent and ancient imperial cities and societies of Alexandria, Damascus, Persian Ctesiphon, and Jerusalem flow into the ranks of the Arab Muslims, bringing with them their tastes, ideas, stories, and tongues. The Arabs are eager to embrace all these new people and their experience, because not only is it necessary to administer the expanding realm of Islam, it seems to reflect the direct instructions of the Prophet, who said "even if you must go all the way to China, seek knowledge."

This initial Arab Muslim strategy of improvisation and assimilation, plus hunger for knowledge and experience, will lay the foundation for the future flowering of the various Muslim golden ages, first in the Arab lands and Andalusia and Persia, then in Central Asia and India, and finally in Anatolia and Mughal India.

And though the map of the world and the beliefs of men and women are being transformed, that is not to say that these first hundred years of Muslim improvisation and consolidation after the Prophet have somehow brought divine behavior into the ways of men. This period, as in all parts of the world, is shaken by political struggles, coups, and assassinations, and resentments and vendettas occasionally break into civil war. But this tumult and assimilation also begin to produce a unique hybrid culture, a nominally Arabic but diverse and rich merger, with the literacy and opulence of Persia, and the learning and styles of Byzantium, along with echoes of Greece and Rome.

This heritage and body of knowledge transmitted from the Byzantines and Persians to the followers of the Prophet will shortly loom large in the flowering of the first Muslim golden age. And just as importantly, the tongue of Arabic classical poetry begins to become the lingua franca of the new realm, the only language for religious discussion and expression, and increasingly important to commerce, literature, and everyday life. Persians, Syrians, Byzantines, Berbers, and many others under Muslim rule begin to learn Arabic.

FOR A HUNDRED YEARS the whirlwind of Arab Muslim expansion continues. The caliphal armies drive the Visigoths from North Africa, and by 711, under the freed Berber slave Tariq ibn Ziyad, a mixed force of Arabs and Berbers invades and conquers Visigothic Spain. A year later, in 712, Muslims advance into Sind in modern-day Pakistan and what we now know as Central Asia, then called Transoxiana.

Some say the invasion of Spain is incited by dissident Iberian Christians trying to draw the Muslims north as allies in a tribal civil war against the ruling King Roderick. Visigothic Spain is already in great turmoil both over factional issues and a campaign by the rulers against the kingdom's many Jews. The minority Visigoths rule in a rough and rapacious way, lording over a restive native population descended from Roman days and before.

The Visigothic rulers have done little to win over their Latin subjects, and Iberia continues in the same civic and economic stagnation brought on by the fall of Rome that most of Europe endures.

Yet the Muslim emir in North Africa, Musa ibn Nusair, is still wary. He wonders if he is being drawn into a trap, and he questions whether Iberia is worth the trouble. He sends over a small force to probe the defenses and finds hardly any. So he sends his loyal commander Tariq to undertake a campaign to establish a foothold.

Foothold would be an understatement. Tariq lands at what will later be known as Gibraltar, christened that day as Jebel al-Tariq, in Arabic the "Mountain of Tariq," on April 30, 711. He has a small army of perhaps 7,000, composed of a few Arabs from Syria plus many of his own Berber compatriots. Upon landing, he is said to have told his men:

O my warriors, whither would you flee? Behind you is the sea, before you, the enemy. You have left now only the hope of your courage and your constancy. Remember that in this country you are more unfortunate than the orphan seated at the table of the avaricious master. Your enemy is before you, protected by an innumerable army; he has men in abundance, but you, as your only aid, have your own swords, and, as your only chance for life, such chance as you can snatch from the hands of your enemy. If the absolute want to which you are reduced is prolonged ever so little, if you delay to seize immediate success, your good fortune will vanish, and your enemies, whom your very presence has filled with fear, will take courage. Put far from you the disgrace from which you flee in dreams, and attack this monarch who has left his strongly fortified city to meet you. Here is a splendid opportunity to defeat him, if you will consent to expose yourselves freely to death. Do not believe that I desire to incite you to face dangers which I shall refuse to share with you. In the attack I myself will be in the fore, where the chance of life is always least.

Remember that if you suffer a few moments in patience, you will afterward enjoy supreme delight. Do not imagine that your fate can be separated from mine, and rest assured that if you fall, I shall perish with you, or avenge you. You have heard that in this country there are a large number of ravishingly beautiful Greek maidens, their graceful forms are draped in sumptuous gowns on which gleam pearls, coral, and purest gold, and they live in the palaces of royal kings. The Commander of True Believers, Alwalid, son of Abdalmelik, has chosen you for this attack from among all his Arab warriors; and he promises that you shall become his comrades and shall hold the rank of kings in this country. Such is his confidence in your intrepidity. The one fruit which he desires to obtain from your bravery is that the word of God shall be exalted in this country, and that the true religion shall be established here. The spoils will belong to yourselves.

Remember that I place myself in the front of this glorious charge which I exhort you to make. At the moment when the two armies meet hand to hand, you will see me, never doubt it, seeking out this Roderick, tyrant of his people, challenging him to combat, if God is willing. If I perish after this, I will have had at least the satisfaction of delivering you, and you will easily find among you an experienced hero, to whom you can confidently give the task of directing you. But should I fall before I reach to Roderick, redouble your ardor, force yourselves to the attack and achieve the conquest of this country, in depriving him of life. With him dead, his soldiers will no longer defy you.

Tariq and his warriors fight their way north and by summer utterly defeat Roderick and his army at the town of Guadelete on the Rio Barbete, leaving the way open for the near total conquest of Spain over the next decade. There are rumors that the defeat of the numerically larger Visigothic forces is sealed when many of them switch sides during the height of battle, presumably because of dissatisfaction with their rulers. Tariq plows north capturing significant booty, and when word of this reaches his patron Musa ibn Nusair back in North Africa, the emir immediately demands an explanation. In a humiliating meeting, Tariq renews his fealty to Musa and turns over the booty, including an emerald- and pearl-encrusted Visigothic table and chairs worth a reputed 200,000 dinars, which many of the Berber soldiers had expected to be shared among them.

These continuing Muslim successes in the Far West are gradually made known by courier and emissary to the caliph in Damascus, and accounts of varying accuracy make their way across the breadth of the caliphate. They report events thousands of miles away and seemingly far from the lives of those who make up the rank and file of this vast new society. But the human meaning is brought home to everyone on one crystal-clear winter day in Damascus in 715.

Two major events mark this date in Damascus: the final completion of the colossal Umayyad mosque and a most memorable visit by Emir Musa ibn Nusair of North Africa to see the Caliph al-Walid. The emir presents to the caliph 40 captured Visigothic nobles and courtiers, and a larger number of hapless followers brought there from Spain. To the cheers of the new Muslims and citizens of Damascus, these captives are made to pay respect to the caliph. In scope and significance, this public ceremony carries deep echoes of many similar ceremonies back in old Rome and in Constantinople.

By 732 in the Far West, only 100 years after the death of the Prophet, his followers have not only largely consolidated their control over the Iberian peninsula, they have established smaller centers under local emirs in southern France. Many of these are built through freelance adventuring rather than any coordinated formal invasion. Quite often the local emirs build loyalty through marriage to local Christian nobility. Although in Spain and everywhere in the caliphate the up-close economic and political landscape seems more like a network of city-states than modern nation states, in fact, in 732 a vast Muslim realm exists with its ultimate seat of power in Damascus. It stretches from Spain in the west to the far reaches of Mongolia, and from southern France in the north to the Indian Ocean and Africa in the south.

TOURS, NEUSTRIA (FRANCIA), A.D. 732—In the tapestry of lost history, there is a strand of conflict, described many centuries later as a war of religions and a clash of civilizations, when, in fact, it is not so simple nor so apocalyptic.

And because the true motivations and actions of men will be lost or reinterpreted over time, a conventional narrative of this conflict will arise, showing these two civilizations as implacable enemies.

Though the history of all the world including Europe, until and long after this time, is a story of unending warfare and imperial ambition and religious conflict, for some reason this particular struggle will be painted in apocalyptic terms, especially by the Europeans.

But in reality, these two civilizations echo with memories of Rome, and these two faiths share many of the same beliefs and traditions and worship the same God. And this struggle will be much more about political and military control, rather than "alien" Islam seeking to destroy "indigenous" Christianity. That unfortunate interpretation will emerge over the next thousand years.

This perceived strand of inevitable conflict can be traced back to a series of battles at the beginning of time.

That tragic moment of first contact and misunderstanding has now come.

Two armies are coming together.

It is a cold, late fall day smelling of onrushing winter, in the evolving place that was once known as Roman Gaul. This land is a patchwork of Frankish fiefdoms ranging from Aquitaine to the English Channel and run by an ever shifting network of nobles in uneasy alliance or combat. It is a dark and disordered time, a time of fear and opportunity.

The sky, too, is dark and foreboding, and the forests are heavy with wet fallen leaves, the fields turning brown after the harvest.

Tours, the old Roman town now become home of the shrine to St. Martin, is really a swollen village whose economy in large part is driven by the commerce of religion. People coming to venerate the dead saint make offerings and spend money and do business. Faith creates jobs.

More than anything, from afar, the scene is marked by its silence. The noises of human endeavor are dwarfed by the sound of wind, of thunder, of nature, which still reigns supreme. Wisps of smoke from huts, dim fire lights in villages break this pastoral scene. The bleating of sheep and goats, the cackling of chickens, are lost in the wind.

While some of the styles and structures of life in these parts are Frankish, the ideal to which all aspire is Roman. Though Rome was brought to them by the lances and legions of Julius Caesar in 55 B.C., the Gauls had become loyal subjects, and long after Rome has gone, these descendants in the eighth century still imitate its forms, almost as if they can bring Rome back by imitating it. And why should they not want it back? The Roman Empire's structure created order and defined the map, as it did for most of the dozens of races and nations who fell to it, and in the final years of the western empire, even Rome's adopted Christian faith had become the faith of most everyone.

The echo of Rome is in the very speech of these descendants hundreds of years later. In this part of Europe, though the Latin is changing into something new, the core root is the old imperial tongue rather than the Germanic dialects from farther north and east.

The foreigner observing all this does not speak the local language nor Latin, but he has heard foreign tongues since he was born. He first heard them in the market of the port in Yemen where he grew up, in the speech of the Byzantines and Persians and Ethiopians trading there. As a boy, on the sun-scorched desert and rocky coast of southern Arabia, he had gotten a taste for things far away.

His name is Abd al-Rahman al-Ghafiqi, and he is now the emir of al-Andalus, headed into battle with the Franks. When he thinks about how far he has come since his boyhood in Yemen, he wonders if he is instead dreaming.

Long ago, he had heard tales of the Romans—tales so fantastical he wondered if they were true. He had heard of Constantinople, of the fallen city of Rome itself. He had heard that the world of Christians outnumbered that of Muslims.

And now, as a grown man, he is so far from home it is almost unimaginable, and he is seeing the source lands of all that he glimpsed and imagined as a boy. Swept up in the fervor of the empire and the surge of the Arab armies north out of the homeland, he has made his way first to what is now Tunisia and then to Morocco, where he becomes acquainted with the new Muslim emirs of Andalusian Spain. In 730, the Umayyad caliph in Damascus makes him the emir of Cordoba.

He has risen from obscurity to become the most powerful ruler in this part of the world. And in fulfillment of those duties, he finds himself in the land of the Frankish Christians, a place of unimaginable greenery and dampness, of forests without end, of game and wildlife beyond number. Though the landscape of men is primitive and poor, the landscape of nature is rich and intriguing.

He counts himself fortunate to have been given this opportunity, to serve and to explore. He knew in the ports of Yemen that he was born to wander. Now he is paid to explore.

But the other part of his job is to govern and protect the new emirate of al-Andalus. When one of his subordinate local emirs in the southern Frankish city of Narbonne turned rebel and made an alliance with

Christian Count Eudes of Aquitaine, al-Ghafiqi took immediate action to break up this alliance. Then, when this same Eudes managed to defeat an earlier Andalusian punitive force in the French city of Toulouse, the problem threatened to get out of hand.

So Abd al-Rahman al-Ghafiqi has been pulled far to the north. He is here to put an end to the rebels and the foreign threats to his northern frontier.

Al-Ghafiqi does not even know the name of his opposite commander. It doesn't matter. The Yemeni knows he far outnumbers anything the Franks could ever muster. He has seen how they fight. Unlike the Hispano-Arabs, the Franks have no horses or cavalry to speak of. Their simple weaponry and light armor resemble what was left by Roman foot soldiers centuries before—a banded iron helmet and neck guard; a lance, bow and arrows; and a simple shield to protect from the chest to the thighs. Men forced to march on foot can't be expected to carry much more, and because of the technological limits of the day, there isn't much more to be carried. He guesses that today, outside Tours, these Frankish men number as few as 15,000.

The Franks see something else altogether. Marching up from the southwest is a vast and organized army, one decidedly from a different world. Yet in a strange way what they see is also Roman. Though they cannot know it, what they see is merely one of the other descendants of and aspirants to the mantle of Rome. In its imperial advance the army inspires awe and fear not unlike what the first Roman legions must have instilled as they marched north from the Alps to subdue the barbarian tribes in the colder climes 700 years earlier.

What is coming toward the Franks is the nearest tendril of an entity that now reaches from the deserts of Arabia, the fabled cities of Persia, and the northern edges of India, to the sweep of northern Africa and the fallen Mediterranean pieces of Rome and Byzantium.

The force coming up from the southwest is only one of many such armies at work across 4,000 miles of Earth. It is really a provincial raiding and stabilization force reporting to the supreme political-religious leader in Damascus, the Caliph of all Islam, Abd al-Malik.

This seemingly awesome army is not an occupation force there to conquer and annex the Frankish kingdom and force everyone to convert to the new faith. No, it is a tactical strike force, sent both to do some old-fashioned plundering and to demoralize adherents and allies of the traitor emir of Narbonne and his ally Eudes.

But the defending Franks have no way of knowing that. They have heard breathless and exaggerated accounts of what has happened farther south, and they have to assume it is now their turn.

Not unlike the Roman legions, this new invader is imperial and multinational and polyglot. Within its ranks are generals and soldiers from distant lands: adventurers from Persia who might have converted to Islam from Zoroastrianism only a decade ago, Arabs from the source land in Arabia and Yemen, Berbers from North Africa, assimilated Christians from Spain and Provence now learning to speak Arabic, and Jews from the diaspora.

The Franks only know Eudes's side of the story. To protect Aquitaine and remain independent of the Franks, Eudes had struck up an alliance with the local emir in Narbonne. That had worked for a while. But then the local emir had declared his independence from al-Andalus and that had triggered this invasion.

They know the Andalusian emir's tactic in dealing with enemies and traitors is simple: He crushes them with overwhelming force. They have heard that as al-Ghafiqi heads north, he has tried to demoralize the enemy by burning churches and towns, sacking villages, ruining the city of Bordeaux, and seizing a large part of the harvest to feed his force which numbers 60,000 or more. They hear that his scouts have told him of the rich shrine of St. Martin in Tours. Much booty awaits the taker. The Franks have heard that the emir will be the taker, unless they stop him.

And what does this advancing force look like, to the Frankish Christian villagers and peasants? The Franks see almost as many horses as they see men, and there are more of both than any of these simple folk have ever witnessed gathered in one place. The hoofbeats, the clanking of weaponry, the whinnying of the horses, and the glottal chanting of the soldiers in Arabic is heart-stopping. These local folk have never heard such a sound. And mounted on the horses are the first armored knights in all of Europe, the first armored cavalry, a vision right out of the biblical apocalypse.

It will soon be lost to history that one of the later ideals of European courtly mythology—the armored knight on horseback, and his weaponry and tactics—will come from this fearsome "alien" invader. Mounted knights and armor are really Muslim imports to Europe.

Lost history will show that this one-way transfer of Muslim styles, ideas, and technologies into Europe will continue for another 800 years. But too often, that strand of technology transfer will be deemphasized, in favor of the strands of conflict between two faiths.

Looking out from their hiding places, the frightened Frankish peasants see Muslim knights dressed in steel from the furnaces of Toledo, swinging swords fired in the foundries of Damascus, dressed in robes and tunics, and holding up their green fluttering flags and glistening shields. In the eyes of the Franks, this is not just an imperial army. This is a force of nature.

While the Franks and their commander, a certain Charles, are seriously worried and desperately strategizing about how to deal with this massive enemy, al-Ghafiqi is not at all worried beyond the usual military concerns at the beginning of battle against a much weaker foe: He is far from his base, it is a constant effort to feed and supply his force, and winter is coming on. His men are from southern lands, and they aren't dressed for the cold and wet. He regrets that this pursuit of Eudes has dragged on so long. Despite all that, he will use his standard approach to overwhelm and defeat his enemy. If the Franks will not abandon their resistance and pledge fealty to him and the caliph, he will punish them.

Charles has a different plan and some tricks up his sleeve. Rather than let the invader set the frame of battle, he has marched to this place avoiding the Roman roads so as to miss any Muslim scouts that might have been about. Having traveled largely unobserved, he is now able to set up his force in a forest, using the advantage of the trees. He forms his men into a phalanx—the classical four-sided infantry formation devised by the Greeks more than a thousand years ago, and adopted and perfected by the Romans.

The Franks do not have horses or armored knights. But they do have some serious fear and motivation to defend their families and homeland. They also see this as a religious battle, a battle to defend Christendom against the warriors of this new southern faith. Already there is a major asymmetry in the two forces, in their perceptions of one another, and in the significance of the coming battle. For the Franks, it is a nightmare. They see it as not only a life or death struggle, but as a defense of Christianity.

For the Andalusian and Arab Muslims and their army, it is not nearly so important. Since their army numbers many faiths and races, the encounter is not so tinged with religion and tribe. And since this is a tactical strike force put out by an empire 4,000 miles wide, it is not life or death, except in the personal sense.

On paper, Charles's plan would seem to be ridiculously futile. Infantries can almost never defeat cavalry, as has been proven time and again—certainly not armored Muslim knights on horseback, chopping away at lowly foot soldiers. So to offset that disadvantage, Charles will choose the battleground first, and make the enemy on horseback come to him where it is weakest, on the higher ground and in the trees.

And so, in position in his forest near the Loire, he waits. And once his advance scouts tell him where the enemy force is, al-Ghafiqi also waits. In the wet falling gloom of late autumn, the emir waits six days for the Franks to come out of the woods. He's no fool. He knows that Charles has shifted the balance slightly. He even thinks about bypassing Charles or turning back to the south.

But because he has been a bit remiss in his military intelligence, al-Ghafiqi assumes that overwhelming Andalusian power and technology, the sheer numbers, cavalry, and the stirrups give him an unassailable edge. He doesn't know who he's up against. He doesn't know that Charles is known for outsmarting stronger enemies.

Charles, too, has a few second thoughts. He agreed to answer this appeal from Eudes only in exchange for Eudes's submission to him, and also to protect the holy shrine of St. Martin. In fact, Charles has begun to make a career of defending Christendom in Europe and building his own empire in the process. The powerless Pope Gregory has already called on Charles to help defend the holy city of Rome against the Lombards:

From Pope Gregory to His Most Excellent Son, Karl.

In our great affliction we have thought it necessary to write to you a second time, believing that you are a loving son of St. Peter, the prince of apostles, and of ourselves, and that out of reverence for him you would obey our commands to defend the church of God and his chosen people. We can now no longer endure the persecution of the Lombards, for they have taken from St. Peter all his possessions, even those which were given him by you and your fathers. These Lombards hate and oppress us because we sought protection from you; for the same reason also the church of St. Peter is despoiled and desolated by them. But we have intrusted a more complete account of all our woes to your faithful subject, our present messenger, and he will relate them to you. You, oh son, will receive favor from the same prince of apostles here and in the future life in the presence of God, according as you render speedy aid to his church and to us, that all peoples may recognize the faith and love and singleness of purpose which you display in defending St. Peter and us and his chosen people. For by doing this you will attain lasting fame on earth and eternal life in heaven.

So not only is Charles protecting a shrine, he feels responsible for protecting all of European Christendom, this time against a much more powerful enemy than the Lombards. He has heard the lists of the Visigoth kings and others who have been destroyed or overthrown. In just his short lifetime, in this part of the world, the Andalusian-Arabs have taken Spain and part of France. They have magnificent armor, they have horses, they have superior numbers and commanders. They land their ships at will on the southern coast of France. They are advanced.

The moment has come. And so now al-Ghafiqi, cold and irritated and a little uneasy, asking the protection of God to aid his men just as He aided the Prophet in his final battle for Mecca, sends his horsemen into the forest, charging ahead into the phalanx. Swords and axes and arrows fly, screams and oaths ring out in many languages, lances and battle-axes crash against armor. Franks and Andalusians fall, but not in huge numbers. Several times the Andalusians break into the square, coming within sight of Charles's central redoubt, but they are not able to go any closer. Christians fall; so do Muslims. The guards of Charles stand their ground. The Andalusians are expelled and repulsed, again and again.

As an unnamed Arab chronicler writes:

And in the shock of the battle the men of the North seemed like a sea that cannot be moved. Firmly they stood, one close to another, forming as it were a bulwark of ice; and with great blows of their swords they hewed down the Arabs. Drawn up in a band around their chief, the people of the Austrasians carried all before them. Their tireless hands drove their swords down to the breasts of the foe.

This goes on for some time. It is a standoff, which for Charles is a temporary victory. But he knows he can't sustain this forever. With the Franks locked into a square in the woods, the Andalusians have the time advantage.

Al-Ghafiqi, puzzled at this outcome, moves forward to better see what's going wrong, how to break the wall of the phalanx. He's angry that an ancient Greek infantry formation is stopping the greatest cavalry in the world. He will definitely have an account of this entered into his journal tonight.

A millennium later, strategists will figure out what went wrong. Military thinkers familiar with horse psychology will theorize that no horse will charge into a solid line of men with shields. The sight creates too unnatural a feeling for the animal and violates too many internal taboos. Trained almost from birth to submit to the master, the horse will not attack the master; this is compounded by the fear of charging into an area where there is no clear foothold, augmented by the off-putting obstacle of the trees.

Now the tricks begin. As autumnal afternoon slides toward dusk, Charles is able to send scouts into the Andalusian rear to set free Frankish prisoners and to circulate the rumor into the enemy camp that the freed men and others are taking the Andalusian booty already gathered in the campaign.

This causes some of the Andalusians to break away, to go back to their hoard to see what is going on. The word spreads among others that they are all in retreat, and they follow those going rearward. In this confusion, the great Emir al-Ghafiqi, too far forward, trying to restore control and communications with his forces now pulling back, suddenly finds himself isolated and surrounded by Charles's men and with hardly any of his own. He is experienced, and he is well armored. Like Charles, he fights as a brave warrior. But in a few swift moments he is overwhelmed, his horse is run through with lance upon lance and falls, and he too falls.

And then he is killed. Lance points drive through the few gaps in his armor, and he is too stunned to fend them off. Gushing blood and uttering his final prayers, the mighty emir in service of the caliph is killed in battle. Expecting to easily win this fight, he has died a martyr.

The news sweeps through both armies. The great and fearsome emir of al-Andalus, Abd al-Rahman al-Ghafiqi, has fallen. This gives a temporary boost to the Franks and a temporary shock to the Andalusians. But in the moment, it does not seem decisive to either of them. Coming back to their rear camp to find prisoners and booty largely intact, the Andalusians realize they have been tricked, resulting in stalemate and in the loss of their great emir. The invaders still have a huge force and much of the power they brought into the encounter. They are embarrassed and angry. Many want vengeance.

Despite this temporary victory for the Franks, they do not think it decisive either. Night falls, and the Franks bed down for a fitful sleep. They expect the fighting to be renewed in the morning. Charles is wondering if he can withstand another direct assault and for how long.

But down in the dark wet fields beyond the forest, something else is happening among the southerners, something unexpected. The dead emir's force is still intact, but shaken. It would seem to be a matter of appointing a new commander, reassessing strategy, either leapfrogging Charles's position, or making another direct assault.

Except the Andalusian subcommanders cannot agree on who should lead. They argue into the night about this point. Only al-Ghafiqi had clear and inarguable authority from the caliph in Damascus. No one else does. Persians, Berbers, Yemenis, Spaniards, Arabs—the patchwork comes apart, without clear leadership.

The next morning, Charles and his men are demoralized to watch day break over the huge sea of black caliphal tents. The tents have not moved from the day before. Another battle will surely come. But nothing happens. In fact, no movement can be seen. No enemy soldiers show themselves at all. Frankish scouts go out and report that the invaders' tents are empty.

Charles's first reaction is fear. He senses a trick, an ambush to reply to his trick of yesterday. Where is the enemy hidden? Will they sweep down this afternoon and tonight, when the Franks have come out of the trees? But scouts going far and wide can find no one. The Andalusians have vanished in the night. The Franks have won. The outnumbered, poorly equipped Franks have defeated the army of al-Ghafiqi, whose men have withdrawn because they could not agree on a new commander. The rest is history.

This surprise French victory will have immediate consequences. Charles will lose no time in assimilating the superior military technologies of his enemy. He and his men strip the fallen Andalusian knights of their armor, their swords and shields, and their stirrups. A few days later he begins to build Europe's first armored cavalry, which he will use in battle only five years later against his Muslim foe at Narbonne in southern France. The armored cavalry based on the technology received from the Andalusian invaders will prove the core of European military power for the next 500 years.

This lucky break also transforms Charles Martel into The Hammer, the sobriquet given him by his men. He and his heirs will now make fighting the European armies of Islam one of their essential missions. His son and successor Pepin III will someday go to the cowering pope in Rome and make the case that since the real power of Europe now rests with the family of Charles, they should be crowned the true kings of France. Desperate for their military protection, the pope will agree and crown the Carolingian dynasty. The seeds of future modern Europe will be planted.

Beyond these immediate shifts, as the years and centuries pass, the perception will also grow that one of the great inflection points of Western history has occurred at Tours. No one can know this in 732, because the full meaning and result will not be apparent in the great and slow-moving drama of history.

From the perspective of the Arabs, for the Andalusians and their Umayyad ruler in Damascus, the Battle of Tours seems no more than a wake-up call. They will now take the Franks more seriously as they stabilize and consolidate their new empire. Their leaders and scholars will begin to focus on their two most formidable foes—the Byzantines and the Franks.

The import for the Europeans is vastly greater, as they rework the victory into the battle to defend European Christendom.

The traditional Western view is that the Muslims—had they won at Tours and continued to press farther north and east—would have gone on to conquer all of Europe. They certainly had the power and, short of Charles Martel, there was no leader or force in Europe that could stop them. These Western traditionalists believe Europe would have become an Islamized culture. The Catholic Church based in Rome could have disappeared. Europe as we know it might have never developed.

A Western traditionalist like Edward Gibbon puts it this way a thousand years later:

A victorious line of march had been prolonged above a thousand miles from the rock of Gibraltar to the banks of the Loire; the repetition of an equal space would have carried the Saracens to the confines of Poland and the Highlands of Scotland; the Rhine is not more impassable than the Nile or Euphrates, and the Arabian fleet might have sailed without a naval combat into the mouth of the Thames. Perhaps the interpretation of the Qur'an would now be taught in the schools of Oxford, and her pulpits might demonstrate to a circumcised people the sanctity and truth of the revelation of Muhammed.

But there is no evidence of the Andalusian-Arab intent to engulf Europe as they had Iberia. After another decisive Muslim defeat in Narbonne in 737, again at the hand of Charles Martel, such a campaign never developed. By 800, Martel's grandson Charlemagne had pushed the southerners out of France and was initiating probes into Spain.

And even if the Muslims had decided to extend the conquest north, it would have been complicated by the rising turmoil in the caliphate itself, which only 20 years after the Battle of Tours would split into separate and mutually hostile entities: the Umayyad emirate headquartered in Cordoba and the Abbasid caliphate in Baghdad. Would Muslim Spain without the support of Damascus and Baghdad have continued—or have had the means—to invade and occupy the rest of Europe?

This debate will never be settled. What is more important is the fact that for the Europeans, the fierce and rapid Arab military conquest of much of the old Persian and Roman worlds right up to central France was resoundingly traumatic for all in its path, leaving a wound that has never fully healed even though the details of it have been forgotten. Yet its memory and the way the event has been portrayed for 1,300 years rest just below the surface.

Said again, perhaps one of the most important legacies of Tours and related events of the Arab conquest of the seventh and eighth centuries is the traumatization of Europe and the shaping of how the Muslim world has been viewed. This perception of Muslims as ruthless invaders created a strange early European lens of fascination and fear that would color how many things were seen long after. That the new religion had echoes of Judaism and Christianity, but was separate, added further complications.

The traditionalist European predictions about the consequences of a Muslim conquest of Europe may well have been proven right, had Charles Martel not resisted. But based on a reading of lost history, which includes the forgotten achievements of the Muslim golden ages and the unique development of Muslim Spain and other hybrid cultures, such predictions could just as likely have been proven wrong. The earlier Roman and barbarian invasions and conquests of Europe yielded a new culture that would one day dominate much of the world and be held up for centuries as an ideal. Why not a similar result from the Muslims?

Based on the largely lost history that the Muslim world surged far beyond Christian Europe in its economic, intellectual, and technological development for 700 years after Tours, wasn't it as likely that such a thing could have happened in France, Germany, Italy, and elsewhere under the Muslims?

The most convincing proof is in how, despite the Muslim defeat, the ideas and styles and forms of the Muslim world did impact the non-Muslim West. The impact was more subtle, less explicit, and because of lost history, not often enough attributed to the correct cultural source. But in the long sweep of time and the distant overview of larger patterns, the best of Muslim thought, invention, and art still managed in its own subtle and circuitous way to seep into the West.

European attraction to Muslim technology and intellect, and fear of Muslim power and religion, would mark the relationship between Europeans and Muslims all the way into the Renaissance and beyond. It would not change until Europe became the global imperial power in the 16th century, and the Muslim golden ages wound to a close. Then a Eurocentric rewriting of history would expunge the greatness of the Muslim golden ages and exclusively credit Europeans for creating modern mathematics, astronomy, medicine, science, technology, statecraft, and a humane, pluralistic society.

Through the lens of lost history, then, the Battle of Tours can be seen as not just a trauma for the Europeans—but also as a unique gift. For the Europeans, led by Charles Martel and then by Charlemagne, did more than simply convert the event into proof of an alien threat used to spur the gradual consolidation of the Roman backwater and the unsophisticated Germanic tribes into the beginnings of a new civilization. They also benefitted from Tours' launch of a 700-year transmission of superior Muslim technology and thought and civic organization into a backward region.

This was proved by the fact that even as Charles Martel and Charlemagne defined their careers by making war on Muslims and pushing them south of the Pyrenees, they were fascinated by and attracted to the intellectual and technological achievements of their enemy. Even as Charlemagne made war against the Umayyads in Spain, he would begin a long-distance correspondence with the Abbasid Caliph Haroun al-Rashid in Baghdad to make common cause against the Byzantines.

Lost history teaches that this fateful first encounter between mainland Europe and the Muslims was much more complicated than a clash of civilizations or a war of religions. For the Europeans it was recorded as a trauma of biblical proportions yet it was also the beginning of their receipt of superior technology and ideas from the Muslims.

And for the Arab Muslims, Tours marked the end of their period of conquest and set them free to turn their energies to invention and creation. Though their military achievements were truly astonishing, their intellectual creations would prove even greater.

DAMASCUS, ISLAMIC CALIPHATE, A.D. 661—The main story now shifts to Damascus, that old biblical city en route to which Saul, the torturer of Christians, had his life-changing vision and became the Christian St. Paul. By now, in the later seventh century, the city's Roman and Byzantine tile roofs are arrayed over sun-parched Syrian hills between rocky stands of shrub, land perimeters and pastures marked by stone walls, and tall cedars yellowed in the relentless battle between life and desiccation.

In 661 the old city of St. Paul has just become the seat of the now 130-year-old Muslim caliphate. Here Islam encompasses millions of people and dozens of tongues. But aside from the immediate concerns of directing conquest and spreading the faith, there are more pressing everyday things, like properly holding and administering this huge expanse of Earth and humanity and creating a sustainable society out of this overnight empire of zeal and courage and pillage.

To complicate this drive, there is now an emerging political rivalry between two old clans sprung from the Prophet's tribe in Mecca, the Quraysh. The two families are, first, the descendants and allies of Abbas, an uncle of the Prophet, known later as the Abbasids, and, second, the descendants and allies of another of the Prophet's more distant relatives Umayya, known as the Umayyads.

Long-standing bad blood simmers between these two clans. Both families carry the blood of the Prophet, but the Abbasids more directly so. Add the fact that one of the patriarchs related to the Umayya, Abu Sufian, was perhaps the most bitter opponent of the Prophet during the early years, right until the final battle for Mecca. After losing the battle, Abu Sufian was spared and joined the Prophet. But many followers never forgot Abu Sufian's resistance.

And when the last of the rightly guided caliphs, Ali the Prophet's cousin and son-in-law, is overthrown in 661 and an Umayya named Muawiya assumes the role of caliph, more bad blood is created.

While Mecca is still the holy city, Damascus will be the seat of the caliph of all Islam. Muawiya I, though he does not claim to be a prophet, is looked to as the leader of the faith and the realm by the Sunnis, whereas the Shiites follow a separate line of caliphs. In this early, improvisational time of young Islam, Muawiya and his immediate successors will have unprecedented power to determine all affairs, including religious issues. Not that they won't listen to others: The Arab tribal way has always been about listening, negotiating, trading, building coalitions and alliances, preserving the honor of the clan, and following a strict code of behavior.

In 711 Tariq ibn Ziyad invaded and conquered Spain with a small force of Arabs and Berbers to expand the Muslim caliphate.

To declare their power and vision and the supremacy of the new faith, the Umayyad successors to Muawiya begin to build what they intend to be the greatest mosque of all Islam. But what should it look like? Should it look like the old shrine of Mecca, that ancient tribal building dating back centuries? Is there something in the architecture of Mecca and Medina, of the Arabian port towns, in the shape of the Bedouin tent that should be declared to the world in this new mosque?

In a telling decision, the Umayyads turn to the brilliant and talented thinkers from all the societies they have absorbed. There is no lack of Muslim architects, even Arab architects to choose from; they have an aesthetic shaped by older, grander civilizations.

Even though the Umayyads and many of their loyal adherents are straight out of the Arabian deserts, the mosque they choose to build, which will stand for 1,300 years, is an astonishing and uncanny testament to that other civilization recently vanished—and to an unborn one that will rise in 700 years. This seventh-century mosque, built at the dawn of Islam, to honor a new and rising civilization, will also honor a dead one, and foreshadow one not yet born: classical Rome and Renaissance Italy.

Even as the shape of this mosque will display the shared architectural heritage of Mediterranean Islam and Christianity, the ground on which it stands also echoes with an interfaith heritage. When the Arab Muslims first conquer Damascus in the seventh century, there is a Byzantine church on the spot to be occupied by the future Umayyad Mosque. John the Baptist is buried here. And earlier, before the Christian church, a Roman temple dedicated to Jupiter had occupied the site. During Muawiya's time, the Arabs share a prayer space in the church with the Christians. This goes on until about 25 years after Muawiya's death, when the Muslim community becomes large and outgrows the original prayer space.

It is not until the reign of Umayyad Caliph al-Walid in A.D. 705-715 that the 200-year-old church is purchased from Christian leaders with the promise of protection of all other churches in Damascus, as well as the construction of a new church dedicated to the Virgin. The old church is then demolished and the Umayyad Mosque is established according to a new floor plan and innovative design. Al-Walid is also responsible for the completion of the other great Umayyad building, the famous Dome of the Rock in Jerusalem, built on the Temple Mount.

When completed, the classical facade of the imperial Umayyad Mosque in Damascus will be pure Greece and Rome seen through the filter of Byzantium. The rounded arches, which will become elements of later Muslim architecture in Spain, are an adaptation of Roman arches, and its columns and capitals, its lintel and triangular roofline also are straight from Athens and Rome. The dome in the center and its interior basilica, with its windows high above the worshippers, echo the Pantheon in Rome. But most astonishingly, the courtyard of the mosque built to honor Allah not only echoes the plaza facing the pagan Roman Pantheon, it foreshadows the Christian Piazza of St. Peter's Basilica to be built in Rome many centuries later, as well as the piazzas of the great future Renaissance cities of Sienna and Florence and Venice.

How is it that this seventh-century mosque in the seat of the new Muslim caliphate resembles both fallen Rome and future Renaissance Italy? Could it be that these supposedly rival civilizations are really one greater expression?

An Andalusian-Arab description from the 12th century will see the great mosque and Damascus this way:

Damascus was the most populated city in the world. Behind the city walls the streets were narrow, lined with three-story houses of mud and reeds. The bazaars were noisy with metal workers and fragrant with spices. There were many public baths. There were twenty colleges for students of law and religion and a large free hospital. The Orthodox Christian church of St. Mary was brilliant with mosaics, and worshippers there were freely allowed to practice their religion. The rich Jewish community of some 3,000, many of them refugees from the Latin Kingdom of Jerusalem, ran their own university.

The most splendid building was the great Umayyad Mosque. Within the three-aisled basilica of the original church, the walls were covered with mosaics representing the great cities of the Muslim world, and overhead was an onion-shaped dome, the Dome of the Eagle, within which was a gilded and painted cupola. From the height of the dome men could be seen in the great courtyard reduced to the size of small children, a dizzying experience. The Mosque possessed a couple of brazen falcons. Every two hours they dropped brass balls from their beaks into brass cups, from where the balls returned to the interior of the device. At night a water clock operated a system of lights behind colored glass. But more important than these marvels was the teaching that regularly went on in the Mosque. The learned scholar with his back to a pillar and his students around him, was sometimes moved to tears of appreciation by the elegance of his exposition.

Muawiya and his heirs like Yazid (680-683), Muyawiya II (683-684), and Marwan (684-685) followed by Abd al-Malik (685-705) and al-Walid

(705-715) must also feed and house the people of the capital, and as is always the case across the new Muslim caliphate, water is an issue. Water enables life; it enables agriculture; it enables cleanliness as specified by the Prophet. To enable the volume of agriculture to feed a new imperial capital, the caliph orders the use of new irrigation techniques. Though they are probably imported from Persia, they will be exported across the empire with modifications, and someday travel in the hands of the Spanish Catholics to the New World. The Umayyads are also responsible for making Arabic the official language of government as well as for changing the coinage from Byzantine and Persian to Arabic script.

As he administers and sets up his court at Damascus, Muawiya I and his 14 successors between the years 680 and 750 also make some fateful political decisions. As sons of Mecca and kinsmen of the Prophet, they ensure that positions of power and leadership continue to be held by Arab kinsmen and a tight group of Syrians. Their army that is surging across the world is largely Syrian. The polyglot majority of foreign Muslim converts—Persians and Turkic people, Byzantines and Egyptians—will remain in a deliberate subordinate position under the Umayyads. In seeming violation of the instructions of the Prophet, they are also forced to pay the "infidel" tax even after they convert to Islam.

These foreign, second-class Muslims known as *mawali*, in alliance with the rival descendants of Abbas, will later prove the downfall of the Umayyads. In the decades after the establishment of the caliphate at Damascus—though the empire continues to expand, the trunks of booty and tribute flow toward the caliph, and Damascus enjoys its greatest period of growth and wealth—the size and administrative burden of the conquests begin to take their toll. Nature also conspires against the Umayyads, bringing deeper drought to already-dry Syria that scorches the fields and new irrigation canals. Drought increasingly forces the Umayyads to depend on food supplies from the better-watered landscape of Iraq along the Tigris and Euphrates Rivers.

This shift of agriculture and commerce from Syria eastward into Iraq changes the political mix greatly. Iraq has always been a buffer area in the sway of Persia; in a way it is the doorstep of Persia, and by depending more on Iraq to sustain the empire, the Umayyads come to depend on Persian cooperation. But the new Persian Muslims aren't given the political status that their rising economic and intellectual importance would suggest, and this engenders even more resentment.

As the Umayyad caliphate reaches its peak of geographic conquest in 732, plots against the Umayyads have been bubbling for decades. This is intensified by a sudden rise in resistance from external enemies in the far-flung corners of the empire. Not only in France, but in Central Asia, Persia, and northern India, enemies begin to push back against the conquering Muslims, while the many internal foreign subjects and new converts resist the narrowly constituted Arab ruling elite in Damascus. One overthrow attempt in 740 fails, but by 750, the rival Abbasids form an alliance with foreign Muslims, primarily Persians, and in a final battle by the River Zab, a tributary to the Tigris River, utterly defeat the Umayyads.

The survivors in Damascus are confronted on a dark night as the victorious Abbasids sweep into Syria and invite the Umayyad nobility to a "feast of reconciliation." In the spirit of the faith and of peace, they offer to work together to find a new way to jointly rule this world empire.

The feast is to be held in the Umayyad palace, and everyone gathers. Not that there isn't Umayyad trepidation to see the victorious black-flagged Abbasids now riding with their swords and armor right into the heart of the Umayyad home. But there is no one left to oppose them. The patriarch has been killed in battle and his army surrendered. This is the new world.

The dinner is made up of the victors and the defeated. And then, when it looks as though this improbable reconciliation of two dynasties at odds since the time of the Prophet might succeed, when most are lulled by wine and food into the quiet of evening, the secret order goes out among the visitors, and the terrible swords begin to do their duty. The Abbasids mercilessly slaughter every man, woman, and child of the Umayyad court, from cooks and servants to the wives of the harem, the sons and daughters, the cousins and retainers. In the ultimate nightmare of betrayal, the victorious new dynasty destroys the old. Nurseries, bedchambers, and kitchens become pools of blood, and the stones of Damascus ring out with a sound no one should ever have to hear.

Two teenaged youths, one named Abd al-Rahman and the other his brother Yahya, presumed heirs to the Damascus caliphate, cower in the palace darkness hearing the weeping and screams as their mother, their siblings, cousins, and most all of the courtiers they have known since birth are slaughtered without mercy. It is a searing experience that would send many people into inconsolable fear and grief or anger beyond retribution. But through the cunning of a few courtiers, these two surviving Umayyad royal youths are spirited out into the night and sent to flee, with only one servant and no money or bodyguards, toward North Africa. They will be lucky to live, much less find any kind of life.

To their enemies it does not yet matter. They do not even know the two are alive. The triumphant Abbasids under the new caliph swiftly consolidate their power after the massacre, and bring the various subordinate Muslim groups, particularly the Persians, into a new, more representative power-sharing arrangement. And they forever turn their back on Umayyad Damascus, deciding to move their capital to a heretofore obscure city on the Tigris River not far from the ruins of ancient Babylon. Caliph al-Mansur chooses Baghdad not for what it is, but for what it could be. The city is equidistant between the power centers of Syria and Arabia and close to Persia, and al-Mansur will lay the foundation for the first golden age of the Muslims in Baghdad.

Despite the brutality of their takeover, al-Mansur and his descendants, free to define political, social, civic, cultural, and religious affairs, will create a 500-year intellectual flowering that is among the greatest in human history, and which will resonate for another 1,250 years. The glories of their achievements are such that no other contemporary can begin to shine as will the reign of the Abbasids and their future world city, Baghdad.

But in one of the great ironies of history, the experience of that night of murder in the Umayyad palace will inspire another, perhaps even more astonishing, achievement considering the odds against it: the founding of a rival caliphate and civilization in a city called Qurtuba, in a faraway place called al-Andalus. Umayyad rule, which will not be restored again in Damascus, will revive in Spain.

And these two competing families and dynasties and visions, born of the same faith and springing from the same holy city of Mecca yet forever split by a night of murder in Damascus, will found two civilizations and two golden ages, no longer focused so much on military conquest and conversion of infidels and the plunder of booty, as on building twin centers of thought, of invention, of creativity.

Their impact on the world will seem the stuff of legend. For these two cultures together will inspire some of the greatest ideas and ideals our world has seen, from European courtly love and the troubadours, to the tales of *The Thousand and One Nights* of Scheherazade, to the Jewish philosophy of Maimonides, to the modern university, to modern medicine, to modern humane pluralistic society.

This is all lost history.

2

LOST CITIES OF GENIUS

My Lord! Increase me in knowledge.
QUR'AN (XX:114)

BAGHDAD, IRAQ, 2007—From high above and far away, 21st-century Baghdad looks like a low geometric earthen maze constructed out of the yellow delta mud of a desert river, not unlike what Babylon might have resembled eons ago, farther north. Only this construction is much larger and shines with the glint of metallic and glass surfaces that would not have existed then. No hanging gardens survive today, despite the dreams of Saddam Hussein.

Vast grids of roads and streets follow certain limits of the landscape, along the green-banked artery of the Tigris and its assorted marshes and green flats, framing a cross-hatched map of nearly six million people brought together to work, to trade, to survive. Tracking the far horizon in a 360-degree turn, the orange glow of the dawn atmosphere fades off into the heliotrope-blue of the west, toward Syria and Jordan. A bluish layer hangs low to the city from exhausts and fires in the still inversion of Iraqi summer, spreading out into the suburbs.

Ali al-Madina—surnamed either for a tiny village north of the city or perhaps the other holy city of Medina in Arabia where the Prophet once found refuge—lets the wind-up alarm clock wake him because the electricity is too uncertain these days. Through the window, beyond the boxy rooflines and swinging clotheslines of his neighborhood of Aadhamiyah, he can see the rising pinkish corona of sunrise just touching the top of the dome of the ancient Abu Hanifa mosque built by the Abbasids 1,200 years ago.

Like the drab concrete houses and the glory of the old mosque, the al-Madina family has always been caught between this dual unclarified heritage, between common obscurity and the hint of something greater. They might have been nobodies descended from an Iraqi village, as his mother would have shouted to her husband in one of those arguments of long ago. Or they might have been warriors in the original army of the Prophet raised in the oasis outside Medina, journeying out of Arabia in the service of caliphs, landing here. His father's mother told young Ali those kinds of stories, sang them to him.

No matter now. Ali eats his breakfast of fried eggs and cheese, hears his children Amina and Anwar chattering about the dreadful television news of the night before: another pair of bombings; another mass shooting in a marketplace; corpses found in warehouses; a kidnapping of an entire government office, men and women blindfolded and taken away by men in police uniforms, put into unmarked vans, and driven away.

It's no proper subject for children, and he tells them to be quiet. As he has thought perhaps a thousand times in the last three years, he wonders how it is possible for children to keep their bearings in this place, which leads to thoughts about emigration to Jordan or Syria, Dubai or Abu Dhabi. He and his wife have had this conversation many times. Ten years ago, his Arab heritage and his language would have given him a certain job. But now those wealthy emirates can attract the best engineers and architects in the world, men and women from Stanford University, Oxford, or the Sorbonne.

Those conversations have always ended in emotional outbursts about the price of leaving home. Baghdad is home. The network of extended family and friends numbers into the hundreds. What would life be like without them?

His wife, Merna, tells Ali with her eyes that it is one of those days. They wonder if it is safe enough to go into the streets, to send the kids to school, to go to their jobs?

They have reason to be concerned. Ali is Sunni and Merna is Shiite, and until last year they have rarely thought about that. They hardly ever go to mosque. Now just the fact of a mixed heritage could be reason for them and their children to be dragged off and shot by zealots on either side.

Will this be the day that lightning strikes? Miraculously, none of their immediate family has been harmed by war and occupation. But at the office, at the market, at the school, nearly everyone has been touched within two or three degrees of distance. The al-Madinas know the streets to take, the houses and buildings and buses and places to avoid, although no one can ever be sure.

Ali kisses his wife and, at the neighborhood square, hails a taxi driven by one of his neighbors. He doesn't have to tell his friend to go to the Ministry of Public Works. It is there that Ali, a civil engineer, is working on rebuilding traffic infrastructure. The whole neighborhood knows that Ali has a job, a good job—more specifically, a job repairing bridges and highways damaged by the invasion and, increasingly, by insurgents. He works fairly closely with a group of engineers from one of the American construction companies.

The relationship was closer in the past, before the insurgency had begun, and the Americans and their contractors were able to travel more freely. Now the Americans stay in the Green Zone, and if Ali needs to meet with them face to face, an appointment must be scheduled days in advance. There is a lengthy delay, a process of approvals, and planning for the hours needed to negotiate the checkpoints and barriers on the outer perimeters of the Red Zone. So mostly they communicate by mobile phone and fax and, less often, by email.

As he rides down Rashid Street, through the boxy concrete neighborhoods and the date palms and the orange haze of summer morning and Tigris dampness mixed with the eternal dust of life here, he nears the only surviving gate of the old city of Abbasid days, the Bab al-Wastani, the gate to Khorasan in northeastern Iran. He tells the cab to pull over at his favorite kiosk so he can buy cigarettes for the day.

His friend at the kiosk sells him Camels, and Ali pauses a moment to unwrap the package. Putting the Iraqi riales back in his pocket, one larger bill blows from his hand and swirls toward the base of a minor monument, a stepped plinth base holding a broken statue of a forgotten hero he has passed hundreds of times and never paused to notice.

Hustling to get the bill before the wind takes it farther, he runs up the cracked steps littered with little dunes of dust, of wrappers and shriveled stems of windblown dead grass, broken bottles, and shreds of newspaper. The bill and the wind take him up to the statue's pediment, where he finally catches his money.

At the top he sees someone has abandoned a box of old books, left out here to weather in the sun and dust. He picks up the top one, leather-bound, entitled *Baghdad's Golden Age*. The pages are largely stuck together, perhaps from the last spring rain, long forgotten. The weathered frontis-piece shows a style of Arabic script from early in the century, perhaps the Ottoman days or the British occupation. It doesn't have the monumental look of the Saddam Hussein era.

Putting the bill in his billfold he lights up, beckoning to the cab driver to wait. He reads.

This book is dedicated to the memory of the glorious and wise Caliph Abu Jafar Abdullah al-Mamun of the Abbasid House, born in the Muslim year 164 A.H., (A.D. 786) and dead 47 years later.

Al-Mamun, inheritor of the Muslim caliphate that stretched from North Africa to Arabia and Persia, Afghanistan and North India, grandson of Caliph al-Mansur who chose a small trading city on the Tigris to be his capital, and son of Caliph Haroun al-Rashid who made Baghdad the capital of the world.

Under the leadership of al-Mamun, Baghdad rose to become the center of world learning and the heart of the Arab Golden Age. His House of Wisdom, where Christian and foreign translators rendered the Greek, Roman, Byzantine, Persian, and Hindu classics into Arabic, helped lay the foundations of modern mathematics, astronomy, chemistry, medicine, and literature. As a result of his patronage and vision, in this city were born algebra and advanced trigonometry, the names of the stars, the mixtures of tinctures and remedies, the heart of philosophy and literature. It was here that Scheherazade told her tales of The Thousand and One Nights.

From this day until the 13th-century arrival of the Mongols, the wealth and learning of Baghdad were unequaled. Palaces of alabaster, gardens of palm and jasmine, avenues of stone, and the greatest market in Asia flourished here.

O Iraqi mortals, remember the greatness of your countryman Abu Jafar Abdullah al-Mamun, and dedicate yourselves to his ideals.

The Historical Society of Baghdad, May 3, 1915.

Ali's first reaction is to laugh. What pomposity is this? Wasn't this more typical of Saddam's time, inflating Iraqi history into something grandiose, always and inevitably reflecting back to Saddam's own greatness? Sure, Ali had heard of al-Mamun in his elementary school days. But the schools of that day hadn't explained the details of his achievements. No, the textbook hero was as dead and cold as this statue.

For a few seconds, Ali lets the image of alabaster palaces, of lush gardens form in his mind, a scene indefinably richer than the vulgar public works of Saddam Hussein, more elegant, sweeter.

Was that our past? he thinks, his eye sweeping across the endless concrete warrens of Baghdad, the far distance punctuated by occasional gunfire, black smoke on the southern horizon marking a distant fire of unintended or terrorist origin. All accompanied by the drone of the American Black Hawk helicopters shuttling their human cargo from the International Airport to the Green Zone.

Was the past greater than the present? What a rude trick of God. So much for the century of progress.

The taxi driver is blowing his horn. Traffic is getting worse. They'll get stuck for hours at the new checkpoint on Rashid Street if they don't leave now. The newspaper and wind and dust whirl around the statue. Ali grinds out his first smoke and runs back down to the cab, ready for work.

This morning he will be working on the plans for the fallen al-Fatah Bridge north of Baghdad. Because of bad decisions by the American prime contractor, this project is years behind schedule and tens of millions of dollars over budget. If it is ever finished, it will be the finest bridge in Iraq and much better than the roads on either side of it. No matter. Ali is being paid well.

Baghdad: the center of the world, he laughs to himself—only in your dreams, only in your dreams.

BAGHDAD, A.D. 813—Under the stars of Baghdad, Caliph al-Mamun tosses and turns most of the night and then fitfully dreams in those last short moments before dawn. He dreams that a figure of light and gold, dressed in the tunic of Greece and smelling of olive oil, comes and stands before him.

'Who are you?' the frightened caliph asks.
'I am Aristotle,' the spirit says.

'And why have you come to me?' asks the caliph, his heart pounding to be in the presence of such a great thinker, someone he has read of since childhood and been told about by the growing circle of his foreign advisers and viziers and wise men, men from Persia and Byzantium and Syria.

'I have come to answer your question,' says Aristotle.

'And what is my question?' the caliph asks, knowing in his heart but wanting to hear the spirit say it.

'Your question is, What is better for the affairs of man and the affairs of society, reason or revelation? What is the righteous way, the best way between these two?'

And the caliph nods, knowing this is the question that has been troubling him for years, growing larger day by day until it seems to be the paramount question of human existence in this new world.

'And what is your answer to this riddle?' asks the caliph. 'Which is more righteous?'

And Aristotle smiles and places his golden hand on the forearm of the caliph.

'My son,' he says, 'they are not in opposition. But to find true revelation, man must first choose reason, because reason is the doorway to revelation. Man must open his mind and use his intellect to find higher truth. In this way, God shows himself to man through ideas.'

And the caliph is both struck speechless and filled with euphoria to hear the wisdom and truth of this. This is what he has believed in his heart of hearts, but has been forced by those who are opposed to reason to consider their alternative view.

'Are you certain?' the caliph asks. 'For there are many claiming to be holy and righteous who say true revelation comes not from the corrupted human mind but from the pure divine heart.'

Aristotle smiles and shakes his head.

'Such men have always been with us,' the philosopher says. 'Be gentle with them, try to reassure them. Try to not have them fear their minds and ideas, which are sacred gifts of God and reflections of his divine mind. Turn all your resources to translating the great works of thought and knowledge into Arabic, whether they be writ in Greek or Latin or Persian or Sanskrit or any other tongue. Knowledge has no borders,

wisdom has no race or nationality. To block out ideas is to block out the kingdom of God.'

The caliph is nodding; he believes this to be true. And before he can say good-bye, Aristotle is disappearing into the glow of dawn, leaving behind nothing but the immediacy of the memory.

Caliph Abu Jafar Abdullah al-Mamun awakens bolt upright from his strange and prophetic dream. Not accustomed to extended periods of inaction or reflection, he takes a few moments before his day of endless action to think and let this dream clarify itself in his mind.

Outside his walls and below his latticed balcony are the sounds of horses and camels, and the low rush of conversation broken by an occasional word, not all in tongues that he knows. He is used to this river of words; the babble hardly enters his consciousness.

He can hear the same from within, behind the curtain that covers the entrance to his sleeping room and in the courtyard. The palace workers are up, some of his wives are stirring, he can hear the cry of his newest child.

He is past 40 years of age, an age that, were he a common man, would mean he was lucky to still be alive. Although he has risked his life in battle again and again, even defeating his own brother to gain the throne of caliph, he has been spared the terrible draining of the laborer's life. He has avoided the destiny of the poor man in the field or on the desert, and so like a lucky few he has lived longer than others. He does not feel old.

He can hear the muezzin call from the minaret of the Abu Hanifa mosque commissioned by his father Haroun al-Rashid, the domed mosque visible through the rising dawn. He unconsciously starts to follow the ritual. But no one but God can see him on his balcony, and his thoughts are more pressing, and so he lets his mind wander away from the memorized prayers. He thanks God for his dream.

This man is the ruler of an empire that has not yet found itself. More than anything else, this man is the ruler of imagination. Because his mind is hungry to know more and more, he is not burdened by the idea of failure or impossibility. He has not learned to avoid overreaching. He believes that the old world of prehistory has been swept away and, rather than barriers and obstacles, the only limits are the ones in his mind and in those set by his enemies.

His city is Baghdad, and he will make it the center of the world. His empire is the Abbasid caliphate, and it will be like no other. The caliphate will be fueled by an assimilation of the intellectual and artistic accomplishments of older societies that have fallen into the Arab fold, all of them adapted to the tenets of Islam. Together, the conquerors and the conquered will reach even higher.

Baghdad, what is it? It is the political capital of Islam, a role its leaders have only recently wrested from Damascus. Not far from the forgotten ruins of Babylon and the marshy Garden of Eden of ancient Mesopotamia and close to the old cities of Persia, Baghdad is an ancient town of river traders and fishermen. But al-Mamun is making it into more.

The Prophet is now dead 200 years, and his words once committed to memory are written down for all to see. In what he believes to be the intent of the Prophet, al-Mamun is carrying the project of Muslim nation-building to its conclusion: extending this faith into a whole new way of thinking and creating.

Even as Rome has fallen and is mourned for more than 350 years, even as Byzantium is tested on all sides to preserve the religion and ways of Rome, even as Persia looks back to its days of greatness, al-Mamun wants Baghdad to be the city of the future. He sees himself as the successor to the caesars, to the Persian kings, and to Alexander the Great. But he has something that they never had. Although he is not a descendant of the glittering courts of the old empires, he sees himself as the Defender of the Faith.

What is the faith? To al-Mamun and many others right now, more than anything else, it is a thirst. It is a desperate desire to swallow all knowledge and tradition, to include everything within the structure of the faith. It is a willingness to absorb peoples, histories, secrets, and behaviors, and let them flourish there. Just as the faith holds that everything around is an expression of God, so is the caliphate a drive to bring everything in, not to exclude.

An ocean of people is being taken in, and some people do not adopt the faith but adopt the life. There are Persians and Egyptians, Berbers and Visigoths, Jews and Christians, Hindus and Buddhists, Kurds and Azeris, Turks and Uzbeks, and Kazakhs and Pashtuns, all coming under the sway of the caliph.

They feel the energy, they see the flow, they want to be a part. Or they acquiesce. Many of them begin to adopt the tongue of the Arabs, learn its calligraphy, and mimic its sounds. Though the Persians do not sacrifice their own language, now they write it in the script of the Arabs.

The Muslims must find a way to rise above the flood they have swallowed. What are they, who are they? Al-Mamun will chart the path. Whether his dream of Aristotle is divinely inspired or invented by the needs of his political situation, it will one day be used in political discourse to support the policies of his political camp.

His political situation is this: Not only must al-Mamun use the administrative and intellectual skills of the Persians, he must prevent them from taking too much. Already some of the old Persian elite are trying to mount a quiet undermining of Islamic legitimacy by resuscitating the ways of the Persian gnostic religions—Zoroastrianism, Mazdaism, and Manichaeism.

Simultaneously, some Muslim traditionalists and common people are growing uneasy with Abbasid dynastic rule and with the increasingly imperial style of the caliphate. They fear it is departing from the intent of the Prophet.

Rather than let a group of Persian aristocrats and Muslim conservatives set the course, al-Mamun will decide what is best, for the faith and for the people.

To provide intellectual justification for his dynasty and his method, al-Mamun has aligned himself with a group of diverse religious thinkers called the Mutazilites. Though they will someday be called heretics and will be suppressed by the traditionalists, in these early years of improvisation, the Mutazilites backed by the caliph are dominant.

Al-Mamun is partial to the Mutazilites both because their theology supports the kind of state and faith he wants to build and because they have been his personal teachers and tutors.

This is their radical outlook: They believe that the Qur'an is created, not His eternal Word. And they believe that reason is the highest expression of God.

The Mutazilites, with the caliph as their patron and champion, believe that reason is the key to wisdom and God. This is the result both of indigenous strands of Islamic thought, as well as elements of Greek philosophy. Greek-Hellenic knowledge comes into ninth-century Islam from three sources: The Persian aristocracy who play an important role as administrators in the Abbasid period; Christian physicians and theologians, who pursue

Greek logic; and the pagan Sabians of Harran in northern Iraq, an ancient Semitic group whose astral religion connects them to Hellenistic astrology, astronomy, and Hermeticism.

Via Persia and Byzantium as well as Syria and Iraq, the outlines of the ideas of Aristotle and Plato and Socrates, of Euclid and Pythagoras, are slowly making their way into Arabic from Latin, Greek, Syriac, and Persian.

In this turbulent and exciting time, the deep intricacies of early Muslim intellectual and theological debate will too often be lost to history. Foreign scholars writing centuries later will oversimplify the political-religious flowering into a battle between the "orthodox" and the "rationalists," when in fact there is no orthodox Islam—there is no guiding patriarch as in Christianity—and the early Muslim rationalists are theologians, not secular philosophers. Foreign scholars will also perpetuate the misperception that Islamic rationalism comes exclusively from Greek sources, and that misperception will continue into the 21st century.

In fact, the native roots of Islamic intellectualism and rationalism can be traced to the writings of Muslim thinkers as early as the sixth and seventh centuries, long before Greek influences arrive. The concepts of *ilm* (knowledge) and *aql* (reason, human intelligence, wisdom) occur frequently in the Qur'an as well as in early Muslim writings.

In the eighth and ninth centuries, Islam dynamically evolves and assimilates a multitude of cosmological, philosophical, and ethnic influences, bringing countless new perspectives into its fold. This cultural shock wave rapidly diversifies Islamic culture and thought into a rich mosaic of ideas. It will not be until the tenth century that this diversity will settle down into the more familiar Shiite and Sunni schools that will survive into modern times.

At the time when al-Mamun's caliphate begins, there are at least several dozen trends and schools of thought. And all of these schools overlap in some way and cross-fertilize each other. They include the traditionalists (some of whom will later be defined as the Sunnis), the Shiites (some of whose ideas influence Abbasid ideology), the *fuqaha* (a rising class of erudite legal scholars on Islamic law), and the *mutakallimun*. The latter are theological scholars who turn to ancient philosophy to articulate and strengthen their ideas. Among those who are attracted by the rigor of Greek logic, the most famous, perhaps, are the Mutazilites. Each of these diverse groups has its own vision for the political, theological, and intellectual development of the state.

Even as al-Mamun promotes his own vision shared by the Mutazilites, the conservative and traditionalist approach to Islam and society is also gaining support, led by certain legal and religious scholars and backed by segments of popular opinion, particularly in Baghdad. But al-Mamun cannot imagine how their way will lead to greatness. Imagine this: Some of the conservatives are beginning to shape an Islamic ideal in which the caliph does not inherit or seize power, but is elected by the faithful. And this kind of elected caliph will be expected to re-create the kind of society that they believe the Prophet really intended.

Ironically, the rationalist Mutazilites have become intellectual allies of the dynastic and imperial Abbasid caliphate, while the conservatives envision something closer to early Islamic democracy.

Al-Mamun finds this dissension threatening, not only to him and his reign but to his vision of the rationalist, elite-driven caliphate that he has instituted. To combat the creeping influence of the traditionalists, he orders a sort of high-level inquisition called the *mihna,* not as broad and harsh as the one that Catholic Spain will institute, but more focused on weeding out the anti-Mutazilites in the clergy, in the political elite of the empire. All of the leadership must undergo an interrogation of their beliefs. If they do not support al-Mamun's version of rationalism, with absolute political-religious power vested in the caliph, they must either change their beliefs or suffer.

One traditionalist group in early Baghdad is the Hanafite school, who argue that human reason plays a crucial role in the development of a legal system for the state. By the 21st century their school of thought will be considered to espouse a more liberal legal interpretation of Islam. In that far future, some people claiming to follow the Hanafite school will even allow consumption of vodka and beer.

Another group in the growing traditionalist movement is a school of jurisprudence led by a determined and austere intellectual named Ahmad ibn Hanbal. Born in Central Asia of Arab parents, ibn Hanbal has traveled throughout Arabia reconstructing the life and thoughts of the Prophet. The antithesis of al-Mamun, ibn Hanbal has no imperial dreams; he is not a politician. Although he believes the Abbasid caliphs are entitled to political power, he is concerned, as are many others, about their increasing involvement in religious affairs. Ibn Hanbal teaches that while a caliph has secular authority to rule the state, his powers in matters of faith need to be curtailed, and that in spiritual matters the voice of the people, of consensus *(ijma),* matters more. Ibn Hanbal wants the caliph's influence to be restricted to the secular domain.

This puts him on a collision course with al-Mamun, who is vying for both secular and religious control of the state. To achieve total control, al-Mamun must eliminate popular scholars like ibn Hanbal.

The message of ibn Hanbal appeals to some in Baghdad, perhaps more than the imperial elitism of al-Mamun. Al-Mamun is aware of this fact. That ibn Hanbal has a following gives him concern, not because he believes there is some innate wisdom in the people that should be honored, but because it is an obstacle to the realization of his own vision of the faith and of society. This appeal is an obstacle to creating a civilization of centralized politico-religious power, of thought and of beauty, of wealth and excellence that will once and for all show the world that the Muslim caliphate is the equal of or even greater than fallen Rome and ancient Persia, or diminished Byzantium.

Like most rulers then and now, al-Mamun will not know how to handle an opponent like ibn Hanbal. He will have him interrogated and imprisoned by the rationalist mihna. Ibn Hanbal will even be tortured in the hopes that he will renounce his own traditionalist vision of Islam. And through all this ibn Hanbal will conduct himself with dignity, dutifully accepting his imprisonment and torture, but refusing to join the Mutazilites. Such persecution will continue into the reign of al-Mamun's successor, al-Mutasim. But this campaign of forced loyalty to Muslim rationalism will ultimately fail, and one day ibn Hanbal will outlive his tormentors and be honored by some as a hero.

Al-Mamun cannot know all this in 830. His dream of Aristotle and his dream of what the Abbasid caliphate could be are fresh in his mind. Even as he is putting pressure on the dissidents and traditionalists, he sees another move he must make. He must institutionalize rationalism by creating a center of learning and free enquiry and invention. It must be the best in the world.

After a decade of living and ruling from faraway Merv, then still part of Persia, while his power in Baghdad was being consolidated, al-Mamun has seen up close the model for what he wants. Although the classical ideas of Greece and Rome and India and China will be his ultimate goal, he will follow the lead of the Persians and Byzantines in bringing those ideas into the mainstream.

And he has no discomfort at all about adopting the model of the Persians. His mother was a Persian slave woman in the harem of Haroun al-Rashid. Persia is the source of half his strength. Although al-Mamun was the oldest heir to Haroun al-Rashid, the caliph's throne had been willed to al-Mamun's half-brother, al-Amin, because his mother was of royal birth. First sent to administer Persia from Merv on behalf of his father and brother, al-Mamun has risen up, and after a fierce civil war has ordered al-Amin beheaded, and has taken the caliphate for himself. It will be ten years after the overthrow of his brother before he will feel safe enough to leave his base in Persia and come to Baghdad to rule from there.

For ten years, Merv, the old oasis city on the edge of the Garagum Desert, a stopover on the Silk Road, has been the de facto Abbasid capital of the Muslim world and al-Mamun's home. The town has been a crossing place of just about every conqueror and religion ever to arise in Eurasia. Alexander's Greeks, Zoroastrians, Christians, Buddhists, Jews, and members of obscure sects and beliefs have passed through Merv long before the Muslims. Al-Mamun has eagerly drunk in the lessons of this place on the steppe. And once back in Baghdad after many years of absence, he has made up for lost time.

Al-Mamun knows that the wariness some Arabs feel of Persia is really a mix of envy and fear: envy of the sophistication and learning, fear of the Persian military and economic power that has risen again and again to challenge them over the centuries, and can rise again.

The model for al-Mamun and his new center of rationalist learning will be the Persian Academy of Gundeshapur in present-day Khuzestan province, established three centuries before by imperial directive to translate Greco-Roman-Byzantine and far-eastern knowledge into the Pahlavi (Persian) tongue and to build on the thoughts of foreign thinkers and philosophers. The Persian academy has been enriched by the entry of exiled, so-called heretics: Nestorian Christian and Syriac scholars and translators from Byzantium. Persians seem not so afraid of heretics; in fact, at times they embrace them. At Gundeshapur, the Persians created a center of invention.

They may well have built the world's first teaching hospital and an excellent university and library.

Using this polyglot, cosmopolitan model, as well as many graduates and staff from Gundeshapur, al-Mamun will build its successor in Baghdad. As the caliph is, in a way, the personification of what the Muslim world has become in his time through the absorption of all sorts of cultures and thoughts, al-Mamun is not afraid of new and radical ideas. He is not afraid of contradiction or mysteries.

But he is afraid of ignorant anti-intellectualism. He believes that if the most gifted men are not allowed to think freely, they cannot create or invent, and so they cannot fulfill the will of God. All of humanity will suffer the consequences.

This is a man who loves learning so much that when he overwhelmingly defeats the Byzantine emperor in battle, as tribute he asks not for caskets of gold but a copy of the *Almagest,* Ptolemy's Hellenistic compendium of thoughts on astronomy written around A.D. 150.

Even in areas of sectarianism, al-Mamun does not fit into a box. Though the Shiite-Sunni split is not as solidified as it will become in later years, al-Mamun has no problem floating between the two, even in aligning himself against Sunni traditionalism with the Shiites and claiming to be the leader of the Shiites. His first designated heir to be successor caliph is the Shiite imam Ali al-Rida, but when the Iraqis rebel, he abandons that plan.

That is the unending and often unwinnable soup of religious politics, and he has more immediate things to do. Just a few moments past dawn on the morning of the dream, al-Mamun calls in his vizier, a Persian.

"Faithful Tahir," he says. "I want to build a great center of learning here in Baghdad to support free inquiry, philosophy, science, mathematics, astronomy. Send out emissaries to find for me all the greatest books held by the Byzantines and Persians. Go to Gundeshapur, and find me the best in all those disciplines, and bring them here to build my center. And bring me the best translators, to translate into Arabic all that has come before. I will call it the House of Wisdom," he adds, and Tahir bows and takes his leave.

The order goes forth. And to the new center is drawn a dazzling array of thinkers. They will include Mohamed al-Khwarizmi, possibly a converted Zoroastrian Persian later considered the father of algebra and the namesake of the algorithm; the Banu Musa brothers, young sons of al-Mamun's astrologer left to the caliph to educate at the House of Wisdom, who will later become mathematicians, astronomers, and engineer-inventors; Hunayn ibn Ishaq, a Nestorian physician remembered as the most influential of the early translators, who would bring the writing of second-century physician Galen and Greek philosophy into Arabic; and al-Kindi, probably the most accomplished of Arab philosophers, who is later to say:

We ought not to be embarrassed about appreciating the truth and obtaining it wherever it comes from, even if it comes from races distant and nations different from us. Nothing should be dearer to the seeker of truth than the truth itself, and there is no deterioration of the truth, nor belittling either of one who speaks it or conveys it.

With the House of Wisdom in the ninth and tenth centuries, Abbasid Baghdad will reach the pinnacle of its intellectual influence, filling out the dream of al-Mansur and Haroun al-Rashid to make it the true center of the world in every way. Out of his predawn dream and his love of intellect, al-Mamun will also lay the foundation for other great discoveries. On the plains of Iraq will rise not one but two stellar observatories, challenging his astronomers not only to read the hidden message of space but to better map and document it. For his astronomical support, the world will later name one of the craters of the moon for him, al-Mamun.

And now with a center of learning to augment the political capital and trading capital and military capital that is Baghdad, the spires of its minarets and the palaces of its merchants and nobles, the roads of its conquest and the walls and gates of its battlements rise ever higher. Even as the enemies of rationalism and intellectual elitism arise among the clergy and the people, from afar and above, the Baghdad of al-Mamun will shine ever brighter.

As the dawn slides into morning, al-Mamun rides out with bodyguards to find the place for his House of Wisdom. Listen to how an Arab visitor in the time of al-Mamun describes what he sees, as recorded by Ahmad al-Ya'qubi, a ninth-century geographer, in his *Kitab al-buldan:*

I begin with Iraq only because it is the center of this world, the navel of the earth, and I mention Baghdad first because it is the center of

Iraq, the greatest city, which has no peer in the east or the west of the world in extent, size, prosperity, abundance of water, or health of climate, and because it is inhabited by all kinds of people, town-dwellers and country-dwellers. To it they come from all countries, far and near, and people from every side have preferred Baghdad to their own homeland.

There is none more learned than their scholars, better informed than their traditionalists, more cogent than their theologians ... more poetic than their poets, and more reckless than their rakes.

The last line is telling. Although Baghdad is the capital of the Muslim Abbasid caliphate, it is also home to increasingly decadent lifestyles of a wealthy, imperial elite. Taverns are open to the masses, and private parties pleasure the wealthy and powerful. Much wine is consumed, sexual escapades go on in veiled chambers, and parties in private homes and palaces are just as lavish and decadent as those in ancient Rome and Byzantium.

But all that is generally hidden from view, though al-Mamun is well aware of it. What does al-Mamun see as he rides through his city? Around him he sees the caliphal enclave founded and built by his ancestor al-Mansur and father Haroun al-Rashid on the site of a 12th-century B.C. Babylonian river town called Bak-da-du. The Babylonian ruins are buried beneath him here, on the west bank of the river Tigris, between Kadhumain in the north and Shaljia in the south. But in this more recent construction, Babylon still echoes, because al-Mamun's Abbasid ancestors have adopted the classic layout of the Babylonians, the circle. The royal enclave is now called the Round City, with an encircling outer wall and two inner walls protecting the royal core. The early Abbasids imagine that this layout is more easily defended against attackers.

Four immense gates named for each of the districts of the Abbasid Empire—Basra, Kufa, Syria, and Khorasan—breach the outer wall, and replicas of the four outer gates open through two more inner-circle walls, which open onto four main avenues that converge at a vast open circular expanse at the center, about a mile in diameter. Within this central space are the caliph's palace known as the Golden Gate and the grand Green Mosque. The palace is a marvel in itself, with a huge green dome topped by a horseman's figure, which turns as the wind changes direction.

But over time, al-Mamun and many of his countrymen have found this round fortress-city to be confining, so a major exodus has begun to the newer town at al-Rasafa on the eastern bank of the Tigris, where al-Mansur's son, al-Mahdi, had built a mosque even bigger than the one in the walled city. This new city is connected to the west bank by a pontoon bridge. This and other Tigris pontoon bridges can be removed to allow oceangoing ships passage and, when in position, they serve as obstacles to attackers coming upriver.

Connected by a series of canals to the ocean at Basra, Baghdad the river city is also becoming a global seaport, its importance pulling in a seagoing commerce that reaches as far as India, China, Africa, and southern Europe. And in this metropolis of two merging towns—Baghdad and al-Rasafa—al-Mamun sees all sorts of progress that is unique to this imperial capital on the Tigris.

He sees the paper mills using technology brought from China a few decades before, where papermaking was an elite art form reserved for the Chinese literary class; now the Muslims have taken the technology and achieved a level of mass production not possible with the parchment or vellum used in Europe, spawning a public literacy that in turn enables the spread of culture-defining epics such as the tales of *The Thousand and One Nights*.

He sees the first major public and private libraries since the time of Rome and Alexandria, including one so large in the ownership of a rich merchant that, one source says, it would have taken 140 camels to move it from one place to another; and another library belonging to a court scholar who reportedly refuses to move to take a better job elsewhere because the catalog of his holdings alone is 10 volumes, and he would need 400 camels to move the books.

Al-Mamun sees the various Houses of Stories, public storytelling centers subdivided into those that tell edifying moralistic tales and those that tell "night stories," or rather popular dramas to entertain at night. He sees the first madrassas, literally "schools" that will evolve into the first universities, providing a model of higher education that will find expression in late medieval Europe.

And amongst all this, he sees where he will place his House of Wisdom, his ultimate institution, which can be the foundation for a society based on reason and invention, for a world empire of faith filtered through the lens of reason. His scientific center will contain an observatory, a hospital, a library, and research programs in rhetoric and logic, metaphysics and theology, algebra, trigonometry, geometry, physics, biology, medicine, and pharmacology.

As his House of Wisdom rises, these subjects and other academic research will not be pursued by specialists operating in separate compartments of knowledge. No. Many of the men excelling in theology will also contribute to translation and mathematics and medicine and more. In these early times, the scholars see all these studies and phenomena as mosaic windows into a much larger connected reality, which is God's universe. More importantly, these men do not see it as their purpose to force their scientific research to fit a preconceived notion of the universe dictated by theology. Instead, they see that their mission is to try to understand the complexity of creation, as hard or even as impossible as it might be to do. And this mission spawns unending scientific debate and discussion. These men are not afraid.

Over the next four centuries in Baghdad, building on the tradition of al-Mamun and his forebears, new institutions will arise to supplement the House of Wisdom, even to replace it. The first major urban hospital anywhere will go up in the tenth century. Two madrassas are established. They will grow into global universities, the 11th-century Nizamiya and the 13th-century Mustansiriyah Colleges. Mustansiriyah will offer free tuition, medical care, and room and board. Observatories will spring up at Shammasiyah, associated with the House of Wisdom, and in the private homes of freelance astronomers like al-Hasan and the Banu Musa brothers. By the 13th century Baghdad will have 36 public libraries and 100 booksellers.

As early at the 900s, Baghdad will be perhaps the most sophisticated and modern city on Earth. Tenth-century historian Yakut describes it this way:

The city of Baghdad formed two vast semi-circles on the right and left banks of the Tigris, twelve miles in diameter. The numerous suburbs, covered with parks, gardens, villas, and beautiful promenades, and plentifully supplied with rich bazaars, and finely built mosques and baths, stretched for a considerable distance on both sides of the river. In the days of its prosperity the population of Baghdad and its suburbs amounted to over two millions! The palace of the Caliph stood in the midst of a vast park several hours in circumference, which beside a menagerie and aviary comprised an enclosure for wild animals reserved for the chase. The palace grounds were laid out with gardens and adorned with exquisite taste with plants, flowers, and trees, reservoirs and fountains, surrounded by sculptured figures. On this side of the river stood the palaces of the great nobles. Immense streets, none less than forty cubits wide, traversed the city from one end to the other, dividing it into blocks or quarters, each under the control of an overseer or supervisor, who looked after the cleanliness, sanitation and the comfort of the inhabitants.

The water exits both on the north and the south were like the city gates, guarded night and day by relays of soldiers stationed on the watchtowers on both sides of the river. Every household was plentifully supplied with water at all seasons by the numerous aqueducts which intersected the town; and the streets, gardens and parks were regularly swept and watered, and no refuse was allowed to remain within the walls. An immense square in front of the imperial palace was used for reviews, military inspections, tournaments and races; at night the square and the streets were lighted by lamps.

There was also a vast open space where the troops whose barracks lay on the left bank of the river were paraded daily. The long wide estrades at the different gates of the city were used by the citizens for gossip and recreation or for watching the flow of travelers and country folk into the capital. The different nationalities in the capital had each a head officer to represent their interests with the government and to whom the stranger could appeal for counsel or help.

Baghdad was a veritable City of Palaces, not made of stucco and mortar, but of marble. The buildings were usually of several stories. The palaces and mansions were lavishly gilded and decorated and hung with beautiful tapestry and hangings of brocade or silk. The rooms were lightly and tastefully furnished with luxurious divans, costly tables, unique Chinese vases and gold and silver ornaments.

Both sides of the river were for miles fronted by the palaces, kiosks, gardens and parks of the grandees and nobles, marble steps led down to the water's edge, and the scene on the river was animated by thousands of gondolas, decked with little flags, dancing like sunbeams on *the water, and carrying the pleasure-seeking Baghdad citizens from one part of the city to the other. Along the wide-stretching quays lay whole fleets at anchor, sea and river craft of all kinds, from the Chinese junk to the old Assyrian raft resting on inflated skins.*

One of the most important flowerings of the city will come in the area of literature. Aside from Scheherazade's tales of *The Thousand and One Nights,* which are heavily drawn from older Persian and Hindu stories, Baghdad will also grow into the world capital of poetry. This will result not only from the city's wealth, diversity, and inventiveness; it will also come from the fusion of two of the world's most poetic cultures and languages, Arabic and Persian. Both have already long held poetry to be the highest form of literary communication, and in Baghdad poetry will fill the role that journalism and fiction will take up 1,300 years later. The leading poets of Baghdad will include Bashshar ibn Burd, an eroticist drawing on the sensual traditions of pre-Islamic Arabia and Persia; ibn Iyas and Abu Nuwas, who troll the dark side of Baghdad, living lives and writing poems drenched in sex and drinking with a touch of blasphemy thrown in; ibn Walid, poet of love and drinking songs; and ibn Ahnaf and ibn Dawud, who rise above the erotic and titillating to write of an exalted kind of romantic love, which experts see as the predecessor to later courtly love and songs of the troubadours.

As ibn Ahnaf writes:

When I visit you, and the moon
Isn't around to show me the way,
Comets of longing set my heart
So much ablaze, the earth is lit
By the holocaust under my ribs.

The literary disputes of Baghdad—sometimes involving a tension between the Persian-leaning camp and the devotees of classical Arabic, sometimes a deeper debate over God and society—will often break out into open warfare. Poet-aristocrat ibn Mutazz will even rise to be caliph several generations after al-Mamun, but will only survive in the job one day until an assassin takes his life.

On and on will go this concentric circle of thought and imagination, as though it could never end. But as with all organisms, even one so huge as a civilization seen from above and afar, the Abbasid world will carry within it the seeds of its own destruction. At the level of thought and faith, al-Mamun's hunger for pure knowledge will embolden his enemies over time. On issues of faith, al-Mamun already senses that trend in his growing rivalry with ibn Hanbal and all the other dissidents and traditionalists, even though he now has the upper hand. In another few decades, his successor, Caliph al-Mutawakkil, will adopt the traditionalist view and overthrow the Mutazilites so that ibn Hanbal will die a hero to some, his funeral attended by thousands. In politics, al-Mamun's love of and dependence on Persia will plant future seeds of revolt, when he grants effective control of huge parts of Persia to the Tahirids, the family of his former general and vizier Tahir to assure their loyalty. His successors will replicate this process until the caliphs become shadows and puppets, with the real power shifting to the provinces.

Al-Mamun will no more be able to institutionalize his fervent belief in rationalism than he will be able to stave off death. The latter happens during his final battle against the Byzantines. This is the narration of his death as told by Abul Hasan Ali al-Masu'di:

During Al Mamoun's last campaign against the Greek Emperor he arrived at the River Qushairah, and encamped on its banks....

All at once a fish, about a fathom in length and flashing like an ingot of silver, appeared in the water. The Caliph promised a reward to any one who would capture it; an attendant went down, caught the fish and regained the shore, but as he approached the spot where Al Mamoun was sitting, the fish slipped from his grasp, fell into the water, and sank like a stone to the bottom. Some of the water was splashed on the Caliph's neck, chest, and arms, and wetted his clothes. The attendant went down again, recaptured the fish, and placed it, wriggling, in a napkin before the Caliph. Just as he had ordered it to be fried, Al Mamoun felt a sudden shiver, and could not move from the place. In vain he was covered with rugs and skins; he trembled like a leaf, and exclaimed: 'I am cold! I am cold!' He was carried into his tent, covered with clothes, and a fire was lit, but he continued to complain of cold.

When the fish had been cooked it was brought to him, but he could neither taste nor touch it, so great was his suffering.

As he grew rapidly worse, his brother Mutasim questioned Bakhteshou and Ibn Masouyieh, his physicians, on his condition, and whether they could do him any good. Ibn Masouyieh took one of the patient's hands and Bakhteshou the other, and felt his pulse together; the irregular pulsations heralded his dissolution. Just then Al Mamoun awoke out of his stupor; he opened his eyes, and caused some of the natives of the place to be sent for, and questioned them regarding the stream and the locality. When asked regarding the meaning of the name 'Qushairah,' they replied that it signified 'Stretch out thy feet' [i.e., 'die']. Al Mamoun then inquired the Arabic name of the country, and was told 'Rakkah.' Now, the horoscope drawn at the moment of his birth announced that he would die in a place of that name; therefore he had always avoided residing in the city of Rakkah, fearing to die there. When he heard the answer given by these people, he felt sure that this was the place predicted by his horoscope.

Feeling himself becoming worse, he commanded that he should be carried outside his tent in order to survey his camp and his army once more. It was now nighttime. As his gaze wandered over the long lines of the camp and the lights twinkling into the distance, he cried: 'O thou whose reign will never end, have mercy on him whose reign is now ending.' He was then carried back to his bed. Mutasim, seeing that he was sinking, commanded some one to whisper in his ear the confession of the faith. As the attendant was about to speak, in order that Al Mamoun might repeat the words after him, Ibn Masouyieh said to him: 'Do not speak, for truly he could not now distinguish between God and Manes.' The dying man opened his eyes—they seemed extraordinarily large, and shone with a wonderful luster; his hands clutched at the doctor; he tried to speak to him, but could not; then his eyes turned toward heaven and filled with tears; finally his tongue was loosened, and he spoke: 'O thou who diest not, have mercy on him who dies,' and he expired immediately. His body was carried to Tarsus and buried there.

Though al-Mamun is gone, the golden age of Baghdad has now begun in earnest. From beginning to end it will last 500 years.

QURTUBA, UMAYYAD EMIRATE (Cordoba, Spain), A.D. 756—A young prince seared with the memory of the night of murder in Damascus now stands victorious on a mountaintop overlooking the old Roman city of Khordoba—renamed Qurtuba by the Arabs—2,300 miles from home.

After that night in 750, listening to his entire family and extended household being slaughtered, Abd al-Rahman had slipped away almost penniless, accompanied only by his brother, Yahya, and servant, Badr. As their world disintegrated behind them, these three survivors had journeyed to Palestine, then Egypt, wondering what the next step would be.

As the victorious Abbasids were scorning Umayyad Damascus and moving their capital to Baghdad, this youth disinherited by murder had to find a way to survive in a brutal new world.

He could not be confident in even revealing who he was, for the black Abbasid flag was replacing the Umayyad white one at every stop. The new Caliph al-Mansur had his agents and supporters everywhere, and the supporters of the fallen Umayyads, if there were any, remained in the shadows. In Palestine, Abbasid assassins had finally tracked them down and killed Yahya. Abd al-Rahman and Badr had fled the killers and then traveled on alone.

Those few who knew who he was and sympathized had warned him to let go of the past, to change his identity, settle in a faraway place, find work as a soldier or teacher or merchant. They took note of the value of his bearing and his speech, which were marks of a good life and a fine education given as only the court could provide. In a faraway place more removed from the intrigues of Syria and Iraq, perhaps he could attach himself to a man of society or remake himself as one of the conquerors extending the faith.

The prince had listened to all this, but he was young and confident and still traumatized, driven by the memory of that night, determined to answer it in his own way. More than anything, he was driven by the long-ago prophecy of his great-uncle Maslama who had told him that one day, after a period of much suffering, young Abd al-Rahman would be the one to restore the glory of the Umayyads. With this old secret deep in his heart, like a shining light that pulled him onward and gave him the will to live, the prince and the servant continued on into the West

They decided that in the chaos of the change of dynasties, remote North Africa was most likely to provide them haven. There, the once loyal

Umayyad emirs had taken advantage of the chaos to carve out individual kingdoms. The emir in North Africa did not offer Abd al-Rahman safe haven and even attempted to kill him. But Abd al-Rahman was not dissuaded. Hearing reports of strife in Muslim al-Andalus, he sent his servant Badr across the Strait of Gibraltar on a reconnaissance mission. And Badr learned some interesting news from a group of disaffected Yemenis. The word was that al-Andalus, now governed by Emir Yusuf al-Fihri in alliance with a northern Arab tribe known as the Qaysites, could be ripe for a coup. The Yemenis, who had been dependable members of Tariq's invading force only four decades earlier, were now excluded from power in the land they helped subdue.

Abd al-Rahman finds 20 supporters, and they sail across the strait in 755. As they move north, more and more disaffected Andalusians defect to his side, and they already call him by the title of emir. Some of their motivations are honorable: desire to be loyal to this sole survivor of the overthrown caliphs, or dissatisfaction with the sitting emir. But in the case of the group of Yemenis, more of it comes from sheer greed, a desire to recapture the right to riches and plunder enjoyed in those early days after the conquest. Many Yemenis and others under the command of Tariq had been given lands in reward for their loyalty. Under Yusuf al-Fihri and the Qaysites, things had gone badly for the Yemenis. Their land-grant farms in northern Spain had failed, and some had wandered back to North Africa.

Against this backdrop, the sitting Emir al-Fihri is uneasy to have the sole surviving heir of the night of murder appear on his doorstep with a gang of surly Yemeni rebels, and he tries to preempt this threat with a generous offer. To the overthrown heir he offers his daughter's hand in marriage, plus an estate and safe haven. Tempting to anyone else who has survived the ordeal of the last five years, but Abd al-Rahman declines the offer.

His army grows until the following year, in 756, when he meets the emir in battle outside Qurtuba.

And against all odds, the ragtag army of the young but fearless Abd al-Rahman is victorious, creating the new Emir Abd al-Rahman I of al-Andalus and the restorer of Umayyad rule, at least in that faraway place. The 25-year-old emir does not even have a flag of his own to fly, so someone hoists a green turban on a lance.

His first task will be to rein in his opportunistic Yemeni allies, who embark now on a long-awaited campaign of revenge and pillage. Abd al-Rahman, who has a vision of himself as a just and fair ruler, can't allow this, and at the risk of losing their support, he stops their uprising.

That is only the first political challenge. If he so chooses, he can easily spend the next 30 years putting down uprisings and plots and rivals. In his first religious service at mosque, he will feel so weak that he pays lip service to the same Abbasid caliph in Baghdad who has murdered his whole family and driven him here. Closer to home, the overthrown al-Fihri will continue to stir discontent and vow to kill or expel the young ruler. And an Abbasid assassination force sent by Abd al-Rahman's enemies in Baghdad will make it to the very gates of Qurtuba in 763, where the new emir will decisively defeat them, chop off their leaders' heads, preserve them in camphor, and ship them back to the eastern caliph. After that, he will never again feel obliged to mention the name of the Abbasids at mosque. And in another 200 years, one of his descendants will feel powerful enough to declare himself the true Caliph of all Islam.

But now in 756, what to do? The royal house and the vision that nearly died out in Damascus are alive again, though precariously so, in this land so far away from home. And yet, this new land is not so alien. Something about once Roman Iberia echoes of once Roman Syria, more than the African and Levantine areas he has journeyed through. The lay of the cedars on the rocky hills, the quality of light, and the color of the soil all echo of home.

As though his just-completed, five-year campaign of survival and political redemption or his future task of surviving and maintaining power are not enough, Abd al-Rahman stakes out an even grander vision. Gazing down at this minor town founded by the Romans, used as an encampment by the warring Visigoths, and set up as the undistinguished capital of al-Fihri, Abd al-Rahman decides something else.

Here in the rocky hills and dry valleys of southern Spain, Abd al-Rahman will re-create his lost Damascus, as though that can bring back his beloved family. He will re-create the glory of the Umayyad city that had been suddenly stalled in its development and evolution, with its irrigation and its distinctive hybrid Romanesque architecture, its wide civic spaces, and its quasi-Roman villa-palaces. Moreover, he will not just re-create the former capital of Damascus, he will continue the full program of development that would have happened in Damascus and Syria and the entire caliphate had he become caliph there. He will build a competing center of learning and invention. In this raw Visigothic town, on this peninsula that has been a backwater, he will create a world city and a world civilization.

It is ironic, looking back and from far away, how these two warring families, the Umayyads and Abbasids, resemble each other more than they differ. While they might have disputes over the ethnic makeup of their courts or perhaps some fine points on dogma, or whether to follow a white flag in Damascus or a black one, in fact they are both committed to intellect and grandeur. They love ideas and invention, they are not worried about breaking the rules and testing the limits.

The first task for Abd al-Rahman, as it was for his forebear Muawiya in old Damascus, will be to build the infrastructure to support such a society. He will need roads and bridges, he will need mosques, he will need schools, and he will need water.

He will implant Damascene and Syrian ways into Spain. Syrian-born settlers will seed and nurture Syrian-style groves of olives and oranges and lemons, irrigating fields with machinery replicating those in Syria. Syrian hydraulics will move the water. The city of Ishbiliya, later known as Seville, will so much resemble Hims in Syria that Arab poets will call Seville "Hims al-Andalus." Later Andalusian travelers to the East will remark that of all the cities of the Muslim world, only the cities of Syria remind them of home.

In the capital, Abd al-Rahman will build a vast and magnificent garden called the al-Rusafah, and in this garden he will build a palace with echoes of home, called the Damascus Palace. In 786, he will begin building the Great Mosque of Cordoba, a construction effort that will last 62 years.

In a poem, the aging emir writes:

A palm tree stands in the middle of Rusafa
Born in the west, far from the land of palms.
I said to it: How like me you are, far away and in exile
In long separation from family and friends,
You have sprung from soil in which you are a stranger
And I, like you, am far from home.

But from that nostalgic and solitary beginning in 756, Abd al-Rahman's vision will be carried on by his descendants for the next three centuries, and the results will be astonishing. Just as he still looks east and into the past to find his inspiration, his successors will never know the old lost homeland directly, and al-Andalus will become their ancestral home. And inevitably over time, though its inspiration is Rome and Byzantium and Syria and Arabia, Umayyad al-Andalus will evolve into its own new form. Muslims will rule all or parts of Spain for nearly 800 years.

During the era of Muslim Spain, the power structure of al-Andalus will evolve from the Umayyad emirate (756-929), to the Umayyad caliphate (929-1031), to an extended period of city-states called *taifas,* of varying Muslim and Christian control.

Late in the reign of the Umayyad caliphs of Spain, the Great Mosque of Cordoba begun by Abd al-Rahman I will be enlarged and embellished, and a new royal retreat called Medina Azahara outside Cordoba will be built. At its peak in the 11th century, Cordoba will be the most advanced city in Europe with a population of half a million, boasting of some 300 baths, 300 mosques, 50 hospitals, and a high public literacy expressed in libraries, public and private, with more books than in all the rest of Europe.

And then, at its very pinnacle of power and wealth in 1090, Cordoba will be sacked by an invading group of North African fundamentalists known as the Almoravids, seeking to cleanse the freethinking and free-wheeling society of the Umayyads. The shock of the fall of the caliphate will cause a slow fracturing of the Muslim state into taifa city-states. Later incursions from North Africa will include the even more fundamental-ist Almohads (1145-1232), followed by the Nasrids (1232-1492), the last dynasty holding out in Granada, Almeria, and Malaga.

Though each invading group will enter Spain with a more severe view of the diverse and tolerant and inventive model of the Umayyads, each will in turn be softened by the experience, and new hybrids will arise.

Miraculously, far from being the end of Muslim creativity and inven-tion in al-Andalus, the fall of the caliphate and the rise of the taifas will usher in a final era of creativity. Each of the rulers of the city-states will feel obliged to compete with his rivals in the other taifas, creating competing courts of knowledge and excellence. Taifas like Madrid, Seville, Zaragoza, and Toledo will add more to the grandeur of Muslim achievement.

The shifting political mosaic of the emirate, caliphate, and taifa will mix with the unique political, social, and religious texture of Spain. Filtered through the relatively inclusive vision of the Umayyads and their successors, both Muslim and Christian, these forces will combine to create a tri-religious society marked by *convivencia,* a unique form of social coexistence and cooperation between Muslims, Christians, and Jews. The People of the Book, or *dhimmi,* are given a fairly secure second-class status as long as they do not proselytize and do not undermine Islam.

Old Iberian Christians still bowing to Rome will learn to speak and write Arabic and will be called Mozarabs. Their linguistic skills, like those of the Nestorians in Baghdad, will help the Umayyads translate the Latin, Greek, and Hebrew classics into Arabic, and will trigger a parallel flowering of ideas, science, and literature to compete with Baghdad and elsewhere in the Muslim empire.

The Jews, present in Iberia from before Roman times, who were being harshly persecuted by the Visigoths just as Tariq invaded, will see in the Muslims better potential protectors and patrons than were the fallen Visigoths. They too will learn Arabic to supplement their Hebrew and Latin. A Jew will rise to the second highest political job in the land when Rabbi Hasdai ibn Shaprut becomes de facto vizier and foreign minister to Caliph Abd al-Rahman III. And Jews will excel in trading and learning, contributing to the future intellectual glories of al-Andalus. As more and more Jews emigrate to al-Andalus from other parts of the diaspora, it will become the single most important community in the array of many scattered communities. This new Jewish homeland will be called Sefarad in Hebrew, and it, too, will survive almost 800 years.

This does not mean that convivencia will not break down periodically, as in the massacre of 150 families of Jews at Granada in 1066, or in the ninth-century killing of 48 Christians—known as the Martyrs of Cordoba—for openly blaspheming Islam and insulting the Prophet. It does not mean that Muslim extremists from North Africa won't recoil at the "impurity" of the Andalusian ways, and try to "cleanse" them. It does not mean that Christian zealots will not attempt to promote the reconquest.

But as much as or more than they are at odds or in conflict, the three groups will also coexist, and sometimes cross-fertilize one another, and quietly respect and even honor their rivals. Even so devout a Catholic

Once the third largest mosque in Muslim lands, the Great Mosque of Cordoba, Spain, was consecrated as a cathedral in 1236, the year of the Christian reconquest of Cordoba.

supremacist as Queen Isabella, raised in a diverse court with Jewish friends since childhood, will dress in Muslim fashion when she calls on the last emir of Granada, and her Catholic predecessors like Alfonso the Wise will adopt the tri-religious model of the Umayyads, with Muslim and Jewish advisors at his side. Arabic inscriptions will continue to adorn Christian churches and Jewish synagogues long after the Umayyad caliphate has fallen. The Mudejar architecture of Spain will still echo of Syria and Arabia, even when the bells of Catholic Rome ring louder. The hybrid language—the old Latin overlaid with Arabic—will echo of this dual heritage and of lost history.

In that long interval between the arrival of Tariq in 711 and the reconquest under Queen Isabella in 1492, the unique mix of al-Andalus will produce marvelous innovations in architecture, music, literature, philosophy, medicine, and science. But, sadly, this is also too often lost history, much of it lost in the terror of the Spanish Inquisition and the fleeing of Jews and Muslims from their old Spanish homeland; in the forced conversions and the excisions of historical fact; in the extirpation of languages; in the burning of priceless libraries by extremists. Five hundred years after the Inquisition, this lost history is slowly being recovered. But it is still not known to many people, even to those who carry the genes and family names or speak the language, all walking embodiments of lost history.

Consider this 16th-century poem written by the exiled Spanish Muslim Muhammad Rabadan during the Inquisition:

God made possible
That the Moors of this kingdom
With so many persecutions
Would be punished and enslaved.
Having lost the books
Without leaving a trace;
Scholars are gone
Some dead, others jailed,
The Inquisition rampant
With great force and pressures,
Implementing with vigor
Cruelty and excesses;
Almost everywhere
The earth is made to tremble:
They apprehend here and there
The newly baptized,
Imposing on them every day
Galleys, torment and fire
Along with other calamities
For which God alone knows the secret.

CAIRO, SAMARKAND, ISFAHAN, DELHI—As the concentric circle of Muslim improvisation and invention spreads away from Damascus, Baghdad, and Cordoba in the coming centuries, other centers of genius will arise to compete with those first incubators. That early Muslim tradition of improvising and creating, of seeking both knowledge and wisdom will spread to new places, many of them ancient places to which invention and genius are no strangers.

One of the first new centers will arise in a place that barely even exists until the first Arab armies sweep up out of Arabia into Egypt. Since the time of Alexander and then the Romans, Alexandria had been the major city of Egypt, the home of Cleopatra, a Hellenic city near the mouth of the Nile. Upriver there was a Roman settlement, not far from the pharaonic city of Memphis, but it was of minor consequence until the arrival of the Arabs in 642. They name the fortress-town al-Fustat, or the encampment, and make it the military garrison for Arab troops.

The fort sits on the eastern bank of the river, and for more than two centuries after the Arab conquest it remains an island lost on the ocean of sand flowing to all horizons. Al-Fustat stands in the floodplain of the river on a narrow strip of land, cultivated since the time of the pharaohs, watered in the annual floods created by the melting mountain glaciers and winter rains deep in Africa. Along the river and in a few scattered oases, date palms rise over the blistering sands.

But this Muslim fortress on the Nile will come to be known as al-Qahira, or Cairo, upon the arrival in 969 of an invading group of the Ismaili sect of Shiites from Tunisia, determined to establish their own world empire. They take advantage of one of the many periods of political distraction and weakness in Abbasid Baghdad to make their move. The conquering Ismailis are called Fatimids because they claim descent from one of the Prophet's daughters, Fatima. And despite their minority status within a minority of Muslims, they partly succeed in their imperial enterprise that initially seems as unlikely as a lone Umayyad prince establishing his new realm in al-Andalus.

At its peak in the 11th century, the Fatimid Empire holds parts of North Africa, including Egypt, and Palestine, Syria, Sicily, parts of Arabia, and Yemen.

It is the Fatimids who create the outlines of medieval Cairo, a major world city and global center of learning. The Fatimids, with occasional exceptions, follow a policy of inclusion and merit-based rule that allow Sunni Muslims and Christians and Jews to hold high positions. But just as importantly, the Fatimids join the Abbasid and Umayyad search for worldly and spiritual knowledge. They found in 972 both a magnificent mosque and an adjacent university known as al-Azhar, which for centuries afterward will be one of the leading universities of the world. Scholars like astronomer ibn Yunus and Iraqi physicist ibn al-Haytham flock to Cairo. Lured from Baghdad by a generous offer from Fatimid ruler al-Hakim early in the 11th century to find a way to stop the annual flooding of the Nile, scholar ibn al-Haytham will fail in that endeavor, but he will later revolutionize theories of light and optics and lay the foundation for insights by Leeuwenhoek in Europe centuries later.

Al-Azhar university was originally constituted as an Ismaili school, but with the arrival of the Sunni Ayyubid dynasty under Saladin in 1171, al-Azhar will be reorganized as a Sunni center of learning and will thus continue its intellectual leadership.

Although Saladin and the Ayyubids will be determined to overturn most aspects of Fatimid rule and religious thought, they will not abandon the Fatimid quest for knowledge and civic achievement. Within the overall mission of Muslim education, Saladin and the Ayyubids ensure that al-Azhar becomes one of the most inventive centers of learning in the Muslim world. And Saladin will become best known for his turnaround of the faltering Muslim resistance to the Christian Crusades in the late 12th century. Not only will Saladin turn the tide for the Muslims; he will become for the Europeans a symbol of Muslim chivalric honor, both for his merciful treatment of Christians when he retakes Jerusalem, and through his long-distance relationship of mutual respect with Richard the Lionhearted.

The fall of Baghdad to the Mongols in the 13th century will do even more to make Cairo the world's leading Muslim political and intellectual center. Assorted thinkers and inventors will make their homes there. In the early 13th century, Syrian-born ibn al-Nafis working and teaching at Cairo's al-Mansuri Hospital will be the first to teach that the Greek physician Galen was wrong in his understanding of how blood moves in the body. Al-Nafis will describe how the blood flows from the heart through the lungs to the body and back again.

In 1250, Saladin's Ayyubids will fall to a dynasty of former slaves known as the Mamluks, and they will rule Cairo until 1517, when they are overthrown by the Ottoman Turks. Despite all these earthshaking political changes between the years 1000 and 1500, during most of this period Cairo will retain its leading intellectual role in the Muslim world.

Meanwhile Persia, the enricher of Baghdad's Abbasid brilliance, will develop its own unique Muslim centers to rival and eclipse the pre-Islamic cities of Persepolis and Gundeshapur. When the Muslims arrive, Persia will be in a period of political stagnation and decline, but in a curious way, though Persia quickly falls to the Arab invaders, the invasion will infuse it with a new cultural energy. The early Persian cities of Khorasan, Qazvin, and Tabriz will be followed by perhaps the most glorious city of Muslim Iran, Isfahan. Isfahan will flourish under the Seljuk Turks in the 11th century. Seljuk ruler Malik Shah and his Sunni successors will attract scholars and poets to their courts.

The Seljuks are a Turkic tribe rising to administer an empire stretching from modern-day Turkey to Pakistan between the 11th and the 14th centuries. Though Turkic in origin, they will adopt and spread a Persian cultural aesthetic that will echo through many successor groups, including the Ottoman Turks. Their cities Nishapur and Isfahan will be homes to poet and scientist Omar Khayyám and his patron, Nizam al-Mulk, namesake of the Nizamiya schools built all across the Middle East. The Seljuk capital of Konya in Anatolia will be home to the 13th-century Sufi saint and poet-philosopher al-Rumi, who will be as revered by Christians as by Muslims, and whose writings will attract new followers around the world for 800 years after his death up to the present.

After the retreat of the Seljuks before the Mongol invasions in the 13th century, Isfahan will be quiet until the rise of the Shiite Safavids and Shah Abbas l (1587-1629). Then the greatest and most lavish architectural and civic improvements will take place, prompting British travel writer Robert Byron to say, when touring the city that the marvels of Isfahan have no rivals in Europe, not even St. Peter's Basilica or the palace of Versailles. The pointed arches of Isfahan will be topped with brilliant, blue-tiled domes, and the vast green expanse of Imam Square will be surrounded by glittering mosques and palaces.

As the great Muslim cities rise in Asia, Persian urban culture and style will probably have more impact than any other national culture, even as Persian political influence remains secondary. From the rise of the Abbasids to the decline of the Mughals in India and the Ottomans in Turkey, Persian culture, in the Middle East and Central and South Asia, will serve the same lofty role as France will for Europe from the Norman conquest of England to the 21st century. Courts from Ottoman Istanbul to Timurid Samarkand and Mughal India will speak and write in Persian, copy the Persian designs of rugs, create court histories to resemble the illuminated Persian chronicles, and build fabled monuments that echo of Persia.

In Central Asia, Islam and its attending culture will arrive in the eighth century in cities such as Kabul, Bukhara, and Ghazni, all of which will give rise to new Muslim cultures, thinkers, and innovations. Heavily influenced by Persia, often speaking Persian languages, those cities on the steppe will be shocked in the 13th century by the Mongol advance of Genghis Khan and his grandson Hulegu, who will bring turmoil and devastation to Central Asia and much of the Middle East as they establish the vast Mongol Empire in 1206, at its peak stretching from China to Iraq and north into Eastern Europe and Russia. Though the Mongols are devastating and brutal with those who resist, those who acquiesce will come into the fold of a new hybrid empire that will gradually reflect the Islam that it has absorbed, supporting intellectual and scientific achievements.

In 1406 as the Mongols are weakening, a successor Mongol-ethnic regime will spring up near Samarkand, led by Timur, also known as Tamerlane. His short-lived dynasty from 1336 to 1506 will be called the Timurid empire, reaching at its high point from deep into Russia to northern India and west into Anatolia. Though the city of Samarkand dates back to before the time of Alexander the Great, with the rise of Timur it will for a time become the center of the world. The inward flood of tribute and booty will contribute to an exceptional architectural flowering in Samarkand, including the establishment of the Registan complex of religious and educational centers. Even though of Mongol origin, the Timurids will fuel another renewal of Persian cultural creation and innovation.

Despite the disruption of the Mongol and Timurid invasions, these conflagrations will have some positive side effects. For generations, thousands of Central Asians steeped in the inventive ways of early Islam will flee west, intellectually enriching places as far away as Anatolia, Egypt, and al-Andalus. As for the Mongols, not only will they bring Baghdad to its end, most will eventually adopt Islam and will absorb both the religion and the best of Muslim culture. Hulegu Khan, the 13th-century destroyer of Baghdad, will found the world's greatest astronomical observatory up to that point at Maragheh in Persia. Timur the Great will later do the same, carrying captured Muslim art and treasures back to his beloved Samarkand to make it a Central Asian center of invention.

The cultural successor to the Seljuk Turks will be the Ottomans, and their dynasty is founded in 1299 in Anatolia by the patriarch Osman. Though the Ottomans will lose ground to the advancing Timurid steamroller in the mid 1300s, they will outlast the Timurids and rise to take control of much of old Byzantium. In 1453 under Mehmet II, the Ottoman Turks conquer Constantinople and rename their capital Istanbul. The Ottoman Empire will reconquer much of the original Arab Caliphate, minus al-Andalus, but adding Greece and the Balkans. The empire will reach its political and intellectual peak under Suleiman the Magnificent, who rules from 1520 to 1566, and is noted at that time for religious tolerance, the use of meritocracy rather than hereditary nobility to administer the empire, and the renewal of Muslim military pressure on Europe, including extended military campaigns into Hungary and a siege of Vienna.

Far to the southeast, the Arab Muslims will have brushed Sind in northern India in the eighth century, and, trading along the Arabian Sea, will have brought Muslim culture to the Hindu ports. By the 12th century, several waves of invasion from Central Asia create more lasting presences in cities such as Lahore and Delhi. The Delhi sultanate in power from 1206 to 1526 will, at its peak, control all of north India from the Afghan frontier to Bengal.

The golden age of Muslim India will come with the arrival of the Mughals from Central Asia in the 16th century, and the establishment of the Mughal Empire from 1526 to 1857. "Mughal" is Persian for Mongol, and the first Mughal conqueror is Babur, a direct descendant of Timur the Great. Though the Timurid empire has disintegrated by this time, Babur from his home base in present-day Uzbekistan has enough military force and prowess to try to reconstitute Timur's empire. He turns south only after many years of winning and losing the city of Samarkand to assorted invaders from east and west. He finally concludes that he will have better luck south of the Himalaya, and so he confronts and defeats the Delhi Sultanate, later expanding across the Deccan Plateau. Patriarch Babur is a uniquely literate and sensitive warrior, leaving behind a detailed biography, the *Baburnama*.

Though the cities of Delhi and Lahore will have their share of glory and wealth, the greatest of Mughal capitals will be Agra between 1526 and 1658.

Babur's grandson Akbar the Great will be the Mughal ruler best loved by non-Muslim Indians, known for deepening the tradition of tolerance

The Umayyad mosque in Damascus, built in A.D. 715, is one of the oldest and largest mosques in the world.

and inclusion and trying to create a new religion by fusing Islam and Hinduism. His descendant Shahbuddin Mohammed Shah Jahan will be the master builder, creating the Taj Mahal in Agra, the Red Fort in Delhi, and many other masterpieces. Shah Jahan will marry the Persian princess, Nur Jahan, and she will invite hundreds of Persian architects, artists, poets, and thinkers to enliven his court. Although the result will be a dazzling intellectual salon, there will be accusations of corruption and decadence, and native Indian resentment of these new foreigners will contribute to the overthrow of Jahan by his son.

At its peak, in the early 1700s, Mughal India will own approximately 25 percent of all the material wealth in the world, and its population of 140 million will dwarf any nation except China.

And among these far-flung centers, despite the disruptions of war and plague and the hardship of travel, a continuing interchange of people and ideas will go on for a thousand years, particularly from East to West. Al-Andalus, Iraq, and North Africa will be enriched by immigrants from Central Asia, Persia, and Arabia. Bukhara and Ghazni will dialogue with Baghdad and Cordoba, with Delhi and Cairo. The 14th-century traveler ibn Batuta will visit most of these centers from his starting point in North Africa. And despite the differences in race, in landscape, and in language, he will find a common awareness born in the early years of invention and improvisation.

Against this now vanished backdrop of an integrated Muslim universe, the various scientists, thinkers, and artists of lost history will play out their roles. They will lay many of the foundations of the modern world. And although, in the early years, non-Muslims in Europe and elsewhere will be in awe of these achievements and will know the players' names and work, later they will forget the names of the authors and creators, and will come to think that they alone have created the modern world.

GOD IN THE NUMERAL

...and He has enumerated everything in numbers.
QUR'AN (LXXII:28)

BANGALORE, INDIA, 2007—From above and afar, the capital city of Bangalore in Karnataka state is a modernistic grid cutting the green savanna and copses of the vast Deccan plateau. The layout of the city is unusual in this part of the world for its crisp regularity. During monsoon season, huge cumulus clouds build into thunderheads in the afternoon and torrential showers pour down over the palms and scrub, over the square blocks and surveyed quadrants of a place that speaks of the new. The haze of exhaust hangs bluish in the tropic heat, evidence of the roar and tumult as traffic pulses in and out of the various centers.

The grid indicates a city atypical for this subcontinent. Bangalore is a 500-year-old center in a country that goes back thousands of years, but most of its growth has come in the last 30 years. The vast civic park in the center hosts the redbrick, neoclassical high court and the state legislature and library, whereas the newer streets and highways radiate out to the exploding suburbs, boxy towers and corporate parks of global capitalism.

In one of those office parks, Fahmida Khan is writing algorithms for software to support commodities trading at several exchanges around the world, including Chicago and Singapore. An algorithm is a set of numerical calculations and instructions, which if carried out systematically produces a desired result. Algorithms are critical to software design, as well as much of modern science and engineering, enabling computers and smart electronics to sort through masses of digital data and text, calculating spatial relationships, encoding and decoding confidential information—all the basic processes of modern computing, technology, commerce, and science.

Founder of her own small software shop, Fahmida's biggest clients are the new behemoths of Indian information technology, like Infosys and Wipro, but she is starting to get contracts from the big multinational firms, too. Originally dedicated to taking on the outsourced back-office business processes from North America and Europe, these new Indian firms are looking to move up the computing food chain, writing the software and designing the devices and circuits that will drive the next wave of global computing.

Fahmida's algorithms create codes that turn financial data into gibberish when being transmitted, and then on the other end reverse the process to decode the information. For a hacker or thief, the algorithms are so complicated that it would take thousands of massive computers years and years trying every algorithmic permutation, out to the 132nd decimal place, to finally hit on the code. So far, it is not worth trying to break the code.

Fahmida learned her skills in Silicon Valley, where she worked after attending the California Institute of Technology. She worked first at Hewlett-Packard, the grandfather of Silicon Valley firms, and later at Oracle Systems. Had she stayed at Oracle, she probably could have become a vice president or even better, and depending on her timing, left the company a multimillionaire.

But in 1998, she made a momentous decision. Having been raised from childhood to look north and west toward the wealthy countries of Europe and America and to the foreign educational centers like Cal Tech, she decided to come back home. Sacrificing income and the prestige of being with more established firms, she came home to found her own company.

Thousands of other Indians who had emigrated to America have made the decision to come home, in particular to Bangalore. Although the reverse migration has been largely in computing and software, others have begun to follow, including doctors and entrepreneurs. While they all sacrifice income, because of India's low labor and living costs they can afford other amenities and servants that were beyond their reach in America and Europe. They can live at the top of society in India, where overseas they were part of the prosperous middle class. For a country that long languished between colonialism and a stagnated 1960s socialism, this new class is starting an economic revolution that the old socialists could not imagine, though no one knows how far it will go.

Fahmida's family, as reflected in her name, is Muslim. Though the details of when and how they became Muslim are lost, her ancestors were long civil servants in the service of the Mughals and then the British, and her great-grandparents settled in Bangalore in the time of the British Raj. As educated and cosmopolitan people living far south, they have been fairly remote from the periodic dislocations and strife between religions farther north. During the period of partition in 1947, they had taken to heart Gandhi's message of interfaith harmony and had never considered moving to Pakistan or Bangladesh, unlike tens of millions who did.

And they have felt vindicated in their decision. Watching Indian Muslims rise to positions of success and power, in Bollywood, in the presidency of the country, in business and entertainment, has made them proud. And it has made them glad that they have not used their religion as the primary definer of who they are. They are Indians first, and they are glad of it.

And Fahmida's family was so proud to see her moving to California to study, and then to hear of her success in business. Though they had the normal worries about a single Indian woman in faraway America—and they have constantly maneuvered to find her the right husband—they have given her the freedom to make her own choices.

Though Bangalore was captured by the Mughals in the 17th century— and the architecture of nearby Mysore and Bijapur reflects the stamp of the Muslim vision, with domes and minarets and pointed arches echoing back to the Abbasids and Persians and Central Asians—the cityscape of Bangalore does not look particularly Muslim, nor does the state of Karnataka. Always a minority in India, though the political elite for centuries, the Muslims have been only part of the cultural and religious patchwork of South Asia. The Hindu foundation of India is the bedrock of Karnataka and elsewhere. All around the state are ancient Hindu temples like Belur and Hampi. Add to that the influence of the Portuguese, who traded along both Indian coasts for 500 years, and their former colony of Goa only a few hundred miles west, and finally the styles and language of the English, who considered India the prize of their colonial crown.

While Bangalore is rich and exploding, the economy of the state, like India, is also an extreme mix of ancient poverty and global capitalism. Even though 600 million Indians have not been touched by globalization and subsist at a level unimaginable to Westerners, as you move up through the remaining 400 million or more you find rising gradations of wealth, including a middle class that is now one of the largest in the world.

India's world-class technical schools have helped create a new techno-elite that feeds into the big new firms, helping transform this ancient country into a global leader in information technology.

Coming home has actually been an issue for Fahmida and her extended family. While at one level these families mourn for those who have gone away and yearn for them to return, some of the Khans, on the other hand, including her mother, had mixed feelings when faced with the reality of Fahmida back in India. Deeply indoctrinated in a sense of inadequacy derived from a fairly limited time in history—the British colonial period—the older Khans had always thought foreign was superior. British was good and American was better. So they had some heated and confused discussions with their successful daughter who was giving all that up to come home.

Although she would never have admitted it to them, Fahmida felt some of that, too. She had been proud of her Cal Tech degree and her work at Hewlett-Packard and Oracle. She realized that she, too, carried some of the prejudice of her parents, especially about education, though not the love of things British. She respected the newness of America and how far the country had come in such a short time. She knew that the top universities, in the aggregate, were without equal.

But then, when she'd seen the same hint of newness in Bangalore on her return trips, the money, the office parks, the same smell and even some of the same people she'd known in Silicon Valley, she had changed her thinking. She had actually thought that by coming home and helping build Bangalore, she would build India. And maybe build herself.

She has another hour before she goes to a client meeting at one of the downtown hotels. This man has flown in from Boston. His firm has done very well. Looking out the window, she sees it will probably rain before dark. That will slow down traffic.

She has one little mathematical snag to solve before she can feel good about leaving for the day. She looks up to her shelf for one of her old standbys from her university days, *Elements of the Algorithm,* with a portrait of the old Arab or Persian mathematician al-Khwarizmi on the cover, namesake of the algorithm. She knows it had been up on her shelf. Did one of her colleagues grab it during lunchtime?

She needs that book. She knows the chapter she wants. She hardly ever refers to other sections. She doesn't remember anything about al-Khwarizmi, and it's irrelevant now. There was a foreword that told about him, maybe she read it 20 years ago in graduate school, but she doesn't remember anything but his name. And what does it matter? Relevant history in the world of information technology only goes back about two years.

Has she lost that book?

BAGHDAD, A.D. 832—There is a thread in the tapestry of lost history made of a string of numbers and calculations, and these numbers, born of the highest imagination will enable many of the tapestry's other threads to materialize.

A pivotal force in creating these numbers and formulas is a Persian man born in about 780 in the faraway town of Khiva, Khorasan province, known as Khwarizm to the Arabs, in Central Asia. He is named Mohamed al-Khwarizmi, literally Mohamed of Khwarizm.

In the eighth century, his birthplace is deep in the steppe, a way station on the Silk Road that stretches at one end from China, at the other end from Rome. Though the two ends of this spectrum have never had direct contact, over the centuries there is a fairly regular exchange between the two worlds. All this passes through Khorasan; at times the exchange is no more than a breeze, a foreign and exotic lost butterfly hanging in the air for a few seconds, then swept away.

The old trading oasis of Khiva lies south of the Aral Sea, the oasis and the sea composing two watery havens surrounded by the Garagum Desert that stretches off into nothingness. Assorted religions and cults have come through and stayed or shriveled, until Islam finally takes root. Caravans of camels and horses come out of the distant nothingness to lay down their wares and bargain, then to drink and rest, to tell stories and look up at the stars. At night the town is swallowed up by space; by day it is a green dot on the face of yellow vastness. Although it will later become part of other countries and empires, Khiva harks back to ancient Persia, and the lean and bearded man with the long black hair carries the soul of Persia within him. And though he is named after the Prophet as many good Muslim boys are, this young man is also known to some Arabs as al-Majusi, literally the Magus or magician, leading some people to believe that his earlier faith, or that of his people, may have been Zoroastrianism, the old fire worship. Because he also draws on ancient Hebrew mathematical and astronomical texts, there are those who think his family had been Jewish.

To be named the magician will prove to be true beyond the knowledge of those who named him. This dark-haired man, with brown piercing eyes set into deep sockets and cheeks creased by leanness and weather, is a magician in other ways as well. Steeped in the tradition of faith and of magic, he yearns to find the secrets of the universe in numbers. He writes mathematical problems; he dreams numbers; he reduces every movement of his day to numbers: the number of steps to the bathhouse, the angle of sun to Earth and the triangle created there, and the curves of the Silk Road wandering across half the Earth.

In numbers and equations and computations spinning out their series, he senses the hidden codes of the universe, the numerical representation of the complexity of God's creation. And as a Muslim, in a time when it is believed that God can be revealed through reason and knowledge, he will help lead a great mathematical revolution, giving the first glimpse of a future day when the age of computers will outstrip the processing speeds and capabilities of the human mind, no matter how brilliant.

At the founding of the House of Wisdom in 832 in Baghdad, al-Khwarizmi is summoned by the Caliph al-Mamun himself to assist in the search for God in the numeral. And when he arrives there, he sees the great interpreters like Hunayn ibn Ishaq gradually decoding the formulas of Euclid's *Elements* based on geometry, of Pythagoras and Ptolemy, the thoughts of Aristotle and Socrates. Others are translating Archimedes's works such as *The Sphere and the Cylinder, The Measurement of the Circle, The Equilibrium of Planes,* and *Floating Bodies,* all of which influence Muslim mathematics significantly. Al-Kwharizmi will help in that effort, because he is able to read Greek and turn its meaning into Arabic.

The Central Asian man sees turbaned mathematician-astronomers working together in rooms using maps, star charts, astrolabes, and other measuring instruments, thinking through problems together, checking each other's work, poring over translations, and discussing endlessly. For a man who has often done much of his work alone and had rarely found thinkers who were his equal, to find so much intelligence and competition gathered in one place is both exhilarating and intimidating. But he knows this is an unparalleled opportunity, and he will make as much of it as he can.

Even as the knowledge of the ancient Greeks is revealed in greater detail with each passing month, al-Khwarizmi is determined to search for mathematical knowledge wherever it can be found. He has heard of the mathematical wisdom of the early Hindus. In the time of the founding of the court of Caliph al-Mansur, there had been an Indian astronomer in the court named Kanka, and he is said to have used a Hindu text written by a long-dead mathematician named Brahmagupta, used to calculate the position of the sun and planets, to predict eclipses and the like. Al-Khwarizmi has heard talk of this book and method, but he cannot find it. He spends days digging through the archives to try to track down the original, and he endlessly tasks the archivists and librarians to find the Sanskrit papers written by the dead Brahmagupta that the dead Kanka had once used.

When the archivists finally return, they bring with them many treasures originally from India. And among them are the kinds of books and papers that al-Khwarizmi and the caliph yearn for, the collected knowledge and ideas of other peoples and civilizations. Among the treasures lies a 200-year-old book called *Brahma Sphuta Siddhanta,* or *Opening of the Universe.* While knowing only a few words in Sanskrit, al-Khwarizmi believes this is almost certainly what he is looking for, and he has the translators set about rendering it into Arabic.

The Arabic name of the Hindu work will be *Sindhind.* The Hindu original will one day be lost, and al-Khwarizmi's Arabic version will also be lost, but a Latin translation of his work done centuries later will survive.

And as the translators decode the old Indian text, its Sanskrit characters like magic and their impenetrable secrets one by one becoming the familiar swirl of Arabic, al-Khwarizmi is at first dumbfounded, then awed, and then gratified to the depths of his soul. Each evening he awaits the new day's revelation of mathematics. He lies awake at night up on the roof of his quarters at the House of Wisdom as he had done when a boy in Khorasan, watching the half sphere of the heavens orbit Polaris, the middle and southern sky shifting off to the south. At the center of the base of the hemisphere of heaven, he ponders what he has learned the previous day, unable to sleep because of the anticipation of what he will find.

While there are countless things now revealing themselves to him from the translators' pens, the one thing that stuns and shakes him the most is the Hindu character shaped as a dot, a pinpoint of blackness like a negative star. This dot is the foundation of an entire vision of mathematics, of science, and the universe. The black dot, which in its basic form means nothingness, is the source from which all higher mathematics can now spring. The nothingness of the dot will grow to become the center of the source code behind the physical universe.

Weak and drunk with the world that is now exploding in his head, al-Khwarizmi knows that mathematics has to be the code work of the divine. From the discovery of the Hindu dot that will one day be represented in much of the world by a circle and known as zero, he sees an infinite number of paths and possibilities streaking out in all directions.

And he is not alone in these kinds of thoughts, for in the House of Wisdom and other mathematical salons that will arise at other courts, dozens and eventually hundreds of astronomical-mathematical thinkers are turning over in their minds assorted issues, each coming at the numeric mystery from a slightly different angle. Unconsciously and intuitively, the early Muslim mathematicians will create a kind of collective intelligence, feeding on each other, borrowing and stealing from one another, competing for the favors of patrons, making terrible mistakes, authoring spectacular breakthroughs.

In a way, the House of Wisdom in Baghdad and similar Muslim centers will be the world's first think tanks, an example of network computing, using networked human brains rather than machines.

And al-Khwarizmi and his colleagues are not alone in time or history, for aside from inventing, they also assimilate and aggregate much of the brilliance that has come before. From the Babylonians via the Greeks, they inherit the sexagesimal measure of time in 60 seconds and 60 minutes. Muslim astronomers and other scientists will translate these numerals into the degrees of the compass and the directions of Earth and sky that will survive into the 21st century. From the Indians they will capture the astronomic importance of numbers. Via the Persians and directly from the Indians, they will capture the zero, and the breakthrough of decimal math, and the first hints at representing numbers as symbols and not as words.

Among other things, al-Khwarizmi realizes as he scribbles that the very process of writing mathematics will need to be revised. In his day there are three different methods of calculating math in the Abbasid world and its environs. There is a universal finger-counting method, which serves certain basic purposes well, as in business transactions of small size. There is a more complicated version using Arabic letter characters, which is better, but still not up to the task.

And there is the Hindu method, a decimal system with characters representing quantities ranging from 0 to 9, and then arranged in combination to reach up and down into positive and negative infinity from the source dot of zero. The Hindu numerals are the best, the only ones adequate to all the possibilities that al-Khwarizmi and his counterparts and successors see dancing in their heads: needs like calculating the area of irregular spaces; finding missing quantities using the relationship of known ones; calculating the relationship of the Earth to the sun and stars, so as to better compute the calendar and observe the holy days as commanded by the Prophet; finding the location of Mecca so that the faithful can pray in that direction with certainty and not guesswork. The Hindu cum Muslim number system will be essential to establishing a new theory about curvature that will show how to resolve the two different universes of angles and curves. The new number system will begin to help answer the mathematical questions implicit in conical space and projections. And the Hindu-Arab numbers will be essential to 21st-century questions such as the behavior of light and the properties of solids. Modern technology and civilization will not be able to rise and evolve without these numbers.

In al-Khwarizmi's mind and in the Hindu system, all spins around the dot of nothingness. Brilliant Brahmagupta had found the zero and tried to represent its emptiness and mystery in a written equation. He was the only mathematician ever to attempt to use the zero in division. He wrote the ultimate truth of zero to be: Zero divided by zero equals zero. And though he was wrong in that calculation, which is impossible, he was infinitely prescient in his willingness to think in new ways, which in turn threw a spark of genius to the Muslims, starting a bonfire of thought.

Two hundred years later up on that Baghdad roof, al-Khwarizmi laughs to himself. The equation of division of and by zero is absurd; it proves nothing. He laughs out loud, risking waking the others. A woman of the night calls up to him, unaccustomed to hearing laughter from this handsome, dark man and wondering if he wants company. But he is off in his thoughts.

The zero, he realizes, must be accepted on pure faith. It cannot be proven. And in a terrible irony, which he considers sharing with his patron al-Mamun, he sees that the ultimate value of rationalist mathematics is pure revelation, just as God was revealed, not quantified.

In another way, the fact that mathematics is based on a revealed unprovable quantity means that Aristotle had been right, as reflected in the caliph's dream. Revelation and reason are the same thing. They begin at the same point. And everything in the universe spins out from that.

A Soviet postage stamp commemorated ninth-century mathematician al-Khwarizmi from Khiva in modern-day Uzbekistan.

From those days of the revelation of the Hindu secrets until the end of his years, al-Khwarizmi and his colleagues and imitators will work to bring Muslim mathematics up to the level of the ancient Greeks and Hindus and then take it beyond. Just as the Abbasid and Umayyad Muslims are absorbing architecture, language, art, style from all the peoples brought into their sway, in the field of mathematics al-Khwarizmi will take the ongoing process of absorption of the Greeks, Byzantines, and Indians and vault this learning into a new level of sophistication.

Inspired by the writings of all those who have gone before and starting from the work of Brahmagupta, al-Khwarizmi begins to write his own works. By his death in 850, he has written a book each on algebraic calculations, on astronomy, and on the astronomical tables, and he has revised and corrected Ptolemy's theories and maps of the world. His major work on geography based on Ptolemy gives latitudes and longitudes for more than 2,400 places including cities, regions, oceans, rivers, and mountain ranges, providing the foundation of a world map. His work is more often accurate than Ptolemy's, in particular in the Muslim realms and Africa and Asia. Al-Khwarizmi writes another two books on the astrolabe and one on sundials, and even a book on the Jewish calendar.

As is common in those days, the evidence of the brilliance of this man is not universally preserved. Things are lost. By the time his writings begin to be translated into Latin for the Europeans, he has been dead for three hundred years. And yet the Europeans have never seen anything like his books building on the even older classics. They are as dumbstruck by this long-dead Persian as he had been by seeing the translation of his Hindu predecessor.

Until about the 16th century, 700 years after his death, the Europeans will honor and dignify everything they postulate with the concluding footnote, "dixit algoritmi," or "so says al-Khwarizmi," meaning that they have built their own calculations on faith in the teachings of the Persian. His translated works will be the core university mathematics and astronomy textbooks in Europe and the Muslim world.

Though his greatest breakthroughs will be in placing the zero at the center of his mathematical universe, replete with both positive and negative values, and in promoting the acceptance of the Hindu numerals as the only way to represent ever more complicated and abstract processes and values, those vast and basic achievements will gradually become so commonly used and taken for granted that they will fade into the landscape. Later he will best be remembered for his work on algebra, the very word for the concept taken from the title of his book *Al-Jabr wa al-Muqabala,* translated as *The Compendious Book on Calculation by Completion and Balancing.*

In the book, he writes that he intends to convey to the reader:

...what is easiest and most useful in arithmetic, such as men constantly require in cases of inheritance, legacies, partition, lawsuits, and trade, and in all their dealings with one another, or where the measuring of lands, the digging of canals, geometrical computations, and other objects of various sorts and kinds are concerned.

He adds:

That fondness for science, ... that affability and condescension which God shows to the learned, that promptitude with which he protects and supports them in the elucidation of obscurities and in the removal of difficulties, has encouraged me to compose a short work on calculating by al-jabr and al-muqabala, confining it to what is easiest and most useful in arithmetic.

Al-jabr means "restoring," referring to the process of moving a sub-tracted quantity to the other side of an equation; *al-muqabala* means "comparing," and refers to subtracting equal quantities from both sides of an equation.

And why will that be associated with his name, when the basics of zero and the advanced numerals are not? It is because algebra will be the first and greatest step in detaching the source of mathematics from the physical and moving it into the purely abstract.

Until his time, the Greeks had been held in reverence for their work in geometry—the Greek word *geometria* literally means "measurement of the Earth"—and geometry was earthbound and tangible. Geometry was about spaces, sometimes rendered in abstract terms, but always reducible to a physical reality, whether a plot of land or the side of a house or the semicircle of a Greek amphitheater.

This mathematician, al-Khwarizmi, creates a system that will provide the key to begin unlocking all planes of the universe. His numbers and new ways of calculating will enable the building of 100-story towers and mile-long bridges; calculating the point at which a space probe will intersect with the orbits of one of Jupiter's moons; the reactions of nuclear physics; the cellular processes of biotechnology and pharmaceutical and marketing research; the calculus of a global economy; the language and intelligence of software; and the confidentiality of a mobile phone conversation.

But one day, many Europeans—and then the world—will forget who he was or what he did even as they still use his name to name algorithms. They will cease to credit the man for what he has done for them. And one day, some European mathematical historians who do remember his name will deny that he had been great.

Lost history can do the strangest things, even in mathematics. It can disenfranchise the inventor and embolden the lucky beneficiary. Like a mathematical formula built on mistaken assumption, history with gaps becomes a confused and mistaken jumble.

But the good part of the story is that, after al-Khwarizmi, the circle of Muslim mathematical invention, like ripples from a stone thrown in the pond, will radiate out from that center in Baghdad, touching dozens and ultimately billions. On and on they will come, the Arab and Muslim mathematical thinkers, from Iraq, from Persia and points east, from Egypt and Syria and al-Andalus, all driven to unlock the giant puzzle of the universe using numbers. As with the work of al-Khwarizmi and the mathematicians in India, higher Muslim mathematics for most of its history will be almost inseparable from astronomy, for the challenges of measuring location and time using the positions of Earth, sun, moon, and stars will stimulate ever more complicated mathematical formulations.

And even as the high thinkers are driven to explain the movements and positions and appearances of the Earth and the heavens, they also look for hidden answers and clues in numerical puzzles and games, looking for symmetrical formulas that reveal equivalences, combinations of numbers that when squared or cubed will reveal patterns and predictability.

ONE INFLUENTIAL FAMILY of calculating stargazers will be the Thabits, three generations of mathematician-astronomers from the ancient town of Harran, then in Iraq, who speak Greek and Syriac. The patriarch Thabit ibn Qurra is not a Muslim, but from a sect known as the Sabians, who worship stars as representations of the infinite names of God. They have also absorbed much of Greek culture and language, so they are instrumental in helping translate the Greek classics.

In an account possibly traceable to the bibliographer al-Nadim writing a century after al-Mamun's death, the Sabian entry into the House of Wisdom is bizarre. In the ninth century, as Caliph al-Mamun with his army marches north against Byzantium, he comes across the Sabians in what is modern-day Turkey. He holds an inquest of their elders about their faith, trying to determine if they are protected "People of the Book," or one more unprotected faith that will need to be converted. To confuse things, they seem to follow elements of Judaism and Christianity, and they even read from a holy text. Al-Mamun tells them that it appears they do not qualify for protection, so they will either need to convert to Islam or suffer death. He gives them until his return from his northern campaign against the Byzantines to decide.

While al-Mamun fights in the north, the Sabians desperately consult with lawyers and holy men. Poring through the Qur'an, they find several verses conferring protected status on the little-known "Sabeans." Although later scholars will conclude that the Prophet is referring to another group in Arabia with a similar name, this group of Sabians swiftly adopts the common name and claims divine protection.

When al-Mamun returns, they make their case, he grants them protection, and he invites their thinkers to the House of Wisdom.

Among those invited to Baghdad is Thabit ibn Qurra, a moneychanger in his youth but later educated in higher math. He will work with parabolas, angle trisection, and magic squares—a square composed of columns of integers that add up to the same number horizontally, vertically, and sometimes diagonally.

Typical of mathematical problems that Muslim-supported thinkers like Thabit ibn Qurra grapple with is one known as the "chessboard problem," often seen in Muslim texts, an example of exponential series. It is told this way: The man who invented the game of chess asks his ruler for a favor, to receive one grain of wheat on the first square, then double that on the next, that is two on the second square, four on the third square, eight on the fourth square, and so on until all 64 squares are filled. The final amount would result in an unfathomable number. The brain-choking result, as al-Biruni will successfully calculate much later, is 18,446,744,073,709,551,615.

Thabit's grandson Ibrahim will do work in areas such as the apparent motion of the sun and the geometric measurement of shadows. This will lead him into his most important work with parabolas, building on the writings of his grandfather and others; in particular he reveals a method of representing curved spaces as squares with the equivalent area.

Another mathematician from the Sabian area in modern-day Turkey is al-Battani, his Muslim given name reflecting the eventual conversion of the Sabians to Islam. His father is an astronomical instrument maker in Harran, and this leads his son into a similar field.

Long before the time of telescopes and computers, al-Battani will do some serious astronomical calculating. Aside from cataloguing 489 stars, he will calculate the length of the year as 365 days 5 hours 48 minutes 24 seconds, only minutes off the length later calculated using atomic clocks and telescopes.

He will also determine the precession of the equinoxes, a slow westward motion of the equinoctal points caused by the greater attraction of the sun and moon on the bulge of matter at the Equator, so that the times at which the sun crosses the Equator come at shorter intervals than they would otherwise do. He will calculate the inclination of the ecliptic, the tilt of the Earth's axis of rotation relative to the plane in which the orbit of the sun cuts the celestial sphere. Rather than using geometrical methods like Ptolemy to calculate these numbers, he will innovate by using trigonometry.

Another Persian man of numbers is al-Nayrizi, born in the ninth century in central Persia. Building on the work of his predecessors and contemporaries, al-Nayrizi writes a book on how to use trigonometry to calculate the direction of the shrine of the Kaaba in Mecca so that the faithful will know in which direction to face for their five-times-daily prayer. This application of higher math will remove the guesswork involved in the correct stance, particularly during travel. More importantly, it will open the door to the use of trigonometry in more complicated processes of geolocation.

A tenth-century Syrian mathematician named al-Uqlidisi working in Damascus appears to be the first to introduce decimal fractions into Muslim mathematics, paving the way for ever more complicated and precise calculations for later digital and computer processing. In their own way, decimal fractions complete the modernization and streamlining of Muslim math begun with the zero and the Hindu numerals. Since al-Khwarizmi, non-decimal fractions have had an increasingly archaic feel about them, dating back to Babylon and ancient Egypt and other early cultures. They were right for their times. But after al-Uqlidisi, non-decimal fractions will begin to fall away from higher mathematics, leaving a cleaner, more precise system.

Just as important, as advanced Muslim math and higher geometry lay the intellectual underpinning for related fields in astronomy and science, they will also lay the foundation for a uniquely geometric approach to Muslim art and architecture. Because the Prophet seems to speak out against representational art, the natural human decorative impulse of the Muslims begins to flow toward the permissible and royally sanctioned area of math and astronomy. The early, tentative, quasi-Byzantine and Roman decorations of the Umayyads in Damascus will now be replaced by the interlocking triangles and hexagons and nonagons and stars of later classical Muslim art begun in Baghdad and then gradually spreading out to the other centers of genius. Muslim mathematicians in Baghdad and elsewhere will hold workshops with artisans and architects showing how geometric figures can be easily reproduced and turned into the tiled explosions of infinity that will adorn mosques, palaces, villas, and other buildings. Muslim mathematics, born from gazing up at the stars, will express itself in art for another thousand years.

A tenth-century Persian working in Baghdad named Abul Wafa introduces guides for artisans and architects to create geometric patterns in their building projects. Abul Wafa also begins to define a new universe of expression, by translating the unfolding mathematical realities, particularly geometry, into a new medium of artistic and decorative expression.

But this is only one of the contributions of the man considered perhaps the best Muslim mathematician of the tenth century. Abul Wafa will author commentaries on al-Khwarizmi, the Greek geometer Euclid and the Byzantine mathematician Diophantos. He will write a book of practical arithmetic and will create solutions to geometric problems done with a single opening of the compass. He will show how to mathematically construct a square equal to other squares, how to mathematically make regular poly-sided figures. Most importantly, he will lay the foundation of trigonometry, and he will show a new, more efficient way of calculating the sine tables. He will apparently be the first to calculate the secant, which he will call the "diameter of the shadow," an innovation that will be lost to history and perhaps mistakenly attributed to Copernicus 600 years later.

All these men, often in collaboration, sometimes in competition, sometimes in near isolation, work at finding the mathematical source codes that will lay the foundation for all future calculations on Earth. Dozens, hundreds of them labor away, the majority of them no better than the others, all aspiring to gain the mantle of al-Khwarizmi, although few will qualify. But the aggregate result is an avalanche of mathematical work, some of it mistaken, some of it derivative, much of it brilliant.

The intellectual underpinning of the first Muslim golden age and much of what follows, including the European Renaissance, is mathematics. This is pure mind work driven by questions about the stars. Everything else will follow.

IT IS NOW MORE THAN A CENTURY since al-Khwarizmi died. Some whisper he was the greatest and cannot be equaled.

But late in the 900s, a young man appears in the southern Iraqi city of Basra. He does not initially choose mathematics; he decides to go to work for the government of the caliphate, which by that point has shifted to the control of a new and short-lived dynasty, the Buyids. They will rule in Baghdad from 945 to 1055.

This young man's name is ibn al-Haytham, and someday he will rival his predecessor al-Khwarizmi, building on the discoveries of all who have come in the century that separates them. He will author as many as 200 books on various subjects, and he will begin to lay the foundation for mathematical and optical theories that will later enable Galileo and Copernicus to understand the true relationship of the Earth to other heavenly bodies, and the shape of the planet itself.

But all that is yet in the future when ibn al-Haytham comes of age.

His hometown lies in the marshy delta of the Tigris and Euphrates, a meeting place of Arabs and all those who sail to the port city. Date palms line the riverbanks and shade the hidden courtyards. Like most ports, Basra is a mixing place, a place where it is hard to hold fast to absolutes and rigidities. Improvisation and mixing are the rules. Yet to a boy watching the city around him, behind the ambiguity of life in Basra lie deeper mathematical codes and rules.

In this meeting place of the plane of desert, mirror of the river, and lines of sunlight angling down at various times of day through haze, through cloud, through clear desert skylight, the young ibn al-Haytham observes all this visual interaction and wonders. These angles, the areas in space they create, the rules that govern refraction and reflection, captivate him.

More than anything he is entranced by the light and wants to know more. What is light anyway? According to Ptolemy's astronomical treatise, the revered *Almagest,* light is a ray that emerges from the eye of the viewer and strikes the viewed object. Is this true? Are the ancient Greeks to be always taken on faith? Are they always the best reflections of the divine light of rationalist truth, or are they sometimes mistaken?

That will be left for another day. After completing his civil service education with the highest honors, ibn al-Haytham advances rapidly in government service. Eventually he is appointed chief minister of Basra, a very important and sought-after job, somewhere between governor and mayor. He must oversee every aspect of this center of commerce. Yet in keeping with the deeply religious nature of the caliphate, as part of ibn al-Haytham's job he must also immerse himself in theological readings, endless religious debates and disputes, and continuous quibbling and theorizing about revelation. He does this dutifully for a while.

Yet at some point, he has had enough. As sometimes happens with men of science, he concludes that none of the various factions and religious philosophers are necessarily correct. How can something as vast and complicated as the divine be known with any certainty by the mortal mind? How can self-appointed experts and their theories about God and faith be proved? Absent the Prophet to arbitrate, the fighting seems to him to be a pointless game. And at some stage he quietly withdraws from the theological meetings.

Instead, the brilliant young government minister ibn al-Haytham finds solace, like Caliph al-Mamun and all the scholars he patronized, in the thoughts of Aristotle. There, in rationalism, will he find the true mind of God revealed. Ibn al-Haytham turns himself to science and resigns his government position. Though many think he has made a terrible mistake to give up such a position of power and influence, he never looks back. Over the coming years, his scientific skills increase, and his reputation spreads far beyond Basra, Baghdad, and even Iraq.

It even goes beyond the Baghdad caliphate, now much diminished in geographic size since the loss of Spain to the Umayyads and North Africa to the Fatimids. Fame of ibn al-Haytham and knowledge of his distancing from the conventional religious factions at work in the caliphate spread to Cairo, capital of the Ismaili Fatimids. The caliph is one al-Hakim, who has been on the throne since age 13.

From afar, al-Hakim sounds like the long-dead Haroun al-Rashid and al-Mamun of legend. Al-Hakim has a vast and grandiose vision. He rules most of the old Abbasid caliphate. He is ravenous to have every great thinker and inventor come to Cairo. Moreover he intends to someday rule the whole world and to make Cairo its greatest city.

But up close, al-Hakim is more problematic. Historians will debate for a thousand years to come whether he is a misunderstood eccentric ruler devoted to intellectual brilliance and religious tolerance, or an increasingly erratic and possibly mentally disturbed leader given to bouts of cruelty and intolerance. Lost history will be clouded by the intense rivalry and distrust between mainstream Sunni thought as embodied in the Abbasids and their worldview and the alternative vision of the Shiite Ismaili Fatimids. The enigmatic al-Hakim will stand in the middle of that dispute. And for most of history, the Sunni version of al-Hakim will be accepted as truth, and he will come to be known as al-Hakim the Mad.

Al-Hakim's critics will charge that although he is unquestioningly faithful to the love of knowledge, he is also a tyrant given to terrible rages, that he becomes a religious bigot and a fanatic. They will say that because the barking of dogs in the village of al-Fustat on the outskirts of Cairo irritates him, he sacks the village and has all its dogs killed. They will claim that he forces his court to sleep by day and work at night. For reasons known only to him, they report, he bans certain vegetables and the staple Egyptian dish *mulukhiyyah* from being eaten by anyone.

Whether driven by his demons or simply out observing stars, the caliph will take solitary late-night horseback rides in the desert outside Cairo, risking life and limb in that politically conflicted time. His critics will report that he coldly slaughters his enemies, never considering the idea of pardon or reconciliation, and that he tortures his enemies before execution. After starting his reign as a friend of Christians and Jews, he turns on them. As evidence, critics will point to his inexplicable destruction of the Shrine of the Holy Sepulchre, commemorating the tomb of Christ's burial, so sacred to the Christians in Jerusalem.

He is said to ban the playing of chess, most likely because he is a bad player. His court becomes a place of fear and intimidation, and the caliph's viziers stop showing up for work for fear they will trigger their leader's wrath and vengeance.

However, a newer view of al-Hakim will begin to emerge in the mid-20th century. Drawing on long-lost Ismaili, Jewish, Christian, and Shiite accounts, some historians will present a more benign picture of the Fatimid caliph. A praiseful Jewish eulogy will make al-Hakim sound like a generous and tolerant leader. Christians will also depict al-Hakim as their benefactor and protector.

These accounts will recall that the mercurial al-Hakim is the son of a Christian mother. Beginning in 1005 he is involved in the construction of one of the most important institutions of higher learning in the Muslim world, the Dar al-Hikmat, or House of Knowledge, in Cairo. The mosque that he endows, the beautiful al-Hakim Mosque, also in Cairo, is a building dedicated to the concept of light, with its esoteric references to knowledge both divine and human. Historians will recall that under the Fatimids, Ismaili philosophy develops into a powerful synthesis of rationalism and esotericism influenced by Greek Platonic-Neoplatonic, Islamic, scientific, and mystical concepts. Al-Hakim himself seems to have favored an ascetic lifestyle, not much interested in the pleasures of the court.

Historians will note that al-Hakim positions Jews and Christians in his government as important decision-makers throughout his reign, often to the consternation of Muslim communities. In a Jewish source from the period labeled *Egyptian Fragments,* al-Hakim is painted in a positive light:

His kingdom was exalted and strengthened and his throne was higher than the throne of his fathers and forefathers. Thirteen years old was he when he began to reign, and he carried on his government with large-ness of heart and a good understanding, and needed neither minister nor counselor. Many plots were made against him, and many enemies rose up against him, but God made them to fall under the soles of his feet: because he loved righteousness and hated iniquity, and set up judges in the land and commanded them to judge and decide in equity and truth. He took away the violent men and removed the foolish: he rejected them that pervert their way and are corrupt in their doings. But he loved men of understanding, and to establish judgment and the way of goodness.

Whether misunderstood mystic-king or paranoid tyrant, the irony of al-Hakim is that his bright side is so bright that it cannot be ignored by a man of learning like ibn al-Haytham. More importantly, any smart person can apply to study at al-Hakim's House of Knowledge, no matter how poor or unknown. It is not just a place for those who are well connected. And al-Hakim is as scrupulous in preserving this new center of rationality as he is personally eccentric. The House of Knowledge is true to its name, and it is the beacon that draws many promising thinkers to Cairo, when the enigma of al-Hakim would otherwise deter them.

Eleventh-century Cairo, with its splendid al-Azhar mosque and madrassa-university, its palaces and riverfront parks and intellectual salons, is becoming a center of genius equivalent to Baghdad, and will someday surpass it. Men who a century before would have gone to Baghdad are now heading to Egypt.

Caliph al-Hakim learns that ibn al-Haytham, still in Basra, has come up with a plan to regulate the flooding of the Nile. This earthshaking possibility catches the immediate attention of the caliph, and he summons the author to carry out his plan.

Though the flooding is critical to renewing the fertility of the narrow strip of the agricultural floodplain that runs nearly to Alexandria, creating the very breadbasket of Egypt since the beginning of time, in fact the flooding is also very disruptive, and the idea of controlling its extent or even its timing is intoxicating to al-Hakim.

Ibn al-Haytham accepts the job offer from al-Hakim. With a team of court-appointed engineers, he begins to travel up the Nile to find the right point to build his flood control system. And though the journey is quite fascinating, taking these Muslim engineers past the timeless pharaonic ruins of Luxor and Abu Simbel, at some point beyond Aswan the thinker from Basra realizes his plan cannot be executed. The river is too wide, the grade of descent too slight, the flow of water too vast, and his resources too limited.

He must go back to the caliph and tell him that the plan won't work.

At this point, the traditional history says that ibn al-Haytham trembles at the thought of going back to the caliph and telling him that he has failed. So to save himself upon his return, he feigns madness, acting crazier than his patron. It is a terrible risk, but better than telling the truth. Ibn al-Haytham babbles non sequiturs and then goes catatonic.

It is lost to history whether ibn al-Haytham actually pulls this stunt; the story is based on possibly biased accounts written two hundred years after the event. What is known is that ibn al-Haytham does not complete the plan and is not visible at court. But he remains in Cairo and continues his own scientific and mathematical research subsidized by a mysterious patron, possibly the caliph's sister, Sitt al-Mulk, reportedly one of the richest Muslim women in history. Whether in confinement for his failure or not, he continues his work at home.

Ibn al-Haytham resumes his own research, now on the subject of light, the subject that has fascinated him since his youth, and he begins the greatest projects in his long and prolific career.

When ibn al-Haytham begins to unlock his destiny, al-Hakim completes his own journey. In 1016 he declares himself the incarnation of God on Earth. He surrounds himself with a cult of worshippers who believe that he is the true savior of Islam and the divinely guided caliph who will cleanse the faith. When al-Hakim disappears one night while wandering alone in a range of desert hills, his followers claim that he has gone into a state of occultation and will return at Judgment Day as the Mahdi of Shiite myth, to restore righteousness to mankind.

The news of Caliph al-Hakim's disappearance and likely death fills ibn al-Haytham with relief and uncertainty. Freed of the continuing unpredictability of al-Hakim, ibn al-Haytham can resume his public work. It seems likely that Sitt al-Mulk, who inherits the Fatimid throne from her brother and rules for the next two years, continues the patronage of ibn al-Haytham. At any rate, the new arrangement involves changes. Ibn al-Haytham leaves the house given him by the caliph and moves into a *qubbah,* a small domed building at the gate to Cairo's towering al-Azhar mosque. There he teaches mathematics and retranslates the Greeks using his knowledge of mathematics, deeper than some of the early translators, and he builds on the insights gleaned in the intervening 200 years.

His new home at al-Azhar is the shining architectural jewel of Fatimid Cairo, but for ibn al-Haytham it is much more. In its minarets, in its domes and Abbasid arches, in the tawny colonnades of columns and arches overwashed by day and shadow, he watches the light. The geometry of the dome, the soft illumination falling on the faithful at prayer from windows on high, the shadows in morning and afternoon as the sun shifts from pearly dawn to near-white at zenith to blue-rose heliotrope at sunset, the chants of the worshippers and the laughter of his students, swirl around him and in his mind.

What better place to bring his theories of light into light of day than this temple of light on the plane of the Egyptian desert?

For all those years of al-Hakim's eccentricity, while ibn al-Haytham may have been pretending to be more unsettled than his patron, he has been scribbling his tomes and hiding them. He knew that, should an enemy come searching, he might lose it all. But he and his writings have survived.

Though he will write as many as two hundred books, and many of them will eventually be lost, his seven volumes on optics will survive—perhaps his most important work. The core lesson of his writings is that science must be based on empirical methods. As far as we know, ibn al-Haytham is the first scholar to absolutely apply this principle of empiricism without mercy. While the Greeks had understood experimentation and empiricism, they were too often prone to proving their point through intellectual theorizing.

Ibn al-Haytham knows better. No human mind, no matter how brilliant, is capable of theorizing the physical world. It must be measured and observed. Throughout his writings, he will make clear that he questions all scientific assumptions until proven by testing. Like the scientists of a thousand years later, he will take no scientific statements on faith.

One of his greatest discoveries, which will seem trivial in hindsight, is his proof that light rays do not emanate from the eyeball of the viewer. Though Ptolemy's claim to the contrary seems silly now, such basic assumptions about laws of physics still stand strong in ibn al-Haytham's time. He will need to swim against the tide of conventional wisdom to disprove them.

From that important and basic starting point, ibn al-Haytham moves deeper into the various properties of light that first intrigued him as a boy back in Basra. He focuses on how light passes through various media: water, glass, paper, smoke. As he does that, he begins playing around with how light is broken down into its component colors. Though his observations will be quite different from later modern understanding of refraction, nonetheless he is beginning to ask the right questions. He takes his discoveries from the laboratory and begins to observe the colors of the sky and the western horizon at sunset and dusk. He spends years puzzling over the interplay of light and shadow, the behavior of mirrors, and the impact of curved mirrors on the play of light.

He ponders eclipses of the sun and moon, trying to reconcile this long-feared phenomenon with the Ptolemaic view of the sun and stars orbiting Earth. It does not add up, but he can't yet figure out why. Just as his discovery of light being an energy source independent of the eyeball contradicts

Ptolemy, he confides to others that Ptolemy's view of the heavens must be seriously reevaluated. He is warned that he is verging on intellectual heresy.

That warning has no meaning to him. The only thing that motivates him is the hunger to know more, to understand the complexity of God's universe, to find its hidden keys in the source code of mathematical formula, to find truth wherever it is, no matter the language or the conventional wisdom or the articles of faith.

A massive rainbow spreads above him after a spring shower in warming Cairo, and he sees the same spectrum in the sky he found in the laboratory as he played with glass and prisms and glasses of water. The mysterious separation of white light into vast and tiny rainbows sends him back to his calculating table.

The very nature of the human eyeball fascinates him, and he studies dissections, trying to understand how light enters the cornea, what happens between the lens and the back of the eyeball. He gives a detailed explanation of how the eyeball works; later scientists will build on this insight to develop a modern explanation of human vision. Inspired by the human eyeball, he starts to build what will later be known as the camera obscura. Five hundred years before Leonardo da Vinci, he delves into things that will later be attributed to the great Italian and to Kepler and Descartes, when in fact they, like some Renaissance and post-Renaissance thinkers are really replicating or building on what the great Muslim scientists had established long ago.

Using his camera obscura, he determines that light travels in straight lines, an understanding basic to any higher studies of light but, until ibn al-Haytham, never proven. In his *Book of Optics*, he writes:

Let an experimenter take a solid body, make a tiny hole in it, then hold it opposite the sun. He will find that light goes through the hole, moving along a straight line. If he tests the light as it extends through space, he will find it to be perfectly straight. It is therefore clear from all this that the light of the sun only extends along straight lines.

Ibn al-Haytham tries to figure out the mechanics of human binocular vision. He wonders why the sun and moon appear so much larger near the horizon than when they are high in the sky, and offers the correct explanations. He obsesses on the mathematical implications of spherical and parabolic mirrors, and these issues take him on whole new flights of mathematical calculation. He begins to understand the magnifying power of a lens, a critical discovery that will later help Galileo and Copernicus and Leeuwenhoek to find the stars and to find microbes.

Ibn al-Haytham's work will also pave the way for an early form of calculus. This work is very influential, shaping mathematics as far away as India. And in one of his greatest and most audacious triumphs, ibn al-Haytham deduces that the curious interval of twilight, something that to the casual observer seems magical and to be taken for granted, has various mathematical and physical explanations. He calculates that twilight only occurs when the sun is 19 degrees below the horizon. Using that fact he comes close to gauging the depth of the atmosphere, something that will not be verified until the 20th century, the century of space travel.

Reaching out to the very limits of higher physics, he seems to be aware of gravity itself, and he writes about the attraction of masses 600 years before Galileo and Sir Isaac Newton.

In one of his more lyrical moments, he attempts to quantify from his emerging visual theories what constitutes beauty in *On Direct Vision*:

> *Sight perceives [beauty] by perceiving each one of the particular properties of which the manner of perception by sight has been shown. For each of these properties separately produces one of the kinds of beauty, and they produce [other] kinds of beauty in conjunction with one another.... Position produces beauty, and many things that look beautiful do so only because of order and position. Beautiful writing is also regarded as such because of order alone. For the beauty of writing is due only to the soundness of the shapes of letters and their composition.... Separateness produces beauty. Thus dispersed stars are more beautiful than nebulae and the Milky Way.... For this reason, too, blossoms and flowers dispersed in meadows look more beautiful than when they are gathered and crowded together. Continuity produces beauty. Thus meadows with continuous and dense vegetation are more beautiful than those in which the vegetation is interrupted and discontinuous. And of the meadows that look beautiful because of their colours, those which are continuous are more beautiful than the others.*

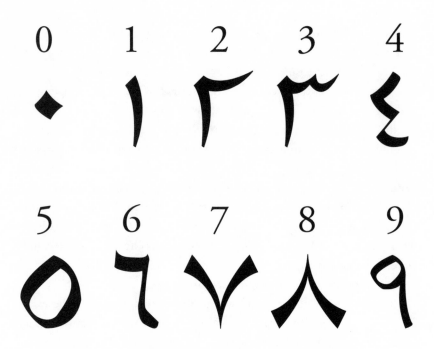

Modern numerals in the West are directly derived from the medieval
Arabic-Indic number system. Similarities can still be seen today.

Many of his questions will not be answered for nearly a thousand years, until the appearance of another genius obsessed with math and light, one Albert Einstein in Zurich. Considering the earliness of his work and the limits of his time, ibn al-Haytham must be considered an equal of Einstein, though largely lost to history.

The light of life goes out for ibn al-Haytham in 1040 in Cairo. He is about 75 years old, and with failing vision and health, this student of light has long known that the next light he would see would be in the spiritual world. It will be several centuries before his voluminous writings are translated into Latin, first about 1270, and printed by Friedrich Risner in 1572; ibn al-Haytham will be known to the Europeans as Alhazen. For a time they will consider him a giant, so far is he beyond the ideas of medieval Europe. And then, by the time of the Renaissance, those replicating or expanding upon his work will eclipse him.

Ibn al-Haytham would probably not have cared. He was much more interested in answering the questions of the universe than in getting credit for his work. He was happy to write and study for himself, locked away in his private asylum.

And if he had been able to see the future after he had departed, he would have been filled with excitement. Because in faraway Central Asia and Persia, things are happening that will produce the next Muslim giant of mathematics, a man who will be remembered in the West not for his math, but for his poetry.

IN 1048 Ghiyath al-Din Abu'l-Fath Omar ibn Ibrahim al-Nisaburi Khayyámi is born in Nishapur, a Persian city in the fertile valley up against the jagged range of Mount Binalud, that has been the capital of a new Muslim state, the Seljuk Empire, for ten years.

This boy, who will grow into a mathematical and astronomical genius, is perhaps unique in the pantheon of Muslim mathematicians, for more than anything else he has the soul of a poet. He will become a philosopher of everyday human existence. He will be both a lover of the sensual and a lover of the ecstatic. He will dare to question the very tenets of orthodoxy in his faith.

He will temper all this with a melancholic sense of the tragedy and futility of life, of work, of achievement. Even as he toils on behalf of his rulers and patrons to unlock the secrets of numbers and the secrets of stars, he will mock his work and will venture that he would have been better off spending his time drinking wine in the tavern, or resting in the arms of a lover. To most of the world he will be known as Omar Khayyám, his last name meaning tentmaker. Members of his family support themselves by that trade.

The Seljuk rulers are the first in a wave of Central Asian conquerors who will gradually begin to destabilize and then overwhelm the old Arab-Persian culture of the Abbasids. The Central Asians will increasingly define the world of Islam, and far from being illiterate barbarians, they will adopt and build on the older civilizations in their path, spawning multiple golden ages along the way.

The Seljuks begin to create a Turkic-Persian world that in varying forms and under differing regimes will last 900 years: in the Seljuk Dynasty and its spinoffs in Persia, Anatolia, and Syria from the 11th to the early 14th centuries; in the Mongol rule in the 13th and 14th centuries; in the era of Timur, or Tamerlane, and his heirs from 1336 to 1405; in the reign of the

Ottoman Turks from 1299 to 1922; and in the Moghul rule from 1483 to 1857.

Long before the birth of Omar Khayyám, the turquoise mines near Nishapur, the ceramics and tile industry, and the caravan trade have made the city rich. The color blue permeates Nishapur, not only from the sky above, but in the tiled domes of mosques and palaces, in the colonnades of arches and around the perimeter of tombs, in geometric patterns playing out the geometric formulas of the Greeks and Arabs. Before Khayyám's time, the wealth of Nishapur from trade may have equaled that of Baghdad and Cairo.

But not everyone in this city knows wealth. The Khayyám family is poor. For young Omar, his richest times are spent on the roof at night, looking up at the sky untainted by anything other than clouds or dust off the distant deserts. In Nishapur in the 11th century, aside from some wood smoke in winter from the fires and oil lamps, man has no ability to impede the glow of the stars. Khayyám looks up at an ocean of stars, the familiar constellations, and the vast and irregular blur of the Milky Way appearing with a clarity common across much of the world in that day. The night sky is by far the most fascinating panorama and the most engaging entertainment available, especially for someone of limited means.

Although the stars call to him, the reality of his earthly life cannot be escaped. At some point, Khayyám's father is gone, and he and his mother must keep the younger siblings alive. But Khayyám's mother knows that her son is exceptionally gifted and meant for greater things than stitching tents together to feed his brothers and sisters.

In those days, if one is smart and ambitious in Nishapur, one goes to study with the imam Mowaffak. The legend is that anyone who studies under the imam will know good fortune later in life, no matter what one's profession. A beneficent man and a Muslim rationalist in the tradition of al-Mamun, imam Mowaffak is probably the only door to greater opportunity for most of the young men in Khorasan province.

At first the imam, besieged with such applications, is skeptical. But he submits Khayyám to a quick math test, which the youth passes with flying colors. And so begins one of the most compelling human and intellectual stories in the lost history of the Muslims.

Though Khayyám does not yet know it, in the madrassa of Mowaffak he will form an unusual triangle of relationships that will reflect the turmoil of the Muslim world for the next thousand years, and shape three lives until their ends.

Documentary proof of this triangular connection will be lost to history, so that it will be treated more as legend than as fact. But there will be a dramatic symmetry to this story that will captivate writers and historians, so that many of them will weave it into their narratives.

In Mowaffak's madrassa young Khayyám is allegedly joined by one Hasan ibn Sabbah, wealthy son of a strange and reputedly fanatical man. And through Mowaffak there is a connection, possibly a personal introduction, to the esteemed teacher Nizam al-Mulk.

Legend also has it that there is a slave girl in Nishapur named Darya and that both Hasan ibn Sabbah and Omar Khayyám compete for her love but that Khayyám is the winner.

Then they all scatter to the winds, in pursuit of different opportunities. Omar Khayyám continues his studies in Central Asian cities like Balkh, the ancient birthplace of Zoroaster and the cultural heart of what will later become Afghanistan, and Samarkand, another Silk Road trading center on the steppe that will later belong to Uzbekistan. In those years, he applies himself to considering certain mathematical formulas, including a work on the rules governing the positive roots of numbers and one entitled *Sharh-i Mushkil min Kitab al-Musiqi,* dealing with the mathematical structure of music.

For many centuries before and after Khayyám, music is seen less as an art and more as an extension of mathematics and science, in particular drawing on Byzantine and Arab-Persian theories of the eight-moded musical scale, the fractional elements of fretting an instrument, and the like. Music is seen as the representation in sound of mathematical formulas. Music, math, and astronomy intersect in concepts such as the music of the spheres originally theorized by Pythagoras, in which he speculated that the distance between Earth and the "celestial sphere" was the most perfect harmonic interval. Following his theory, the Muslims interpreted that to the supposed extraplanetary sound of the heavenly bodies spinning in space, a musical representation of their movements reducible by mathematics to the formula of their orbits, inclinations, speeds, masses, and sizes.

Early in this intellectual journey, Khayyám becomes aware of the continuing theoretical battles between the Muslim rationalists and the textual literalists over theology, philosophy, the sciences, and the political struggle between Sunnis and Shiites over power. Khayyám begins to shape his own personal philosophy, not unlike what will arise in Enlightenment Europe 700 years later. While he professes to believe in God, he believes that the observable universe is governed by scientific rules that can only be discovered through study and research. He ventures the daring and futuristic concept that God does not intervene in the physical world.

The festering debate between textual literalism and rationalism touches everyone. Luckily for a man like Khayyám, in his day the ruling Sunni Seljuk and Abbasid powers lean toward rationalism. Ironically, the rival Shiite Ismaili also incline toward rationalism. More often than not, the various Muslim rulers and conquerors seem to know instinctively that a society cannot innovate and be great, if the mind is not free. Though by Khayyám's time the Abbasids are much weakened and the Umayyads are far away in Spain, their shared method of endowing and supporting invention and inquiry has been noticed and adopted by many successors, from the Fatimids of Egypt to the various conquerors in Persia and Asia.

In his work in Balkh, Samarkand, and Nishapur, Khayyám authors methods for solving cubic equations that are intelligible only to the most advanced mathematics students a thousand years later. A cubic equation is a polynomial equation in which the highest occurring power of the unknown is the third power. An example is the equation:

$$x^3 + 200x = 20x^2 + 2000.$$

Omar Khayyám's method works, in fact, by intersecting a parabola with a circle.

In addition, Khayyám discovers the binominal expansion, an important formula giving the expansion of powers of sums. He also critiques Euclid's theories of parallels. His writing in this area gradually makes its way to Europe, where it helps the gradual development of non-Euclidean geometry. And his work in astronomy is just as important and as complicated. His methods hold potential applications such as refining the calendar, which leads to more efficiency in government and trade.

But life is fairly uncertain for Omar Khayyám. Despite periodic assignments by the wealthy and powerful, he is still dependent on the needs and requests of his patrons to survive. In Samarkand, he is supported for a time by Abu Tahir, a prominent judge, and this allows him to do much work on algebra. But that is only temporary. As he later writes:

> *I was unable to devote myself to the learning of this algebra and the continued concentration upon it, because of obstacles in the vagaries of time which hindered me; for we have been deprived of all the people of knowledge save for a group, small in number, with many troubles, whose concern in life is to snatch the opportunity, when time is asleep, to devote themselves meanwhile to the investigation and perfection of a science.*

Finally, mention of Omar Khayyám and his intriguing new books catches the attention of the Seljuk court, now relocated to the Persian city of Isfahan. But Khayyám is not a provincial unknown to the court. In another stroke of good luck, Mowaffak's old friend, educator Nizam al-Mulk, has risen to become grand vizier to the Seljuk ruler, Malik Shah. In 1073, both because of his accomplishments and his connections, Khayyám is invited by the sultan to Isfahan to be a court mathematician and astronomer.

Journeying to the imperial city of Isfahan, Khayyám sees the blue domes of its mosques and palaces glinting in the Persian sun, and the world suddenly explodes with promise. How lucky he has been to have come even this far. The son of a tentmaker, now he has been summoned to work for the ruler of half the world.

At Isfahan, Khayyám is given the assignment of building an observatory and recalculating the calendar. Malik Shah, though the patron of intellectuals, is not an intellectual himself. His real motive in the project is astrology, not astronomy. As a conqueror and ruler, he wants to know what the stars are saying about his future and his world. Khayyám must carefully educate the sultan, cautioning that in his opinion the stars do not predict the future.

Instead, leading a research team of mathematicians and astronomers, Khayyám begins the effort of creating a new, more accurate calendar. He rightly believes that this will give a more precise measurement of time, allowing not only for more faithful observance of religious holidays, but for more accurate record keeping and improved tax collection.

For 19 years, Khayyám will enjoy the most secure and stable period in his long life. Even as the forces opposing his patrons gather strength only an arm's length away, he is at his most productive.

In 1079 in an astonishing feat of computation without computers, Omar Khayyám will calculate the length of the year to be 365.24219858156 days. In the 21st century, using the Hubble telescope, atomic clocks, and computers, the year will be calculated to be 365.242190 days. Khayyám's error in the sixth decimal place will amount to an inaccuracy of fractions of a second.

And in another achievement, Omar Khayyám will demonstrate to an astonished audience how the Earth revolves on its axis, rather than having the heavens orbit it. He will prove this to an audience, which is said to include the eminent philosopher al-Ghazali, by building an elaborate construction of stars, a revolving Earth, and candles representing the stars and the sun.

But back down at Earth level, things are beginning to happen that will upend Khayyám's two decades of security. And one of the key actors is his schoolboy friend Hasan ibn Sabbah, who has also held a Seljuk government position, possibly as a minister.

Lost history and the diverging accounts from Sunni and Ismaili historians will obscure much of the story. By conventional accounts, Hasan ibn Sabbah has attempted to kill his onetime patron Nizam al-Mulk, but fails. He has fled into exile and joined a Persian group of Ismailis by going underground. The group presents political resistance to the Sunnis, and as some would charge, makes targeted political killings. Aside from resisting the Seljuks and Abbasids, ibn Sabbah's parallel mission and that of his successors is to physically preserve the Ismaili faith in the face of rising antagonism led by the Seljuks.

Ironically, ibn Sabbah's faith, though in political and doctrinal opposition to the Sunnis, has absorbed some of the same mix of Greek rationalism, Qur'anic guidance, and esoteric beliefs, until it declares that human reason is on equal footing with religious piety. But this philosophical bridge is not enough to overcome the doctrinal gulf between Sunnis and Ismailis.

Nizam al-Mulk, in the name of Sunni tradition and Seljuk power, will be one of ibn Sabbah's strongest antagonists. The Seljuks see the Ismailis as rivals and enemies, as well as heretics. Whether in self-defense or to promote subversion, ibn Sabbah establishes a network of mountain castles in northern Persia, near-impregnable mountain fortresses where the leaders and adherents of Ismailism can ride out the rising wave of Sunni hostility to their faith. Ibn Sabbah's Persian strongholds will now serve as a haven for the Ismaili doctrine to thrive and evolve for the next century and a half. To protect their mountain communities from the continuous Seljuk threat, ibn Sabbah's small "secret order" of elite soldiers resorts to various strategies to hold off the much larger Seljuk armies. One tactic is to limit bloodshed and retaliation by merely intimidating army commanders and governors into leaving Ismaili territories alone.

This broad political-doctrinal struggle will directly impact on Omar Khayyám's life, putting him on opposite sides from his childhood friend Hasan ibn Sabbah. And this strange triangular destiny now plays itself out. In 1092, the wonderful friend and patron, the wise vizier and namesake of the universities called Nizamiya that spread across the Muslim world at his initiative, Nizam al-Mulk, is assassinated. Only a month later, Sultan Malik Shah falls in battle. And although his wife briefly succeeds him, she was never a friend of Nizam al-Mulk or his court favorites. As a result, Khayyám is out of favor, then forced to leave the court of Isfahan.

That is not indignity enough. Alarmed at his irreverent and increasingly nontraditional views, Sunni clerics interrogate Omar Khayyám about his faith. In a foreshadowing of the trials that Galileo will endure 500 years later, Omar Khayyám is questioned about his own beliefs.

The two camps are arguing at different levels. Omar Khayyám, the scientist and the mathematician, cannot espouse conventional statements of faith. He tries his best to explain, but his explanations inflame or disturb as many as they assuage. Finally, to prove his belief, he is obliged to make a pilgrimage to Mecca. It keeps him alive but does not restore his former position.

From that dark point, it would seem that the long journey of Omar Khayyám is over, but by a final stroke of good fortune, it is not. In 1118, after a long hiatus, Malik Shah's third son, a supporter of Khayyám's, becomes sultan, moving his capital to Merv, the Persian city where al-Mamun had been Abbasid governor and then caliph three hundred years before. In the final four years of his life, with a new patron and an unfailing belief in science and research, Omar Khayyám resumes his work.

He tells someone in his final days that he will be buried in Nishapur, in a grave covered by rose petals. A visitor centuries later claims that the gravestone in Nishapur is so covered by rose petals that it cannot be read.

Despite the brilliance of his insights into mathematics and astronomy, most non-Muslims will know Omar Khayyám by the rose petals of his poetry. The debate about the true meaning and intent of his words is still raging. The 19th-century translation of the *Rubaiyat* by Edward Fitzgerald, though inspired, is badly flawed.

In his *Rubaiyat*, Khayyám says this of human existence in the 20th-century translation by Omar Ali Shah and Robert Graves:

What we shall be is written, and we are so.
Heedless of God or Evil, pen, write on!
By the first day all futures were decided.

Writing around 1120, only two years from death, Omar Khayyám writes what he calls his *Profession of Faith:*

The temple I frequent is high,
A Turkish-vaulted dome—the sky,
That spans the world with majesty.
Not quite a Muslim is my creed,
Nor quite a Giaour; my faith indeed
May startle some who hear me say,
I'd give my pilgrim staff away,
And sell my turban, for an hour
Of music in a fair one's bower.
I'd sell the rosary for wine,
Though holy names around it twine.
And prayers the pious make so long
Are turned by me to joyous song;
Or, if a prayer I should repeat,
It is at my beloved's feet.

They blame me that my words are clear;
Because I am not what I appear;

Nor do my acts my words belie—
At least, I shun hypocrisy.
It happened that but yesterday
I marked a potter beating clay.
The earth spoke out—Why dost thou strike?
Both thou and I are born alike;
Though some may sink and some may soar,
We all are earth, and nothing more.

STAR PATTERNS

It is not for the sun to overtake the moon nor doth the night outstrip the day.
They float each other in an orbit.

QUR'AN (XIV:39)

NASA JET PROPULSION LABORATORY (JPL), Pasadena, California, 2007—Robert Bailey is at his workstation in greater Los Angeles, monitoring the latest radar feeds from the Cassini spacecraft as it flies past Saturn's giant moon, Titan. Peering through the distant moon's smoggy atmosphere of superchilled hydrocarbons, Cassini has found wide lakes of liquid methane at the planet's north pole, not unlike the geography of lake and tundra in Earth's Arctic region, though totally different in chemical composition and temperature. Each Cassini flyby is better than the previous one, adding detail to the heretofore hazy image of Titan.

Elsewhere on Titan is an Australia-size continent called Xanadu, its surface shaped and eroded by ice-water volcanoes, ethane winds, and methane rain and rivers. The moon hangs in perpetual blue twilight, the distant sun and reflections of nearby Saturn cut by frozen haze and clouds.

Bailey loves this job. He's been on the Cassini project for more than a year, after an unhappy but career-necessary stint at NASA headquarters in Washington, D.C. There he had helped the administrators prepare for congressional briefings. Though the long hours and high pressure led to several promotions, Bailey would rather be dealing with the fog of Titan than the fog of Capitol Hill. Living in the city was expensive, the traffic terrible, and though, he was glad for the kids' sake to spend a time in a racially tolerant and diverse city, he was and is a man of science, not of politics and policy.

The Washington experience had become so wearing for him that he had considered taking a job with a private company, before this NASA assignment came open.

Bailey is a native of Georgia, the second generation of his family to get a college education. He won his doctorate in astrophysics at the Georgia Institute of Technology, in Atlanta. His parents were both public school teachers in coastal Georgia. His grandparents were farmers, and his great-great-great-great grandparents were African captives brought from the Yoruba area in Nigeria to the Georgia coast, where they were forced into slavery. Spared the dislocations forced on other slaves, the Bailey family had remained intact and close to where they had landed in America for almost two centuries.

Bailey has had to deal with the reality of ethnic and tribal lines all his life. His wife is of another race. They met and married at Georgia Tech. That was one reason he valued the time in Washington, at least for his children. Although he had spent much time in Atlanta, another diverse and tolerant city, by the time the kids were born, they were living in Cape Canaveral and then Houston. His older son was stopped several times in his car by Texas police for no apparent reason. His little daughter had seen racial slurs written on graffiti walls in Florida.

But Bailey feels fortunate. After 20 years with NASA, he earns a good six-figure income, and he has accumulated savings and investments and a retirement account. He kept his homes in Florida and Texas after they moved and made them rental income properties. His wife has built up an expertise in real estate, and between the two of them, they have a net worth of over a million dollars.

While he knows he has worked hard to get where he is, Bailey also understands the importance of luck. He was lucky to have parents who valued education; he was lucky to be given the time and money to study all those years.

He peruses the radar images of the far distant blue ice-moon spinning with the rings of one of the most dazzling objects in the solar system, this frozen satellite named after the Roman deity who fathered Jupiter and all the Roman gods. Saturn's moon Titan was named after the giants spawned in the first wave of the planet's procreation. To clear his eyes, he looks out at the dim hydrocarbon haze of Pasadena with its Lombardy poplars and eucalyptus and palms, its freeways and cars spinning off at the JPL exit. He realizes how much he loves being freed of the bonds of Earth in his work. The world of politics and everyday human affairs just brings so much confusion. Religion, ethnicity, tribe, ego—he really wishes all that could be left behind, so people could just be their own selves, not bit players in a group destiny.

When Bailey's mind is out in space, the insignificance of human division is utterly wiped out in the grandeur of the cosmos. Out there, among the greater and lesser spheres, in the vast blackness between the stars and planets, man becomes pure energy, one more identity riding the radio and radar waves, one more tiny note joining the galactic symphony of space, the hums of the planets, the bursts of sun and star noise, the lingering roar of a faraway star falling into a quasar at the beginning of time.

Back down on Earth, in his NASA cubicle, is a clipping from *the Atlanta Journal-Constitution* sent by his 80-year-old mother still living on the Georgia coast. In the cubicle he has photos of his parents and wife and kids, mixed in with big color posters of Mars, Saturn, and Jupiter.

The newspaper article is about a group of cultural anthropologists who have been studying the little Georgia island town where the Baileys have lived for 200 years. The researchers have focused on the African ancestry of the town, even of his own family. It turns out that the African ancestor of the Baileys is a Yoruba man named Bilali, and he was most likely a Muslim. At least a third of the slaves coming to America were Muslim, and possibly all of those who had ended up on the same island as the Baileys.

The anthropologists have also studied the old Sunrise African Baptist Church, where most of Bailey's ancestors are buried. They have found that it and the other old churches on the island dating back to slave days all point east, in the direction of Mecca. The old-timers of the town also face east to pray their Baptist prayers. The implication is that these African Baptists turning east to pray are Christianized crypto-Muslims. They have forgotten who they are.

On top of that, the Bilalis were Anglicized into Baileys long before the Civil War. Their namesake is the seventh-century African Bilal, one of the first converts to Islam and followers of the Prophet, who first uttered the call to prayer on the Arabian desert 1,400 years ago. Though unlikely, the Baileys of Georgia are possibly descended from the first Muslim muezzin ever to cry out in the desert dawn.

Bailey has read all this but hasn't responded to his mother. What does she want him to say? Express joy that, on top of being descendants of the world's worst institutionalized slavery, they are also descendants of the religion that some Baptist preachers are railing against every Sunday morning?

Shall he bring the kids into this one? Shall he lay another one on them? It was hard enough telling the little innocents that there were certain people in the world who would judge and reject them for their skin color. He will let this one go. This is his mother's thing. If she wants to become a Bilali Muslim at the age of 80, let her.

He will let this go. It is one more thing pulling him back into the past, away from the stars. What possible relevance does it have for him?

BAGHDAD, A.D. 780—As much as mathematics, astronomy will trigger significant scientific outpouring throughout the various Muslim golden ages. In fact, eighth-century Muslim astronomers are almost indistinguishable from Muslim mathematicians, and astronomers begin to flourish in Baghdad even before the House of Wisdom is established in the times of city founder Caliph al-Mansur, and then in the reign of Caliph Haroun al-Rashid. These men consider themselves as much mathematicians, and sometimes philosophers, as they are lovers of stars.

Questions of the heavens are driving many of the mathematical inquiries during the time of the Abbasid caliphs. Scholars are computing the movements of the stars, the phases and timing of the lunar year, explaining and predicting lunar eclipses, trying to gauge and understand the very nature of time itself, as tracked out by the seasonal positions of the sun, moon, and stars.

Why is this? Much of this goes back to the revelations of the Prophet and his statements about key ritualistic issues. He has conveyed that the faithful must pray five times a day, at specific times, beginning at dawn and moving on through day into night. He has communicated that the faithful must face Mecca when they pray. He has taught that there are 12 months in a year, including four sacred months, one being Ramadan, which commemorates the time that Muhammad received his first revelation from God.

Until the Muslim era, an assortment of religion-based calendars have competed for attention in the Middle East and Central Asia. The two religions closest to Islam, Judaism and Christianity, are using similar calendars with enough built-in inaccuracies to require the insertion of a 13th month every 19 years to bring the dates and sun position back into harmony.

But the Qur'an clearly states that there are only 12 months per year:

... the number of months in the sight of God is 12 [in a year]—so ordained by Him the day He created the heavens and the earth; of them four are sacred: that is the straight usage. Qur'an (IX:36)

Additionally, after the Prophet's death, the community decided that the Muslim calendar will be defined by the lunar year, which is 11 days shorter than the solar year. On top of that, Muslim astronomers will be tasked with a unique challenge: the Muslim months do not begin with the new moon, but with the crescent moon.

Predicting just when the crescent moon will appear is a special challenge to Islamic astronomers. Initially, when the early Muslim community still lacks a well-developed astronomical-mathematical approach to mark the passage of time, people use the moon's phases to develop the calendar. They rely on moon sightings—the first visible crescent—to mark the first day of the month. Later on, once the astronomical-mathematical approaches become more acceptable, people will rely less on human sightings and more on calculations of the moon's position. By the 21st century, some countries will practice the traditional method of moon sighting, while others will follow mathematical calculations.

In other calculations, to compute the time of day, for example, the mathematical challenge is to determine the unknown sides or angles of a huge triangle composed of the Earth and the celestial sphere, from the known sides and angles. The Muslim astronomers must form a triangle whose three points or vertices are the sun's position, the zenith of the sky and the north celestial pole. The known quantities are the sun's position and the north celestial pole. The time is the angle at the intersection of two arcs: one through the arc of the zenith and the pole, and one through the arc of the sun and the pole.

While the early Greeks had been using a cumbersome method of repeated calculations to gauge time, their system was impractical: By the time they got an answer, time had moved on. Over a span of several centuries, the Muslims are able to simplify the process by using more efficient trigonometric formulas. Though one of the trigonometric functions, the sine, had come to them from India, the astronomers in Baghdad are able to determine the remaining five, and so unlock the full power of trigonometry: cosine, tangent, cotangent, secant, and cosecant.

Finding the direction to Mecca for prayer and building the full Muslim calendar will push spherical geometry—the study of spheres, which goes well beyond plane geometry—to great heights and will be the driver of much of the work of Muslim astronomers and mathematicians.

But the Prophet and the faith are not the only motivators of Muslim astronomical research. At the everyday administrative level, there is also a good reason why an empire, stretching from the Atlantic Ocean, into Africa, far into Central Asia, and along the coasts of Arabia and India, looks to the stars. The caliphate needs to be able to navigate and find its way from point to point.

And finally, there is the lingering practice of astrology, an ancient pre-Islamic practice of the Zoroastrians, Hindus, Jews, and others, that will fall in and out of favor over the coming millennium. Astrology will even be accused of violating Islamic doctrine, but never will quite disappear. While some astronomers will reject astrology, others will keep their feet planted in both camps.

The earliest Muslim astronomers are deeply influenced by Brahmagupta's text brought from India, the *Brahma Sphuta Siddhanta,* or *Opening of the Universe.* This book of astronomical knowledge is used in calculating the Hindu calendar, and, although its origins and computational methods are presented more as assertions rather than supported by scientific explanation, for the early Muslims, challenged with their own issues of time tied to celestial events, it is invaluable.

But the most important foreign source document is Ptolemy's astronomical work. Originally called *Syntaxis* or *The Great Treatise,* in its Arabic translations it will be called *Almagest,* meaning "the greatest." When the *Almagest* later moves from Arabic into Latin via the Catholic and Jewish translators in Spain in the 12th century, the name *Almagest* will stick.

THOUGH FLAWED IN SERIOUS WAYS, including the geocentric structure of the universe—which erroneously describes the universe as having the Earth as its center—Ptolemy's theories will hold until Copernicus's calculations. The Muslims will consider Ptolemy's work to be the best overview of the way the heavens work, and they will devote great energies to checking, verifying, critiquing, and improving its formulas. Some will begin to find flaws and inconsistencies, and a few will question the geocentric approach.

There is growing evidence of a long tradition of discussions on the Earth's motion among Muslim philosophers and astronomers. This debate will include scientists like 11th-century al-Biruni and 13th-century al-Tusi. Al-Biruni—likely inspired by Indian heliocentric, or sun-centered, theories —will also question the motionless Earth of Ptolemy's model, arguing that it might be possible for the Earth to turn on its axis. By the 13th century, Islamic astronomers question the proofs provided by Ptolemy, claiming that his arguments do not decisively prove the Earth is stationary.

Working out the implications of a rotating Earth while demanding decisive observational proofs for Earth's motion will become one of Islamic astronomy's most heated controversies after the 13th century, reaching well into the Copernican period, and perhaps even feeding it.

Parallel debates will take place in Europe among intellectual theologians like the Frenchmen Nicole d'Oresme and Jean Buridan. While Muslim astronomers will be open to the idea of a rotating Earth, they will refuse to believe so until much stronger evidence for its motion is available. Discussions of a moving Earth will spread farther into Europe, although there such issues continue to be firmly located within theological deliberations, whereas in the Islamic world the argument will be part of a purely scientific discourse.

There is some evidence to suggest that Copernicus will inherit these important astronomical questions from Arabic astronomy. Copernicus uses similar arguments to refute Ptolemy's proofs of a stationary Earth, while developing a mathematical edifice for the motion of planets that, in many important ways, was like those designed by al-Tusi and other Muslim astronomers—although Copernicus's brilliance will rest in the fact that he not only understands the rotation of the Earth on its axis, but also how the Earth revolves around the sun. Science historian Thomas Kuhn, in his book *Copernican Revolution: Planetary Astronomy in the Development of Western Thought*, will demonstrate that this "astronomical revolution" occurs as a result of many factors including social, economic, and philosophical reasons, and is not just a revision in scientific thinking resulting from unambiguous scientific proofs.

A prominent 15th-century Muslim astronomer, al-Qushji, was more open to the idea of a moving Earth. According to professor Jamil Ragep of McGill University, al-Qushji argued that if a more compelling physics based on certain premises and on observational evidence could be derived, he would be prepared to accept the rotation of the Earth. This makes al-Quishji "almost unique among medieval astronomers and philosophers."

One area where Ptolemy is correct, and which early Muslim thinkers also accept, is the concept of the Earth as a globe. By the medieval period, physical proof of the Earth as a sphere has been available for centuries to certain people, although European maps of the time will show a flat world, marking the edge with the words "Beyond this point, there be dragons." But since ancient times, sailors must have noticed the Earth's spherical shape. Calculations of longitude depended on the fact that the Earth was round. Otherwise spherical geometry would not have developed.

The Muslims also draw from the Sassanian [Persian] star charts called the *zij,* a distinct system of observing and charting the heavens. Masha'allah ibn Athar, who will be renamed by later Latin translators as Messahala, is a Jewish astrologer of Persian origin working with al-Naubakht in the Baghdad courts of al-Mansur and Haroun al-Rashid. Among other things the men are consulted by al-Mansur for the astrological aspects of locating the new city of Baghdad.

Ibrahim al-Fazari, a Persian from Kunduz in what will one day be Afghanistan, is also summoned to the court of Haroun al-Rashid. There he authors a treatise on the astrolabe, the sky-based navigational tool of Greek and Ptolemaic origin, but brought to its highest development in Muslim times. The astrolabe is a pre-digital analog computer, a device of increasingly rich and complex construction that allows a trained user to determine latitude, by first noting which constellations are nearest the sun at daybreak, then at noon measuring the degree difference between sun and horizon, using a movable needle. By comparing these measurements to a chart, the user can calculate latitude. The astrolabe is the staple of navigation until the 18th century, when it is replaced by the sextant. The astrolabe helps in determining not only location, but the precise times of day to pray.

Muslim astrolabes, reaching their full glory in the ninth and tenth centuries, will make their way to al-Andalus, and from there to England in the 13th and 14th centuries. Fourteenth-century English poet-author Geoffrey Chaucer, creator of *The Canterbury Tales,* will be drawn to the power of the astrolabe and will write an essay about it. Scholars at Oxford University will be fascinated by this device and, as they build their own instruments, will incorporate the old Arabic script and Arab names of the stars into the design.

Those star names, which will endure until the time of space travel and beyond, will echo of the days at the House of Wisdom. Even as probes continue to move deeper and deeper into space, they will orient themselves on stars named in Arabic by forgotten Muslim astronomers. Not only do terms like "zenith" and "azimuth" come from Arabic, the very names of the stars will sound of that old desert language of poetry: Vega, Altair, Deneb, Betelgeuse, Rigel, Aldebaran, Fomalhaut, Algeuze, Elfeta, Alferaz, and Mirac.

Al-Fazari, followed by his son, Muhammad, continues his investigations by beginning to translate Hindu numerical texts into Arabic, a task that will be completed by al-Khwarizmi in the ninth century.

Al-Khwarizmi's own zij star tables will be updated by the Andalusian astronomer al-Majriti in Madrid two hundred years later, and translated into Latin by Abelard of Bath in 1126. The joint al-Khwarizimi–al-Majriti tables will form the core of European and Asian astronomy for hundreds of years to come.

Despite all the astronomical breakthroughs under al-Mansur and Haroun al-Rashid, the first golden age of Muslim astronomy will not come until the ninth-century reign of al-Mamun, under the auspices of the House of Wisdom. Not only will al-Mamun draw astronomers to Baghdad, he will subsidize a network of Muslim observatories. One will be located most appropriately in Gundeshapur, the home of the old Persian learning center. Working at these observatories, Muslim astronomers will develop a new method to measure more accurately than the Greeks a degree of meridian—the theoretical north-south line on the Earth's surface.

Al-Mamun will have other observatories constructed, including one at the Shammasiyah gate in Baghdad, and another on Mount Qasiyun overlooking Damascus. The Shammasiyah observatory will be run by a Jewish convert to Islam, Sid ibn All. Other observatories will be built at Wasit in Iraq and Apamea in Syria.

At all these centers, astronomers and mathematicians apply themselves to translating and proving and critiquing Ptolemy's assertions, trying to measure the length of a degree of meridian, calculating the dimensions of the Earth, and understanding eclipses, equinoxes, and comets.

Without telescopes and using only the application of their ever more sophisticated trigonometry to spherical geometry, the Abbasid astronomers will calculate that the diameter of the Earth is about 7,909 miles (actually 7,932 miles), and that the distance around the Equator is about 24,835 miles (actually 24,906 miles). They will calculate the length of an average degree of meridian on the Earth's surface within 2,800 feet of accuracy—little more than half a mile off. They will calculate the angle of Earth's tilt on its axis, known as the obliquity of the ecliptic; latitudes on the lunar surface parallel to its equator; and the wobble of the Earth on its axis, known as the precession of the equinoxes. These are among the most important calculations of the Middle Ages.

Also summoned to the House of Wisdom is a Persian mathematician and stargazer named al-Farghani, from the ancient Central Asian city of Farghana in modern-day Uzbekistan. As is fitting, al-Farghani springs from the heartland of the Zoroastrians nearly at the western gates of China, where men have been looking up at the skies in search of meaning and message since the time of the three Persian kings, the Magi, who journeyed to Bethlehem drawn by a dazzling cosmic event. The Persian-Asian love of the stars is entwined with magic and hermetic knowledge, with a need to divine the secrets of life and the universe. It is this rich mix of the emerging discipline of astronomical science with the lingering old schools of astrology and magic that will produce so many wonderful astronomers born on the steppes of Central Asia. And it is telling that even as the science grows more advanced, the love of astrology will persist, even when countless thinkers and rulers point out that the Qur'an certainly denies that destinies can be affected by any supernatural force other than that of God.

Al-Farghani creates an appealing Arabic summary of Ptolemy's *Almagest* around 833. The summary will be rapidly circulated through the Muslim world and will eventually make its way into Latin in several versions beginning 300 years later, translated both by John of Seville and Gerard of

Cremona. Al-Farghani's Latinized name will be Alfraganus, and one day a crater of the moon will be named for him.

Long before the European Renaissance, the 13th century Italian poet Dante Alighieri, writing not in Latin but in the vernacular Italian of the everyday, will describe in the *Divine Comedy* his ascent through various spheres of the heavens. This celestial structure will come to him from the Latin translation of the Arabic translation of the *Almagest,* and taught to him at university, as well as from Arabic sources describing Muhammad's celestial journey *(mi'raj)* through the seven heavens.

At the House of Wisdom in the early 10th century, the mathematician al-Battani, later known to the Europeans as Albategnius, will compute his own zij. These revised astronomical tables will make their way into Latin and Spanish in the 12th and 13th centuries. Though for some unknown reason this work achieves little resonance in the Muslim world, in its European versions it will be greeted with acclaim. Seven hundred years after it is written, Copernicus in his work *On the Revolutions of the Heavenly Spheres* will refer to al-Battani's zij a total of 23 times.

Then, as the Abbasids in Baghdad fall into turmoil in the 11th century as the Fatimids rise in Egypt, the Muslim astronomical scene will shift to Cairo. And it will be marked by a celestial event that few humans have ever had the good fortune to see, then or now. Yet it is so colossal and strange that most see it as a portent of bad fortune to come, not good.

In the year 1006, when the mercurial yet far-seeing Fatimid ruler al-Hakim is only 21, a year after the founding of his House of Knowledge, a dazzling new star appears in the southern night sky, shimmering just above the walls of al-Azhar university and the minarets of the al-Hakim Mosque, above the wide copper flow of the Nile, above the pyramids at Giza just south of the city. Listen to how a young amateur astronomer named ibn Ridwan describes it:

The sun on that day was 15 degrees in Taurus and the spectacle in the 15th degree of Scorpio. This spectacle was a large circular body, two and a half to three times as large as Venus. The sky was shining because of its light. The intensity of its light was a little more than a quarter of that of moonlight. It remained where it was and it moved daily with its zodiacal sign until the sun was in sextile with it in Virgo, when it disappeared at once.

This event will be seen and recorded from Switzerland to China and points in between and understood by no one. Not until one thousand years later will astronomers, in the age of space travel, realize that what ibn Ridwan has witnessed is a supernova, the explosion of a star.

And although many observers will have noted the appearance of this celestial event, only ibn Ridwan will have made clear enough notations of location and duration so as to be used by scholars a millennium later. Using ibn Ridwan's account, scientists in a place later named the United States will gradually locate the remnants of the exploded star that ibn Ridwan had seen. They will name it Supernova 1006, after the year of discovery. It is 7,000 light years from Earth, its interior plasmas still burning at one million degrees Celsius in the 21st century. They will calculate its brightness in the year 1006 to have been –7.5, making it the brightest supernova in recorded history, a hundred times brighter than Jupiter.

Though ibn Ridwan will not follow up on his youthful interest in stars but become a physician—his account of SN1006 is written when he is only 18 years old—Fatimid Cairo will produce several of the greats of Muslim astronomy. Ibn al-Haytham, author of the *Book of Optics*, will be one of the best, merging his interest in empirical science, optics, light, and the skies to create perhaps the most scientific and accurate view of the physical universe until Copernicus and Galileo. Another stargazer in Cairo is ibn Yunus, who creates star tables under the auspices of al-Hakim, known as the Hakimi zij. His comprehensive zij will be the core of sky-based timekeeping for almost 800 years throughout the Muslim world, though Europeans will be unaware of it until the 19th century. His zij will be unique not only for its accuracy, but because he prefaces it with one hundred commentaries explaining the celestial phenomena such as conjunctions between the planets and lunar and solar eclipses.

In the 10th century the Abbasids in Baghdad lose real power to the Buyid dynasty, originating from the Persian province of Daylam south of the Caspian Sea. But the short-lived Buyid caliphate will continue its patronage of astronomy and the sciences. One Buyid ruler will support Abu Mahmud Hamid ibn al-Khidr al-Khujandi, who is born in what will one day be Tajikistan, descended from one of the noble tribes of the area.

Al-Khujandi will be best remembered for his construction of a giant tenth-century astronomical device on a mountaintop at Ray in Persia,

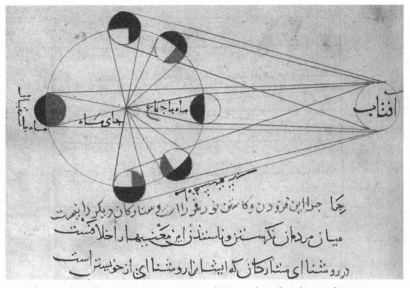

A diagram by 10th-century Persian scientist al-Biruni shows how lunar eclipses occur—when the Earth blocks the sun's light from reaching the moon.

not far from Tehran. This giant structure will approximate the work of a sextant, another Muslim invention. His project is driven by the Muslim belief, valid at the time, that the larger the measuring device, the more accurate the measurements and resulting astronomical calculations will be. His structure seems to have been a giant camera obscura similar to one described by ibn al-Haytham. It is a structure with an aperture at the top that admits sunlight that transects a wall mural of lines and calculations. Taking measurements of sunlight angles at the summer and winter solstices enables al-Khujandi to calculate the latitude of Ray and the angle of the ecliptic. His huge structure is also the first astronomical instrument capable of measuring arcseconds, a more precise fractional measurement of angles than degrees and arcminutes.

The diffusion of astronomical and scientific knowledge from Baghdad will also reverberate as far away as Umayyad Cordoba, by the 11th century at its peak of wealth and sophistication. Although the first two centuries of the intellectual development of al-Andalus are primarily the story of an ambitious province struggling to catch up with faraway Baghdad, by the 10th and 11th centuries, enough scholars and thinkers have been enticed from the far ends of the Muslim world by rich stipends from the Umayyads to make Cordoba competitive with its rival city. Foreign astronomers bringing their star wisdom west include ibn Taimiyyah from Baghdad. But the first major astronomer to spring from the soil of al-Andalus is Maslama al-Majriti, hailing not from the capital of Cordoba but from another proud Spanish city that will one day be the imperial capital of the Catholic kings: Majrit, or Madrid.

Built on the dry high plains of north-central Spain and protected from the worst of the damp northern winter by the wall of the Pyrenees, Majrit is founded by the ninth Umayyad emir, Mohamed I. He orders the building of a small palace and a mosque near the Manzanares River, which flows down from the Guadarrama Range. Al-Majrit, which in Arabic means "watering place," will flourish until the reconquest by Christians led by Alfonoso VI in 1065. After the reconquest the mosque will be rebuilt as the Cathedral of Almudena, and the emir's palace will someday disappear beneath the Royal Palace so that the Muslim architectural memories in modern Madrid will be lost history. But until the time of Isabella, under both Muslim and Catholic rule, Madrid will be one of those fertile places of intermingling of peoples. Living in 10th-century Madrid are Arabized Christians descended from Romans and Visigoths, learning the newest tongue of Spain; Arabic-speaking Jews; and Muslims of all ethnicities. Until the Inquisition, all these groups will live and work in relative peace.

Al-Majriti as a boy will look up through the dry clear air of Castile to see the same stars and planets as seen in the far eastern sky, only with the panorama and movements different from his position far in the West. Surrounded by olive groves and orange groves and lemon groves, al-Majriti will be equally interested in vistas of both Earth and sky. Looking out on the fields and the orchards in neat rows, at the roads heading to the points of the compass, at the walls circumscribing the plots of land held by rich and poor, by royalty and commoner, he will think about the geometry of the land; he will see the plane of Majrit broken up into squares and circles and rectangles. His eye will travel to the more irregular plots, to the parallelograms and rhombuses, to pentagons and plots curved by the river, and he will think about the mathematical implications of all these shapes.

Later, in the service of the Umayyad caliphs, he will study and analyze al-Khwarizmi's and other Arabic translations of the *Almagest,* and add further commentary. He will correct the astronomical tables of al-Khwarizmi about 150 years after the caliph of numbers has died. In this far western outpost of Islam, he will devise an ingenious way to convert the old Persian calendar to Islamic dates, for the first time enabling a more precise and accurate calculation of pre-Islamic Persian dates and events.

But perhaps even more important than those personal innovations and contributions, al-Majriti through his rising fame at home and north of the Pyrenees will help start one of the greatest cross-cultural transmissions of ideas in human history. It will begin in a small way, with the translation into Latin of his own work. The translation will trigger a European hunger for the ideas of all his distant mentors and predecessors, from Ptolemy to al-Khwarizmi and al-Battani. A century after his death in 1006, the curious and fascinated Catholic monks and thinkers will be regularly traveling to Muslim Spain. There al-Majriti's works will be the starting point for many of them, opening the doors to the universe of Muslim astronomical, mathematical, and philosophical works. Not only will Sylvester II, the first French pope, study in Spain and learn of al-Majriti. Abelard of Bath, Gerard of Cremona, Robert of Chester, Plato of Tivoli and many others will enter the secret world through the door of al-Majriti.

Aside from transmitting history, al-Majriti's ideas will have direct impact on the ground. Taking eastern Arab improvements on the astrolabe, he will apply the astrolabe to measuring plots of land, the same plots he saw reduced to a pattern of geometry when he was a boy. With the astrolabe, he and a colleague named ibn al-Saffar will provide the first improvement in European land surveying methods since the Romans. Not only will the astrolabe be used to divide up the olive and orange and lemon groves, it will be used to outline the Syrian-style irrigation canals that will water the dry expanses of al-Andalus.

Al-Majriti's inventive soul and vision will ring out across the peninsula, and the echoes will not stop until the days of the burning of libraries and the forced expulsion of races in 1492.

About 20 years after the death of the stargazer of Madrid, a new boy is born with questions of time and the stars ringing in his ears. And this boy, whose name is Abu Ishaq Ibrahim ibn Yahya al-Zarqali, who will be known in Latin as Arzachel, will flourish in Toledo, city of Andalusian steel on the banks of the Tagus River.

Toledo is much older than the Muslims. The story has it that this city was founded in the sixth century B.C. by a group of Jewish colonists who were part of the Phoenician world based in faraway Lebanon. These Jews named their city Toledoch, meaning "the mother of peoples." By the time of the Romans the city was already known as a place of both beauty and arms-making. And it was important enough to be the capital of the Visigoths under King Roderick in 709.

Under the Muslims, Toledo, while not the capital, flourishes nonetheless. They call it Tulaytulah. The town is rich and productive. Its foundries turn out the best swords in the world. For its adherents, Toledo is considered the cultural and spiritual and intellectual heart of Spain. Some day in the future, it will be the city of Alfonso the Wise and Miguel de Cervantes and El Greco.

And this is the world that al-Zarqali is born into in 1029. He is not from a family of scholars but rather of artisan-mechanics. They make instruments and devices at the direction of scholars and wise men. Al-Zarqali attends no House of Wisdom; he simply apprentices with his father and uncles to learn the various aspects of metalwork. His Arabic nickname means "engraver of metals."

One of his patrons commissions him to make an astronomical device for the use of a group of respected astronomers. His work is so precise that he arouses the attention of the astronomers, and they quiz him on his astronomical and scholarly education. He laughs and says he is a craftsman, not a scholar. He claims he has never opened a book.

The astronomers decide that his approach and techniques are so clever that they indicate greater talents hidden within. They urge him to go to school, which he does at the age of 31. When he returns two years later, they are so impressed with his progress that they make him a member of their center of invention and later the director.

Al-Zarqali designs and builds a sophisticated astrolabe. More important, he writes an essay on the astrolabe that spawns a whole genre of astrolabe writing. More than 200 years after al-Zarqali's death, Castilian King Alfonso X personally makes two translations of al-Zarqali's essays.

Now al-Zarqali turns himself fully to building time machines. In the same year, 1062, that he completes his studies and joins the group of astronomers, he also designs and builds the legendary and phenomenal water clock of Toledo that can tell not only the hours of day and night, but also the days of the lunar calendar so important to Islam. An observer describes it thus:

The clocks consisted of two basins, which filled with water or emptied according to the increasing or waning of the moon. At the moment when the new moon appeared on the horizon, water would begin to flow into the basins by means of subterranean pipes, so that there would be at day-break the fourth of a seventh part, and at the end of the day half a seventh part, of the water required to fill the basins. In this proportion the water would continue to flow until seven days and as many nights of the month had elapsed, by which time both basins would be half filled. The same process during the following seven days and nights would make the two basins quite full, at the same time that the moon is at full. However, on the fifteenth night of the month, when the moon would begin to wane, the basins would also begin to lose every day and night half a seventh part of their water, until by the twenty-first of the month they would be half empty, and when the month reached her twenty-ninth night not a drop of water would remain in them. It is worthy of remark that, should anyone go to any of the basins when they were not filled, and poured water into them with a view to quicken its filling, the basins would immediately absorb the additional water and retain no more than the just quantity; and on the contrary, were anyone to try, when they were nearly filled, to extract any or the whole of their water, the moments the hands are raised, the basins would pour out sufficient water to fill the vacuum in an instant.

This mysterious device will work into the 12th century, until a less talented Muslim inventor asks King Alfonso VII, now ruler of reconquered Christian Toledo, if he can take the water clock apart to understand its workings. The king agrees, only to have the inventor not only fail to understand it, but be incapable of putting it back together again.

Al-Zarqali will also contribute to the computation of the Toledan Tables, one of the most accurate calculations of astronomical data up to that point. He will write one of the world's first almanacs ("almanac" being an Arabic-based word for "climate") called the *Book of Tables*. This ingenious work has a series of tables allowing the user to determine when the Muslim, Persian, Roman, and Coptic months begin. The tables also predict eclipses of the sun and moon and allow one to determine the positions of the planets on any particular day.

Omar Khayyám—11th-century Persian poet, astronomer, and mathematician—compiled astronomical tables and reformed the calendar.

Even as al-Zarqali reaches his zenith of greatness, he will be driven from his beloved Toledo because of the instability and violence generated by the Christian reconquest. Toledo will fall to Alfonso VI in 1085, not long after Madrid. And although the initial groupings of Christian-run city-states, with their loose tri-religious *convivencia,* will be nothing like Queen Isabella's land of religious and ethnic purity 400 years later, it means that Muslim invention in the Christian taifas will now be done under Christian patronage.

Only decades after the death of the timekeeper of Toledo will come the birth in nearby Morocco of Nur al-Din ibn Ishaq al-Bitruji, whose Latin name will be Alpetragius. He will eventually make his way to the dazzling city of Seville, known to the Arabs as Ishbiliya.

Muslim Seville is as old and storied as Toledo, a port city on the Guadalquivir River, a city also possibly founded by the Phoenicians, later home to Greeks and Romans. For the Umayyads and later Muslim and Christian kings, it is one of the jewels of Spain. The Muslims adorn it with a magnificent mosque that the Christians will later destroy to build a cathedral. The mosque's towering, sand-colored minaret, which also serves as an observatory, is later reused as the bell tower for the cathedral called La Giralda. The Moorish palace and gardens of the Almohads facing the central plaza will one day become the Alcazar of the Christian kings.

Though Seville is not the political capital of Umayyad Spain, it is the richest and largest and most powerful city of the Ibero-Muslim realm, grown rich on the crops of olives and citrus, and on sea trade.

Al-Bitruji, using the eastern advances in trigonometry and spherical geometry, will join ibn al-Haytham in attacking some aspects of Ptolemy's work, though al-Bitruji will focus on Ptolemy's irregular orbits of the planets and the sun, and will not question the geocentric model. He will labor mightily to restore the orbits to a pre-Ptolemaic series of perfect concentric circles, and though his approach will one day prove as flawed as Ptolemy's, at the time and for long after, his methods will remove some of the mathematical anomalies of Ptolemy's approach. Al-Bitruji's major work will be translated into Latin by a Scotsman based in Muslim Sicily known as Michael Scot. Al-Bitruji's work will also draw the attention of Seville's vibrant Jewish intellectual community, and two men will translate his work into Hebrew, first Moises ibn Tibbon and then Yahuda ben Solomon Kohen.

Al-Bitruji's work, developed in the late 12th century, will surge through Europe in the 13th century and will be studied, adapted, and even plagiarized repeatedly. Copernicus, writing his revolutionary heliocentric theory in the 16th century, will quote from al-Bitruji.

Now the flavor of Andalusian astronomy becomes more complex. The history of Muslim astronomy in al-Andalus—as with the history of all of the sciences, medicine, and philosophy in this western outpost of Islam—is also often a Jewish history. By the ninth and tenth centuries, the Jewish intellectual communities and economies of Muslim Spain, in cities like Cordoba, Seville, and Toledo, are at their peak. Not only have Jews risen to hold the second highest political position in the realm, under Hasdai ibn Shaprut working for Caliph Abd Al-Rahman III; they are also producing their own rich literature, music, philosophy, and scientific thought, sometimes independently, sometimes in collaboration with those of other faiths. Their favored position under the Umayyads, and later under the Almoravids, becomes the talk of far-flung Jewish communities across North Africa and elsewhere, and by the tenth century, an immigration of Jews to Spain further enriches and energizes the caliphal cities.

The greatest of Spanish Jewish thinkers will be Musa bin Maymun, known in Europe as Maimonides. He will be remembered best for his medical work and for his philosophy and focus on tolerance and civic virtue, reconciling the same Aristotelian thought so important to the Umayyads and the Abbasids with his own Jewish heritage. But he will also delve into astronomy. Born into a Jewish intellectual family in Cordoba in 1135, equally fluent in Arabic, Hebrew, and Spanish, Maimonides will spend much of his youth in this capital of Spanish Judaism that has flourished under the caliphs of Islam. In this center of tolerance and inventiveness, the three faiths descended from Abraham live and work together. But all that will be upended when the fundamentalist Almohads take Cordoba in 1148. Their ultimatum, uncannily like the one that Catholic Queen Isabella will utter in 1492, is a terrible choice for a devout Jew: Convert to Islam or go into exile or die.

Musa bin Maymun, then only 13, will wander with his family, seeking refuge in far southern Spain for nearly 10 years. Finally the family will move to North Africa, and after studying medicine at the university in Fez, Morocco, Maimonides will make his life in Cairo. He will work as court physician to the grand vizier there, and also for Sultan Saladin, enlightened and tolerant leader of the Muslim forces against the Christian Crusaders.

It is no coincidence that Maimonides, trying to escape the strictures of a harsh strain of Islam, will seek refuge not in Christian Europe but in

Muslim North Africa. He and his family know that the people of major urban centers of Islam are more tolerant and intellectually open than anyone in 12th-century Europe.

Maimonides, like most of his contemporaries, will dabble in astronomy. He will address himself to another of the inconsistencies of the Ptolemaic calculations. In particular he will question Ptolemy's equant of Saturn, which seems flawed because it falls directly on the orbital path of Mercury. The equant is a mathematical device created by Ptolemy to explain the somewhat irregular movements of the planets around the Earth. The equant of Saturn, like that of all the other heavenly bodies, is a circle—according to the model of the time—around the circumference of which the planet is moving.

Maimonides is not the only multitalented philosopher who will be drawn to the movements of the planets and stars. Another Andalusian thinker, who will deeply influence scholars from all three Abrahamic religions and over hundreds of years, will be wondering about those planetary orbits, too.

Ibn Rushd—in Latin Averroes—is born into turbulent 12th-century Cordoba and will be better known for his philosophy than his astronomy. His core beliefs are a freethinking and unorthodox system once again centered on the rationalist Aristotle, a philosophy not unlike that of his far eastern counterpart Omar Khayyám, and so powerful that it influences his Jewish countryman and counterpart Maimonides, as well as Christian thinkers like Thomas Aquinas. He will be depicted in the fresco "The School of Athens," by the future Renaissance painter Raphael, as one of the greatest philosophers of all time.

Like all daring thinkers when competing with convention and tradition, ibn Rushd will dance right on the edge of danger. His freethinking rationalism will continually alarm the conservative clerics in Cordoba. Some later observers will even theorize that he sounds more like a Buddhist than a Muslim. But in one of the great feats of political footwork, he will for a time enjoy the patronage of certain key Almohad rulers, the same puritanical dynasty that is otherwise forcing conservatism on Spain. Ibn Rushd is so smart that he is often able to overwhelm the less impressive arguments of the conservatives. But finally, his detractors are too many, and he is banished to Morocco, where he winds up his life in writing and reflection. Despite the turmoil around him, nothing escapes his sweeping mind, and so ibn Rushd will also delve into Ptolemy's writing and find fault.

He gradually develops a harsh attack on the ancient Greek astronomer from Alexandria, writing:

> *To assert the existence of an eccentric sphere or an epicyclic sphere is contrary to nature.... The astronomy of our time offers no truth, but only agrees with the calculations and not with what exists.*

Ibn Rushd joins al-Bitruji in rejecting many of Ptolemy's mathematical constructs and advocates a concentric model of planetary orbits around the Earth.

Out of the background of Andalusian intellectual ferment and questioning and political unrest, enhanced by the cross-fertilization of subcultures, will rise the main transmission points of Muslim astronomical and other knowledge into Europe beyond the Pyrenees. In the 13th century, King Alfonso the Wise will for the first time commission translation of the important work of ibn al-Haytham into Castilian. The work will later be translated into Latin, and European astronomers and mathematicians will clamor to see a copy of his writings.

The three greats of 12th-century Andalusian higher thought and astronomy—al-Bitruji, ibn Rushd, and Maimonides—will all die within eight years of one another: Ibn Rushd in 1198, Maimonides in 1204, and al-Bitruji in 1206.

Their deaths mark a passing and the beginning of even more turbulence in the coming times. As al-Andalus fragments into city-states called *taifas* and undergoes centuries of conflict between the Christians and invading forces from North Africa, the far east of Islam will also be experiencing its own conflicts, and its own new wave of astronomical invention.

This far eastern unrest and ferment is part of a drama driven by an Asiatic invasion force capable of sweeping across entire continents and empires and peoples, far beyond the incursions of the Almoravids or Almohads from North Africa.

FORTRESS OF ALAMUT, PERSIA, 1256—They are coming, and the stories of their onrush and power reach back for half a century, for two generations. They have been on the move for enough time that their earlier deeds have become myth and have been forgotten in the lulls of decades, only to be rudely awakened by the latest nightmare tale. For a lifetime or more, thousands of people have been fleeing their advance, fleeing west, south, wherever their feet and their resources can take them. Houses and farms have been sold, businesses and old friends abandoned, homes left empty to be swept only by rats and wind before the wave arrives.

Every city in their path, whether in China or Russia or Transoxiana or Persia, has fallen to them. In the stories of survivors, the attackers seem not human, rather a murderous hybrid of horse and man that seems without limit, so numerous that they are an ocean, an unstoppable rolling wave rippling west. They are the Mongols, born on the grasslands north of China, and they are driven by war.

From the devastation being inflicted all across China and Korea and Central Asia, thousands of refugees stream to Cairo, to Moscow, to cities in Turkey and India, enriching the recipient societies in the process, but draining the intellectual wells of Central Asia of many of their thinkers.

Just what is so fearsome about the Mongols? They are an alliance of Asiatic tribes probably not numbering more than two million people, plus several times that number of Siberian ponies. Stripped of any of the refinements of urban, pacified society, they are an efficient conquering machine. They take few prisoners.

In the secure and tiny nerve center of this rolling empire is the mobile battlefield encampment of Genghis Khan, known to the Chinese as Temujin, and his family and retainers. He is attended by a small cadre of Nestorian Christian holy men and thinkers.

What strange irony is this? The Mongol hordes have a Christian bent? Lost history reveals that the Nestorians had continued their eastward migration when they were finding new homes in the Middle East and Persia. By the seventh century they had made their way to the gates of China. By the tenth century, some of the Turkic-Mongol tribes accepted Nestorianism as one of their state religions. By the 13th century, the mighty Genghis will marry one of his sons to a Nestorian princess of Mongolian-Turkic origin, and she will be the mother of Hulegu Khan, who later ravages Baghdad; Kublai Khan, who rules as emperor of China; and a third son.

Kublai Khan will help the Nestorians enter the heart of China, where they will hold sway at court and coexist with Taoists and Buddhists. Franciscan missionaries from Europe will be impeded in their own proselytizing by the brief political power of the Nestorians. Not until the fall of the Mongols in the 14th century and the rise of the Ming dynasty will the Nestorians also fall from favor and Christianity virtually disappear from China until the 19th century.

Some historians will question the lurid image attributed to the Mongols. They will say that the Mongols give their opponents the chance to surrender and be left in peace, with the burden of paying tribute to the Khans.

Their defenders will later say the Mongols are doing what they do in order to survive. With nothing else to their names but horses and courage—no cities, no ports, no iron mines, no rich farmlands, no good rivers, no water—they are conquering in order to avoid starving to death.

Arrayed into widely dispersed columns of 10,000 men and horses, called *tumen,* the Mongols advance at horse speed. For those who do not surrender in advance, there is little or no mercy. Shock and awe originate with Mongol techniques. Target cities are leveled and burned. Aside from a few cadres of traitors, plus local craftsmen and others who can help the war machine move forward, the Mongols kill everyone. Witnesses after the battles describe huge piles of bodies and burned bones, stenches that drift for miles and miles, towering columns of smoke from burned bodies and clothing.

Historian ibn al-Athir later writes of the fateful year of 1221 when Persia is being engulfed:

For some years I continued averse from mentioning this event, deeming it so horrible that I shrank from recording it and ever withdrawing one foot as I advanced the other. To whom, indeed, can it be easy to write the announcement of the death-blow of Islam and the Muslims, or who is he on whom the remembrance thereof can weigh lightly?... Yet, withal a number of my friends urged me to set it down in writing, and I hesitated long, but at last came to the conclusion that to omit this matter could serve no useful purpose.

For even Antichrist will spare such as follow him, though he destroy those who oppose him, but these Mongols spared none, slaying women and men and children, ripping open pregnant women and killing unborn babes. Verily to God do we belong, and unto Him do we return, and there is no strength and no power save in God, the High, the Almighty, in face of this catastrophe, whereof the sparks flew far and wide, and the hurt was universal; and which passed over the lands like clouds driven by the wind. For these were a people who emerged from the confines of China, and attacked the cities of Turkestan, like Kashghar and Balasaghun, and thence advanced on the cities of Transoxiana, such as Samarqand, Bukhara and the like, taking possession of them, and treating their inhabitants in such wise as we shall mention; and of them one division then passed on into Khurasan, until they had made an end of taking possession, and destroying, and slaying, and plundering, and thence passing on to Ray, Hamadan and the Highlands, and the cities contained therein, even to the limits of Iraq, whence they marched on the towns of Adharbayjan and Arraniyya, destroying them and slaying most of their inhabitants, of whom none escaped save a small remnant; and all this in less than a year…remaining only for so long as their march required and no more.

The coming centuries of Mongol and Central Asian invasions will seriously shake and transform the Muslim world, putting the Indians on permanent military alert, as well as the Europeans, who will watch the Mongols thunder into Poland and Hungary and get their scouts as far as France. But Muslim thought, including astronomy, will not be squelched. Muslim civilization will quite possibly be enriched. How is that possible? The answer is in lost history, revealing other strands of Mongol culture too often obscured by their mighty war machine. By the time the Mongols arrive in Arabic lands, they have a large and well-established empire that has absorbed sophisticated cities, cultures, and ideas of the time—including the high cultures of China, Tibet, Northern India, Central Asia, and Persia. For example, their code of law developed by Genghis Khan, known as the *Yassa,* although severely harsh at times, also codifies meritorious ideas like religious tolerance, peace, trade, and rule of law to protect communities against theft and crime.

Moreover, Mongol military campaigns are not as haphazard as the stories told. They are carefully and strategically calculated by the *Kurultai,* an assembly of aristocrats and rulers, who govern the Mongol empire from the cities of China. Likely relying on older Islamic trading networks, the Mongols also develop a sophisticated system of trade with foreign lands and set up laws to protect traveling merchants. The Mongols value scholars, scientists, and artists, often absorbing them into their administration. Also important are the complex and sometimes fruitful alliances they maintain with Christians, Buddhists, and Muslims as they conquer vast territories. Soon after conquering the Muslim world, the Mongols create magnificent new cities in Persia, Central Asia, and India, leading to intellectual renaissances in these parts of the world for centuries.

In doing so they create a rich, dynamic melting pot of Chinese, Islamic, and European ideas and cultures.

ONE OF THE ACTORS IN THIS DRAMA of Mongol conquest and assimilation is a brilliant thinker named Muhammad ibn al-Hasan al-Tusi. He is born in 1201 in Persian Khorasan, in the ancient city of Tus. Tus echoes with the memory of many great men. Nizam al-Mulk, the enlightened Seljuk vizier and patron of Omar Khayyám, was born here. Probably the greatest and most beloved Persian poet of all time, Firdausi, made Tus his home in the 11th century. The Abbasid Caliph Haroun al-Rashid is said to be entombed there.

Al-Tusi is a mainstream Shiite, and his father and uncle are both respected Shiite educators and religious jurists. In Tus he learns the basics of theology, as well as algebra, geometry, and physics.

For the first 13 years of al-Tusi's life, Genghis Khan is busily devouring China, 4,000 miles to the east. But in 1214 he turns west, triggering the steady streams of Central Asian refugees and their horror stories of the Mongols. About this time al-Tusi is sent to Nishapur, 50 miles west of Tus, to continue his higher studies there.

By 1220, the Mongols have reached Tus, and they ravage it and much of Khorasan, though Nishapur is temporarily spared. Genghis Khan at this point decides to resume his campaign to the east, and leaves the west to his sons and relatives. The result is a confused, stop-and-start, multipronged Mongol assault that will go on for decades, leaving some parts of the eastern Muslim world relatively safe and obliterating others.

By this time, al-Tusi has built up a following and reputation as a mathematician among thinkers and scholars in Nishapur, and his reputation spreads beyond. Like his predecessor Omar Khayyám a century before, al-Tusi desperately needs a patron who can give him the stability and security to work. But no one in the Muslim world can offer that security in the 13th century. Far to the west, al-Andalus is undergoing its own turbulence. The Mongols are already in parts of Iraq. Egypt is relatively peaceful, but it is also within striking distance of the Mongols.

Making a fateful decision, al-Tusi decides to stay closer to home. And to do so, he accepts the patronage of the Ismaili governor, Nasir ad Din Abd al-Rahim. To show his sincerity, al-Tusi asks to become a novice in the Ismaili faith, and is accepted. Some will later charge that his conversion is opportunistic. The truth is lost to history.

Al-Rahim welcomes the young thinker to his court at a mountaintop fortress at Alamut, the crossroads between ancient Persia and the endless grasslands and deserts of Asia. Al-Rahim not only controls Alamut, he has a network of mountain fortresses throughout the Elburz Range in Persia that would seem to offer protection from the Mongol armies, who are at their best on flat ground.

And so, in an unusual alliance conducted in a mountaintop fortress, driven by the nightmare of the Mongol advance, al-Tusi finds the resources and security to pursue his many interests—philosophy, mathematics, science, medicine, and astronomy. His output includes more than a hundred works on these subjects. For about the next 25 years, al-Tusi stays at Alamut, using its rich library to write some of his most important scientific and philosophic works. One of his works, entitled *Memoir on the Science of Astronomy,* has a deep influence on the subsequent history of astronomy, both in and beyond the borders of Islam. His studies on planetary motion will shake up the foundation of Ptolemy's universe and bring the world one step closer to its overthrow by Copernicus. Al-Tusi is also known for his outstanding work on plane and spherical trigonometry and his efforts to establish trigonometry as an independent field of mathematical research. In 1232 he publishes a book on ethics and dedicates it to his Ismaili patron.

As seen from this unique ivory tower, an uneasy balance exists between Mongol rule on the Persian steppe and Ismaili refuges on the mountaintops. In 1228 the Ismailis even send a delegation to the Mongols proposing an alliance. For almost three decades, the answer continues to be a de facto peace, though legend has it that Genghis Khan harbors a deep suspicion of the Ismailis, seeing them as an obstacle to his dominion over Persia.

The final answer comes one morning in 1256, when the Ismailis and attendants and courtiers awaken to see the full force of the Mongols arrayed in the valley below them. The fortress of Alamut is surrounded. This fortress that has been impregnable for centuries is facing its ultimate challenge. The outcome will be life or death.

Hearing reports of the Mongol advance, the Ismaili ruler has already smuggled his young heir out of the area and sent him to faraway Anatolia, where his line of imams will spend several generations in hiding. Only that desperate move will prevent the extinction of Ismailism.

The commander of the approaching Mongol force is Genghis Khan's grandson Hulegu, who has inherited the grandfather's mantle of Khan. Hulegu is an *Ilkhan,* meaning a deputy ruler. By 1256, the Khans control what is perhaps the largest empire of human history in sheer area, by one estimate encompassing two-thirds of the Earth's landmass and at least 100 million people. Hulegu is as ruthless as his grandfather and blessed with the energy of youth. Through his experience in fighting the Muslims he has acquired their love of the sciences, though he is far from becoming a Muslim. His family will convert some 50 years later, when Ghazan Khan chooses the faith. Hulegu will float between Nestorian Christianity and Buddhism, an unlikely religious foundation for a war machine.

Religious or not, Hulegu has rightly concluded that he will never have total dominion over Persia until he eliminates the Ismailis in the hills. The Ismaili fortresses have been attacked before. But never like this. These Ismaili warriors, unafraid of death, nonetheless suffer a few shivers on that fateful morning. While they cannot escape, they believe they are protected by the secrets of the mountain. And so it looks like a long standoff is taking shape. The Ismailis wonder if their stores and water will hold out longer than the Mongols can sustain a siege.

Now dual histories come into play. One account says that Ismaili ruler Rukn al-Din Khurshah decides to peacefully surrender Alamut. Another account says that someone now totally lost to history betrays the secret passageways into the mountain. Whatever the truth, all agree on what happens next. The end of the Ismailis comes swiftly and without warning. One moment, they are watching the unmoving Mongol enemy from over the fortress parapets. The next moment, they find the Mongol enemy charging into their inner sanctum.

The Mongol slaughter of the Ismailis is swift and almost total. The Ismaili leader is killed—and most of the court. But as is typical, a few are spared: possible spies and those whose unique skills can be of greater use.

Al-Tusi is one who is spared. Though the truth of why he is spared is lost to history, the whispering begins. His acceptance of rescue and his willingness to meet Hulegu cause the whispers to grow. When the imperial meeting comes, accounts vary on what happens. Some claim that al-Tusi renounces Ismailism and swears he has always been a loyal mainstream Shiite. At some point soon thereafter, al-Tusi marries a Mongol woman.

Who is the real al-Tusi: the one who asked to be an Ismaili initiate and won the patronage of the governor, or the one accepting the rule of the conquering Mongol prince, who has the power of life and death over millions? Only al-Tusi knows. His reward for joining the Mongols is great. Hulegu, who is just as interested in knowledge and research as the Ismaili leader he has just slain, appoints al-Tusi as his chief science advisor and also puts him in charge of religious affairs.

Some people claim that al-Tusi will accompany the Ilkhan Hulegu as his forces move farther west, targeting the intellectual heart of Islam, Baghdad, the city of the caliphs and the home of the House of Wisdom. In joining Hulegu, al-Tusi will be undoing his very own intellectual heritage.

By 1258, when the Mongol armies draw up around the magnificent city on the Tigris, when Hulegu and the imperial entourage gather for the final rout of the city that once ruled so many, Baghdad is weary with 500 years of greatness. The Abbasids have survived in name only; real power has gone to the Buyids and Seljuks and a group of former slaves known as the Mamluks. The dynasties are too many to remember. The nominal caliph, the inheritor of the proud mantle of al-Mamun, is al-Mutasim, a foolish and decadent man of artistic bent, much more comfortable with poets and artists and his court jesters, than with soldiers and the battlefield.

At first, al-Mutasim refuses to submit, saying that the entire Muslim world will come to his aid. When he sees the arrayed power of his enemy approaching the city, he offers to name Hulegu the sultan of Baghdad, but it is too late.

The battle with the Mongols is pitiful. First the forces of al-Mutasim are swiftly dispatched. Then his court of 300 is slaughtered, and the caliph is strangled a few days later. The Mongols enter the city and, by some accounts, march 800,000 inhabitants out onto the desert plain. Under the beating Iraqi sun, men, women, and children are butchered and then heaped up in great piles. The structures of the city are pillaged, battered, and burned, many reduced to rubble. The destruction of the city is so complete that, though some will try to rebuild it in coming centuries, it will never regain any prominence in world affairs until its oil-funded rebirth in the 20th century.

The fall of Baghdad will rank with two other defeats in degree of cultural impact and symbolism. It will rank with the final loss of Byzantine Constantinople to Ottoman Turks in 1453 after 600 years of sporadic Muslim attacks, and with the conquest of imperial Mexico by the Spanish in 1521.

What is al-Tusi thinking about this debacle and slaughter? Does he believe that it was better for him to survive and join a conquering foe? Does he wonder what it would have felt like, to be one thrown on those heaps of bodies?

His thoughts at that moment are lost to history. What we know is that the conqueror Hulegu is jubilant at having destroyed this symbol of Muslim resistance. He is so happy that he is open to just about any project that the brilliant al-Tusi can propose to him.

And in that moment of tragedy and symbolism, al-Tusi is ready. This philosopher, mathematician, and physicist will have a grandiose astronomical project such as the world has never seen. Even as the Muslim world bleeds from its wounds from the Mongols, a hybrid, new golden age of Muslim science is already being seeded.

AL-TUSI'S PLAN IS TO BUILD the largest observatory ever constructed. Fittingly, it will be built at the city of Maragheh in what will someday be the Persian province of Azerbaijan, in the city that Hulegu has made his capital. Construction begins in 1259, the year after the fall of Baghdad. The observatory will rise on a hill of basalt west of Maragheh, built to double also as a fortress, with walls at least six-feet-thick and measuring about 1,000 feet by 400 feet,

Completed in 1262, this massive new center of sky study possesses things never before seen. It has huge astronomical instruments, such as a 12-foot wall quadrant made of copper and an azimuth quadrant invented by al-Tusi. The azimuth is the direction of a celestial object, measured clockwise around the observer's horizon from the north. Thus an object due north has an azimuth of 0°, one due east 90°, south 180°, and west 270°.

And just as al-Mamun and the House of Wisdom drew on the wisdom of the Indians, the Persians, and the Greeks, al-Tusi has at his disposal the astronomical wisdom of the faraway Chinese, that other epicenter of global civilization.

Though Chinese wisdom has come trickling westward for millennia, it has been an uneven transmission along the Silk Road or via the Indian Ocean, rather than in any sustained and comprehensive effort.

But because Hulegu's brother Kublai is the Emperor of China and the Khan of the Earth, the intellectual riches of Chinese astronomy now pour west to Persia. It is now all one system. It is all part of a superstate.

The intellectual flow will be two ways, not only from China west but equally from Muslim lands to China, a flow that for many Chinese will also be lost to history. The Maragheh observatory is where centuries of Greco-Arabic-Persian learning in astronomy will be centralized by the Mongols, empowered by the likes of al-Shirazi, who first gave the correct explanation of the formation of a rainbow; the Syrian astronomer al-Urdi, who constructed planetary models; and al-Futi, the Maragheh librarian in charge of some 400,000 books. These scholars will be brought together from various parts of the Muslim empire to enrich the center headed by al-Tusi. The rigorous astronomical work done at observatories in Damascus, Antioch, Baghdad, Ray, Cairo, Fez, Cordova, Seville, and Toledo will come to be focused at Maragheh, with centuries of Islamic knowledge ready to be transferred into China.

In 1267, the Muslim scholar Jamal al-Din brings to the court of Kublai Khan a Persian calendar to cover 10,000 years, seven astronomical instruments, and a magnificent wooden terrestrial globe, possibly designed by al-Tusi. The instruments will likely serve as inspiration for the royal engineer Kuo-Shou-Ching to develop similar ones for the Khan. In the 1270s, Kublai Khan will employ Muslim engineers and astronomers, and maintain two astronomical boards, one Muslim and one Chinese. This spurs the development of new techniques and observatories in Beijing and of sophisticated mapmaking techniques, which will ultimately lead to China's supremacy in navigation in the 15th century, under the Muslim admiral Zheng He.

Less than 20 years after the construction of the Maragheh observatory in Persia, the royal Beijing observatory is built and placed under the directorship of Persian astronomer Jamal al-Din, with similar instruments designed by the engineer Kuo. Several historians will note the likely influence of the Islamic observatory on the Chinese during the 13th century. In this period of rich intercultural exchange between Muslim lands and China, Jamal al-Din also heads an extensive geographic-cartographic survey of Kublai Khan's territories.

Al-Tusi's observatory also has adjacent libraries and research centers, and he will allow his Chinese and Persian and Arab scientists to pursue almost anything remotely relevant to science. The witness to the destruction of the House of Wisdom will have created his own, grand house of science.

Out of this thought center will come a stream of treatises and discoveries. Al-Tusi will produce a vast star catalog. He will plot the most accurate tables yet done of planetary motion. They will be called the Ilkhanic Tables, in honor of his patron Ilkhan Hulegu, and will be the result of 12 years of hard observation and calculation. In his *Treatise on Astronomy,* he will articulate the most comprehensive and advanced adaptation of Ptolemy's planetary system, illustrating an astronomical-mathematical breakthrough called the Tusi couple, which will resolve linear motion into the sum of two circular motions. His theorem will be repeated 250 years later by Copernicus, and it will be debated whether he takes it from al-Tusi or another intermediary source.

Al-Tusi will calculate the precession of the equinoxes—the wobble of the Earth's axis of rotation—at 50.3 arcseconds per year, or one complete cycle in 25,700 years. He will write deeper treatises on the astrolabe. He will pour out commentaries and theories on spheres and cylinders and assorted issues of higher math. He will lead the world as the first to separate trigonometry as an independent field of math and not an appendage of geometry or algebra. In a display of his brilliance at higher math, he will be the first in the world to calculate all six cases for a right-angled spherical triangle. And he will turn out volumes on minerals and a theory of coloration. He will write about medicine. He will write about ethics and philosophy.

And the sum of all this—even as Baghdad is lost, as Cairo fears a possible Mongol attack, as al-Andalus is fading into the Christian reconquest, and as Persia becomes a Mongol province—is that al-Tusi will be credited by some with doing more to revive and sustain Muslim science in his time than anyone else.

Al-Tusi grows old. Like the exploding star on the southern horizon in 1006 seen by young ibn Ridwan, al-Tusi will flare, and then he will be lost to the eye.

But like the supernova now numbered SN 1006, its interior plasmas still pulsing at one million degrees Celsius a thousand years later, the glow of al-Tusi and all his Muslim colleagues will endure. No matter that their names will be forgotten to Europe and China and elsewhere. No matter that many of them will never have a Latin name. Despite being largely lost to history, they will be there, in places like the Palomar Observatory in California and the Hubble Space Telescope. Muslim astronomic and mathematical calculations will help drive massive computations one day done by thinking machines. Had they never lived, would astronomy and computation have evolved in quite the same way?

Their contributions to modern astronomical knowledge and technology are almost beyond counting. In the field of astronomy alone, they will help develop modern astronomical theory, modern instruments, large international observatories, and a climate of research and discovery that will be the model for Renaissance, Enlightenment, and even 21st-century astronomy.

In star theory, they will articulate important critiques of Ptolemy's ideas. They will also develop important instruments. As scientific historian David King will one day write,

> What only recent research has shown is that ... virtually all innovations in [astronomical] instrumentation in Europe up to ca. 1550 were either directly or indirectly Islamic in origin or had been conceived previously by some Muslim astronomer somewhere.

This does not rule out independent developments in European instrumentation, but demonstrates the important contribution of Islamic instruments to the history of science.

Muslims will develop large observatories carrying out big-budget projects. The influence of the Islamic observatories on China, India, and Europe has been extensively documented. In 1576 Tycho Brahe's observatory in Denmark will contain instruments very similar to those found in Taqi al-Din's observatory in Istanbul of a few years earlier. China's royal Beijing observatory will resonate with the Maragheh observatory. India's five Jantar Mantar observatories, built by Maharajah Jai Singh in the 18th century, will in part re-create the magnificence of Timurid ruler Ulugh Beg's observatories of the 15th century in Samarkand. Over several centuries, information flow from Muslim countries to Europe and China and India will shape the nature of these observatories up to the early modern, pre-telescopic period.

For centuries, Arabic astronomy will be at the epicenter of global knowledge. Astronomy advanced by Muslim scientists is not only a crucial element of Islamic culture, but it plays a central role in how today we measure the Earth, map the continents and their territories, navigate the oceans, calculate time, measure the year, develop architecture, position places of prayer, and locate cities. Islamic astronomy charts new avenues, poses new questions, develops new techniques, sets new standards, and creates new disciplines.

And from these twinned starting points, God in the numeral and the patterns of the stars, all the other Muslim sciences will ripple outward. Muslim engineering, chemistry, architecture, and medicine will all find some foundation in the numbers and the stars. If nothing else, the love of empirical science espoused by the likes of ibn al-Haytham will enable them all.

The rest is also lost history.

5

INVENTORS AND SCIENTISTS

*O, company of jinn and men, if ye have power to penetrate [all] regions
of the heavens and the earth; then penetrate [them]!*

QUR'AN (LV:33)

DOHA, QATAR, 2007—From above and afar, the peninsular nation
of Qatar is caught between the dun color of endless desert and the ceru-
lean mixing of ocean and sky. From above, through the orange haze of
enveloping summer humidity, the capital Doha is an abrupt cliff of office
towers and shopping malls and luxury hotels where the edge of the Arabian
Peninsula falls off into water and emptiness.

Doha is one of the newest cities in the world, its grid of streets and
highways laid out only in the last two decades echoing an aesthetic of pure
modernity and globalization. Its Science and Technology Park, one of Jon
Hasda's projects due to open soon, is intended to put Qatar in the forefront
of high-tech invention and stem the tide of the brain drain by emigrating
knowledge workers, drawn from their country where they are badly needed
by more developed countries. The project is intended to bolster the technological capabilities of a nation with less than a million people, on the
edge of one of the harshest deserts on Earth, and a thousand miles from
Mecca on the other side of the peninsula, where the Prophet received his
revelations from God.

Jon Hasda is regional director of engineering for one of the world's
largest contractors headquartered in Europe. He has lived and worked in
Doha for five years, building relationships with the political powers that
be and all the domestic and international companies that do business here

in Qatar, and up and down the coast of the Arabian Peninsula. He and his expatriate colleagues travel constantly, from Kuwait in the north to Bahrain, Abu Dhabi, Dubai, and the big Saudi cities of Riyadh and Jeddah in the south.

Jon looks out from his office on the Doha Corniche, seeing the rush hour take shape through the afternoon haze. Around him are large photos of all the projects his company now has in operation in the Persian Gulf. He has pictures of himself with CEOs and heads of state and government ministers, with assorted dignitaries he has met, both in substantive meetings and on ceremonial occasions, at the signing of a major agreement or the completion of a new building.

There's also the picture of his ex-girlfriend, Yasmin. She's now in Malaysia, and they haven't seen each other in a year and a half. She had wanted to get married and have children; he wasn't ready.

It has been a great assignment for a man still in his thirties. But having been out in the field for so long, he is beginning to have fears that his career will never go beyond where it is now. Accustomed to moving around, he was excited when the opportunity in Doha opened up. But after five years, he has begun to wonder.

Doha and other coastal cities like Dubai are curious places, created almost out of nothing at what had been Arab fishing and boatbuilding towns. The city leaders are now vying to compete with Singapore and Hong Kong. They want these cities to be hubs of the Middle East, gateways to and for the world. And they have partly succeeded, leaving older, more cosmopolitan cities like Cairo and Damascus behind. With dozens of five-star hotels completed or under construction, tourists are starting to come in from India and Pakistan, from the Arab countries, from Iran and Russia and Europe to spend on imported duty-free jewelry, clothes, cars, condos. Beach resorts and golf courses reach off into the distance, out toward the United Arab Emirates in the east or the emptiness of interior Saudi Arabia to the west. Doha is a magnificent place to do business, but it seems almost devoid of history. The tiny enclave of Old Doha is being preserved and enhanced, a nice place to go for drinks or dinner, but it is dwarfed by the ocean of modernity around it. Doha feels like a combination of Las Vegas and Miami Beach, though with many more men and women in traditional Arab and South Asian garb, all chattering into mobile phones.

The religion that is so much more visible across the border and across the water is quietly in the background here. That is deliberate, because the city fathers do not wish to dampen the surge of business with the religious-political disputes only a few miles away. Jon is comfortable with that. He is not a religious man.

Traveling and relocating are quite natural for Jon. His grandfather had been a Dutch businessman working in the Dutch East Indies when World War II broke out. They went to the Caribbean during the war. His grandparents passed on, his parents divorced and died young. He has no siblings. After a stint in Paris, Jon is now a certified Middle Easterner.

But like the new cities of the Persian Gulf, his heritage does not go back that far. He is very new. The Hasdas appear out of nowhere in Amsterdam and Jakarta in the 1920s. No other families spell their name that way that he knows of. People outside the Netherlands always accept that the name is Dutch, but there are no Hasdas in the Netherlands.

The question had come up once with his girlfriend, Yasmin, a beautiful Chinese-Malay Muslim girl he'd first met in Dubai when she was taking a customer service flight attendant's course at Emirates Airlines. She had been in Dubai for a year, and they had been quite involved; then she'd been transferred to the Emirates base in Kuala Lumpur. She'd visited him, even flown him to a beautiful island off Malaysia on a free ticket. But then when he didn't reciprocate, things had started to go cold. Her parents were already scandalized that their daughter was leading an independent life. And to be carousing with a foreign man on island trysts was too much.

Once, on a lonely winter night after the relationship had broken up, when the Doha hotel bars were empty, he'd drifted back home and gradually ended up at the computer. Originally thinking he'd hit one of the dating websites, he'd started playing around with other things. And then he'd found himself doing a search on the Hasda family, to see if there was any history to this family, or if he was truly an orphan, alone in the world and stuck with a name that was some clerk's typographical error.

He hadn't needed to search long. There were indeed other Hasdas in the world. They were a branch of a larger, older family who spelled their name Hasdai. The Hasdais and the Hasdas were Sephardic Jews originally from Spain. One group of Hasdas had had a huge family reunion in Orlando, Florida, a few years ago. The reunion had drawn Hasdas from New York and Sao Paulo, from Buenos Aires and Istanbul, from Casablanca and Cairo and Athens, from Tehran and Lisbon and Los Angeles and Tel Aviv. At the reunion, someone had laid out the family saga.

After more than a millennium in Spain, the families had faced the ultimatum of Isabella: Convert to Catholicism or face exile or death. Some of the Hasdas had remained behind and were now lost to memory, their names converted to the names of their Spanish Catholic godfathers. The others had taken the offer of the Ottoman Turkish sultan to bring their skills and what belongings they could carry to Istanbul. And they had all been Turks for several generations. A few ancestors had gone east to Iran, others to the Americas. Most all of them still consider themselves Sephardim, the Jews sprung from Sefarad during the Muslim rule of Spain.

Jon had sat and looked at all this in disbelief. But it made some sense. He'd been told his grandfather had moved them to the Caribbean to get away from the war. Maybe he'd been escaping the Holocaust.

And except for that brief time in the Netherlands, his forefathers had spent 1,300 years interacting with the Muslims. He'd almost let himself fall in love with one.

Or it could all have been a mistake. Maybe his ancestors had made up their name, or someone had inadvertently created it by misspelling it. It doesn't matter anymore. It's ancient history. And it's quitting time. He's invited to fly down to a reception tonight in Dubai at the Burj al-Arab, the hotel that resembles a ship's sail built out into the Gulf waters. It's a reception for the Ministers of Science and Technology from all the Gulf countries.

Suddenly he's missing Yasmin, he's missing his parents, he's missing something he can't identify. He needs to get transferred to Europe. He feels like he's losing out on something.

QURTUBA, AL-ANDALUS, A.D. 852—While documentary proof of many aspects of Muslim science will be lost to history, some accounts will be talked about for a thousand years.

In one story, a crowd has gathered in the square facing the Grand Mosque of Qurtuba to see a man either kill himself or make history. High up on the parapet of the minaret, high above the cantilevered tiled Romanesque-Syrian rooftops, on the tiny balcony where the muezzin normally sings his call to prayer five times a day, now stands another man, definitely not a muezzin. A buzz rolls through the crowd and a few shout up to him, some in encouragement, others in derision.

"Get your crazy rear end off there," someone shouts. "Jump!" scream a few others.

"Does he have permission from the imam to do this?" a woman asks. Nervous laughter ripples through the group.

"I hear he bribed the imam," ventures another, and giggles break out.

This is Qurtuba, one day to be known as Cordoba, the jewel of Umayyad Spain. Nearly a hundred years have passed since Abd al-Rahman I wrested this city from the previous emir. The young Umayyad restorer is long dead, and the city is now ruled by Emir Abd al-Rahman II. In the next century, the Umayyads will declare Cordoba to be the seat of the rightful caliphate.

In 852 the Spanish Umayyads are fast closing in on Baghdad in importance. Cordoba is now by far the largest and most technologically advanced city in Europe. Even now, in the middle of the ninth century, Cordoba is deep in the grips of a surge of high fashion, new music, and urbane sophistication spurred by an Iraqi musician and arbiter of taste, one Abu al-Hasan Ali ibn Nafi, known as Ziryab. This multitalented man has been lured away from the court of Haroun al-Rashid by the Andalusian ruler with an annual salary of 200 dinars and an annual bonus of 1,000 dinars plus additional bonuses on Islamic holy days, along with a "modest" palace and some villas in and about Cordoba. Transformed from an Iraqi slave musician into a wealthy Andalusian man, Ziryab is teaching people how to dress, how to cook, how to make music, how to live life in as sophisticated a way as those in the rival city of Baghdad. Cordobans and other Andalusians are imitating Ziryab's clothes, his haircut, and his manner of speech. He has brought the women of Cordoba the first beauty parlor; he has introduced them to new perfumes and cosmetics. To the men he has presented the first toothpaste. He has improved the technique of playing the *'ud,* which with his addition of a fifth string may evolve into the Spanish guitar. He has spurred the first serious overhaul of everyday life since the arrival of the Muslims. He has transformed the western capital of Islam from a rough town of Visigothic crudity to a place of fashion, manners, and style.

"Jump!" someone cries. "You chicken!" another screams, and the crowd laughs. But an undercurrent of nervousness and sympathy sweeps through them, too. They empathize with the poor daredevil up there.

His name is Armen Firman, and he makes his living taking risks. He makes bets; sometimes he is lucky enough to get a subsidy. If he survives and comes anywhere near his goal, he gets to go on to the next challenge.

In the crowd, made up largely of the common people of Cordoba, is a most uncommon observer. His name is Abbas ibn Firnas, and he has taken some time from his scientific work done in the employ of the emir to observe Armen Firman's latest stunt.

Ibn Firnas had originally come to the court to teach music, under the watchful eye of Ziryab. But by now, in middle age, he has branched out into other areas. He is drawn to mechanical devices, to timepieces, and to the qualities of glass and crystal. He is an astronomer and will someday build a mechanized planetarium with revolving planets for the emir.

His interest in crystals, quartz, and sand will lead him to find a way to melt sand into glass, enabling the creation of Andalusian drinking glasses, experiments with lenses and their magnifying qualities, and everything else that comes from glass. Until his time, Spanish drinking vessels have been made out of wood, clay, metal, or animal skins. He will even come up with a formula for artificially creating crystals.

But his interest in 852 is above and beyond. He has heard of the Greek myth of Icarus and Daedalus. And now, to know that someone is really attempting to replicate the myth is deliciously exciting.

Up atop the tower, stuntman Armen Firman is having some serious second thoughts. It is a long way down, and the stones of the plaza will give no comfort. To make his flight he has constructed an odd suit of silk with wooden reinforcing rods. He has done it fairly quickly, based on cursory study of the mechanics of flying things created by nature, such as birds and leaves, seeds and squirrels. It has been a hasty effort, because he is not a scientist but a stuntman.

Ibn Firnas is down below, watching quietly, his face partly hidden by his robes so as not to reveal who he is. Will the scholars of Cordoba question the judgment of the great ibn Firnas, to know he is watching the crazy stuntman in the plaza?

Finally the moment has come. The crowd is growing impatient and even hostile. Some are beginning to drift away. The bettors are beginning to think that Armen Firman has lost. There is no turning back for a stuntman, if he wants to eat. It's now or never. So, spreading his arms, Armen Firman opens his "wings."

He jumps out into the air. And he plummets. But his strange suit inflates just enough to slow his fall, so that when he hits the ground, it is in a controlled fall, not a full-speed drop. The crowd gasps, the women scream, the men cheer. More than a few of the dignitaries and merchants of Cordoba crack open their shuttered windows to watch the end of the spectacle.

Hitting ground, Armen Firman is mildly hurt and stunned. But he is not crippled, and he is not dead. He has enough of his senses to be able to call out to those who have bet against him. He has won, for now.

Though the word will not even exist for another millennium, Armen Firman will have undertaken what is probably the world's first parachute jump. He could not care less. All he wants is his money.

Not far from where Armen Firman hits, ibn Firnas is taking account. The suit was crude, the attempt silly. But the result impressed him more than he would have expected. It has opened up a whole new train of thought. He has a momentary image of the flight of birds, Icarus and Daedalus over the Aegean. He imagines mortal men, like himself, flying in the realm of the divine.

As the cheering crowd gathers around Armen Firman, ibn Firnas is making an important decision. He has decided that his work with glass, with music theory and timepieces, and with planets, will be expanded. He will now take a very hard look at aeronautics.

IT TAKES HIM A LONG TIME, with assorted detours and distractions, plus the effect of the passing years. He isn't getting any younger.

But finally, one beautiful Cordoba day in 875, some 23 years after Armen Firman's stunt, the 70-year-old ibn Firnas confidently summons his friends and scholars from the court, plus those others who are curious, to watch his own attempt at flight. He has long gotten over his embarrassment about being a stuntman. He is now a true believer, and he wants to try his dream while he still has breath and strength.

He calls his followers to the same low range of mountains west of the city where, one day, Caliph Abd al-Rahman III will begin to build the caliphal city of Medina Azahara. On these sun-drenched and partly wooded hills, the air rushes up from the valley floor, and ibn Firnas has watched the birds hanging there, riding the updrafts, being carried up, dropping down, only to climb again.

He has spent all those years intermittently studying the flight of birds, the creatures closest to the ideal of human flight that he envisions. He has constructed a pair of wings out of silk and wood, and onto the silk he has sewn actual feathers. He has practiced a little, without an audience; now he feels ready to make it public.

Standing on the hillside, the wind rushing up at him, his friends and associates watching, perhaps as bemused and skeptical as the crowd in the plaza many years before, he has a moment of apprehension. The day is windier than most. Although it should help his flight, the wind could also wreak havoc. Finally the air feels calm enough for him to launch. He takes a slow run and jumps off a cliff, out into the clear blue air of al-Andalus.

The crowd gasps. Because unlike Armen Firman, ibn Firnas does not fall. In defiance of all knowledge and experience, he flies like a bird. Out into the air he glides. Turning and descending in slow birdlike circles, ibn Firnas flies for what seems to the audience below a full ten minutes. He flies out above the valley of the Guadalquivir, a mixture of bird and man, for what feels like a long time.

For ibn Firnas out in the sky, the city and river and valley spreading out below him, the blessed interval seems both endless and the blink of an eye. He has attained his dream, flying in the divine realm of the angels and the jinn, or spirits, freed from the bonds of Earth. He marvels at how quiet it is, the air rushing through his ears, the sun blazing above his head and illuminating the irrigation canals between the rows of olive and orange and lemon trees, the fields of asparagus and parsley introduced by Ziryab to make the tables of Andalusia richer and more varied. O God, he prays, thank you for allowing me this experience.

When he begins to descend to Earth he is brought back to reality. He had not thought that hard about the landing and was much more focused on takeoff and flight. But now, rushing close to ground, the ground going by him faster than anything ever encountered by man, the stones and stumps and orchard walls spinning by, he realizes he has made a mistake. He has forgotten something critical. O God, he says in his final prayer, I am such a stupid mortal.

He hits the ground so hard and fast that it knocks the wind from him. He falls tumbling head over heels, not really feeling the impact so much as hearing it in his ears, the cracking of his bones and the smacking of his flesh and skull against the Earth, the impact being so great and painful that he is outside his body, watching, remotely sensing the jolts and crashes.

He spends time in a place of darkness, lost only in a dark cloud of anger at his own stupidity. When he comes to, assorted people are around him, some who have chased him on horseback, others who had gathered below the mountain to help if need be.

"Abu Abbas," someone cries. "Are you alive?"

"I am alive," he says, his voice sounding distant and far away and disgusted.

"Are you hurt?" they ask him.

And he nods. Yes, I am badly hurt.

The pain for him is concentrated in his back, and so it will remain for the rest of his life, another 12 wretched years. The remainder of his time will be like punishment and retribution for those brief moments of stolen ecstasy.

His pain and suffering are so great that some will, indeed, whisper that he has reached too high and been brought low by God. What man is meant to do, he will do. When he goes too far, he will be stopped.

Ibn Firnas hears such mutterings and whisperings for the rest of his time. Though he will recover enough to build his mobile model of the planets for the emir, complete with simulated thunder and lightning, and his water clocks and time machines, though he will melt sand into glass and formulate artificial crystals, he will be tempted to turn to illicit things like wine and narcotics to ease his pain.

Many times he will pray out for relief, anything to stop the pain. And all the while, he will be running over and over in his mind what he had done wrong. And he will conclude that his mistake was not offending God by reaching too high. No, his stupid mistake was to have omitted some way to slow his descent and achieve the control of the bird alighting. For the bird does not come speeding into the ground like a lightning bolt. The bird has an essential element called the tail that gives it balance and control. The bird uses its wings, tail, and feet in unison to slow its speed and bring it into a stall just above the ground so it can land with minimal forward speed.

I forgot to design a tail, he will think until his dying day. I stupidly forgot to design a tail.

BAGHDAD, ABBASID CALIPHATE, A.D. 805—In the Iraqi city of Kufa, 90 miles from the capital, an old man sits in his laboratory. He is surrounded by heaps of manuscripts and tables crammed with instruments, dishes, metal implements, and vials and containers of powders, extracts, tinctures, and solutions. They are all labeled in his own cramped script, words that only he can decipher. He doesn't really need to read the labels; he knows the locations in the chaos of his workplace by memory.

His hands are discolored and scarred from many chemical burns and cuts; he coughs for all the gases and mixtures and steams he has inhaled, both intentionally and by accident. His eyes are weary, his eyebrows only now growing back from the dozenth singeing explosion. Again he coughs.

The water pump, above, is one of the many machines 13th-century inventor al-Jazari sketched in his Book of Knowledge of Ingenius Mechanical Devices.

Outside on the street, a group of Abbasid warriors stand guard at his entrance. Seeing them he feels secure. But in fact, they are not there to protect him. They are there to restrain him. Only out of respect for his lifetime of achievement has his life been spared.

He is 81 years old and a political prisoner, under house arrest by order of the Caliph Haroun al-Rashid, although he couldn't care less. He no longer needs the pomp and groveling of the court. He is glad to be alive and reasonably safe. As long as he has breath in his body and a place to do his work, he will be playing with his powders and mixtures. That is his whole purpose in life.

This coughing old man's name is Jabir ibn Haiyan, and he will be known to the ranks of European alchemists as Geber, the father of alchemy and chemistry. Both words are derived from Arabic, yet these two intellectual descendants of the old mixer's art in Kufa will go very different ways. One will eventually be corrupted and wander off into the dead end of magic and the occult, while the other will become a respectable science, unleashing a worldwide revolution of discovery and invention. For Jabir, alchemy and chemistry are one and the same. Later thinkers will create the artificial distinction.

This old man has had a long and challenging life. An Arab of Yemeni extraction, he was born deep in Persia at Tus in Khorasan, the son of an apothecary. But Jabir's father was doing more than making headache powders. He was dabbling in politics. Though the Umayyads still reigned in Damascus when Jabir was born about 722, their reign would only last another three decades. Meanwhile, out in the bubbling intellectual centers of newly Muslim Persia, the Persians had already made common cause with the disgruntled Abbasids from Mecca. Together they plotted, they lurked, and they muttered in discontent about the little clique of Umayyads, plus some Syrian allies, who were holding all power to themselves. Even as the Persians were providing much of the intellectual and financial power of the new caliphate, they were treated as second-class citizens. The Abbasids understood where the real future of the caliphate lay, and it was not in excluding everyone except the tribes of Mecca.

Jabir's father had allied himself with the Persians, in particular with a family called the Barmakids. One day, when the Umayyads are deposed, the Abbasids and the Barmakids will be triumphant. The Abbasids will be the caliphs, and the Barmakids will be their grand viziers. And Jabir's family will find itself vaulted from the provinces into the court of the new caliphal dynasty.

Going to the court of Haroun al-Rashid as a physician, Jabir will later become the court chemist. Politics are only an earthly necessity for ambitious young thinkers like Jabir. As a chemist, his heart and love are wrapped in layers of mystery and code. He, like the first Muslim mathematicians and astronomers, believes that the secrets of the universe are buried deeply in the physical world around him. It is a matter of unlocking the codes. Like other Muslim thinkers, he believes that these divinely created secrets can only be unlocked by those few who are willing to undertake the long quest and deserving in the eyes of God to succeed.

This Arab son of an apothecary raised in Persia has drunk deeply of the old Persian fascination with the magical, drawing on a well of occult knowledge stretching back to the Zoroastrian magi and the priestly caste, as well as the Egyptian occult thinkers like Hermes Trismegistus. Throughout his life, Jabir will be drawn on one hand to the pole of magic and mysticism, on the other to rational science. His writings will be in elaborate and multilayered code, because he will want to veil the knowledge he is revealing so that only certain of the elect, those intended to have this esoteric knowledge and capable of managing it, will get it.

Jabir will not only be drawn to the mystical spirituality of physical matter and processes, he also will be drawn to Sufism. This movement toward high mystical ecstasy holds that the ultimate truths are not necessarily found in reason, but rather in the obliteration of the self.

Jabir's mystic-scientific side will find expression in alchemy, and according to some the ultimate goal for Jabir will not be turning lead into gold, it will be instead the quest for *takwin*, literally the creating of artificial life in the laboratory. His audacious quest will find an eerie echo among the Europeans some centuries later, in the Faust legend of the lonely searcher bringing life to his homunculus in the test tube in medieval Prague, and in its cruder and more popular form, the Frankenstein story of Mary Shelley. It is one of the ironies of lost history that the uniquely medieval Central European legend of Faust, so important to fiction and drama, to philosophy and the worldview expressed by Christopher Marlowe and Johann Wolfgang von Goethe, will not arise first in Europe. Rather it will come from a man living in classical Baghdad and will be based on ancient practices of magic in Persia and Egypt.

No one will know for sure whether Jabir really intends to create organic life in his experiments, or whether his words are just a Sufi metaphor for approaching divine knowledge.

Aiding him in this mysterious ambiguity will be the Arabic language itself, for in mystic poetry and sacred writing, the Arabic letters and words that define things, processes, and concepts are tied to numbers, and thus to the source code of existence that drives a unified, complex universe.

Jabir's method of encoding his concepts will also have a more practical use. Because he is pushing scientific and philosophical concepts beyond the limits of the day, some say he writes in his particular manner to protect himself from charges of heresy. One day the word gibberish will be derived from Jabir's name.

In the time of Jabir, when none of the intellectual disciplines have really separated out from the core study of numbers and stars, his attraction to the mystical and spiritual component of chemistry will be fairly representative of the day's unitary, holistic thinking. Everything fits together in God's universe; nothing happens randomly or without purpose; and spiritual chemistry, and its corrupted European mutant alchemy, fit perfectly.

But these ninth-century subtleties and nuances will be lost to history and lost in translation, for someday, in about a thousand years, those seeking to denigrate Muslim scientific thinking will resign Muslim "alchemy" to the realm of hocus pocus, while Europe will be refashioned as the birthplace of modern empirical "chemistry." They will ignore the fact that such European fathers of science as Sir Isaac Newton will be proud alchemists. Nor will honest scientific history be helped by those at the crude end of the intellectual spectrum, who abuse higher alchemical practices in a selfish quest to get rich, as in turning lead into gold.

How wrong and confused the writing of intellectual history can be. For Jabir is not only a spiritual and mystical searcher, he is perhaps the world's first real chemist. While one group will remember him for his mystical side, others who are intellectually rigorous will remember him for a titanic list of scientific achievements.

Just as ibn al-Haytham will one day enshrine the empirical method over faith and unsubstantiated theory, so will Jabir pave the way 200 years earlier. Jabir is reported to have said,

> The first essential in chemistry is that you should perform practical work and conduct experiments, for he who performs not practical work nor makes experiments will never attain to the least degree of mastery. But you, O my son, do experiment[s] so that you may acquire knowledge. Scientists delight not in abundance of material; they rejoice only in the excellence of their experimental methods.

Is there any clearer expression of the experimental method and empiricism than that? With this premise as his working method and philosophy, Jabir will open a torrent of chemical and scientific discovery as important to its field as al-Khwarizmi's insights to the birth of modern mathematics. During his years in service to the Abbasid caliphs and the Barmakid viziers,

Jabir will write more than 200 books and undertake innumerable experiments and innovations that will prepare the path for modern chemistry.

He will invent the first alembic, a simple apparatus that will be in use 1,200 years later to distill alcohol. He will discover hydrochloric acid, one of the strongest acids and a major component of the human digestive tract. He will discover nitric acid, another powerful and quite toxic acid, and he will combine the two chemicals to create a substance later known as *aqua regia,* or royal water, which though unstable can shortly after its mixing dissolve a number of precious metals, such as gold and platinum. He will also discover the three different acids found in citrus fruits, vinegar, and wine.

His experiments will not be idle games, because he will always be looking for ways to turn his discoveries to practical application. Out of his discoveries will come ways to rustproof iron and steel, to remove the greenish tint from glass products, to dye and waterproof cloth, and to etch on gold. He will also stumble upon a flammable vapor created by boiling wine, a discovery that will be elaborated by his successor al-Razi, and which the world will one day know as ethanol, an alternative fuel derived from sugar that can replace petroleum products.

He will invent the word and concept of "alkali," a base substance that when combined with an acidic substance will neutralize the acid.

He will publish books on chemical properties, weights and measures, chemical combinations, and dyes. He will construct a precise laboratory scale, the most accurate of its time. In an intuitive glimpse of atoms and molecules, he will theorize that when chemicals are combined, tiny components combine with one another at the microscopic level, still retaining their original character. He will invent a form of flame-retardant paper and a kind of fluorescent ink for reading in the dark.

Jabir will not stop there. He will fabricate hair dyes and find a way to use iron pyrite to write in gold letters. He will take a hard look at magnetism. He will categorize greases, paints, and salts, and his breakthroughs will later be used in the first foundries and ceramic glazes.

Surrounded by the memories and records of all that as he ages, he keeps going as long as his eyes and lungs will let him. Like his counterparts, despite all he has done, he feels as if he has only scratched the surface. In the foul humor of old age, he wonders if anyone will carry on his work. He looks out at the guards holding him prisoner. No great thinkers there, he believes. Who will it be? Will it be one of my students? Will it be someone who has found favor with the Abbasids in Baghdad, someone not tainted by the Barmakids? Will it be someone in faraway Khorasan?

Not long after, as he lies dying still under house arrest, unknown to him, there is a successor. Though the answer is none of the ones that have coursed through his head between experiments. His successor is not a student, not a Persian, but an Arab like himself.

He's a little boy, just learning to read and write, but not far away, right there in Kufa, from a household that will not deign to speak to the old chemist from Tus so out of favor. Jabir's successor will be known as al-Kindi, and his father is the Abbasid governor.

LUCKY ENOUGH TO LIVE and work much of his life in the time of al-Mamun and his rationalist successor, al-Kindi will, indeed, build on Jabir's work and will apply himself to even more fields than his predecessor did, working with music, medicine, philosophy, mathematics, and astronomy as well as chemistry. He will write an astonishing 361 works in all these fields. Al-Kindi will manage to take the first stabs at answering some serious questions of matter, physics, and the universe that will keep great minds at work for the next 1,200 years.

And in the strange irony of time, this scientific successor to Jabir will be a devout anti-alchemist, taking aim not so much at Jabir as at the deluded charlatans who go off in search of magic elixirs to make gold.

Al-Kindi will be a prized member of al-Mamun's House of Wisdom. A devout follower of Aristotle, he will be as well positioned politically and intellectually as Jabir was not in his later years. But as al-Kindi will later theorize and then learn first-hand, nothing is absolute and forever, not even time and good fortune.

In the area of chemistry, al-Kindi will apply himself to both the mundane and the sublime. For the down-to-earth, he will author a massive tome on perfumes and other aromatic compounds, and oils, salves, and lotions. He will work very hard at what will one day become pharmacology, studying substances and their interactions with living organisms. At the high end of that, he will come up with a complicated numerical system for creating and organizing drugs. And at the low end, he will come up with the first low-cost alternatives to important but costly remedies.

Watching countless objects fall to Earth—leaves, dates, stones from building projects, the writing pen from his desk—he will wonder about terrestrial gravitation.

But perhaps his most profound and prescient work will come in the form of thoughts about relativity, about the relationship between matter, time, and space. He will even use the Arabic version of the word "relativity," which a thousand years later will be made famous by a young Jewish mathematician working in obscurity in Zurich. While this shared use of the word separated by language and a millennium seems pure coincidence, is there a hidden linkage of thought to explain the parallel development of these great minds? Al-Kindi says,

> *Time exists only with motion; body, with motion; motion, with body,...*
> *if there is motion, there is necessarily body; if there is a body, there is*
> *necessarily motion.*

This counterintuitive view of time, space, and matter may have been accidental and coincidental in the context of ninth-century Baghdad. It will be ignored or disputed by most of those who follow him, not only by Muslims but also by Isaac Newton and René Descartes. Al-Kindi will have no way of mathematically proving his thesis.

Al-Kindi will also venture into the esoteric area of cryptography. Though simple forms of secret writing have been around for centuries, with the arrival of higher mathematics after al-Khwarizmi, cryptography will become more sophisticated; it will be especially important to leaders and governments and spies from the time of al-Mamun forward.

Al-Kindi will be the first to describe frequency analysis in cryptography:

> *One way to solve an encrypted message, if we know its language, is to*
> *find a different plaintext of the same language long enough to fill one*
> *sheet or so, and then we count the occurrences of each letter. We call the*
> *most frequently occurring letter the 'first,' the next most occurring letter*
> *the 'second,' the following most occurring the 'third,' and so on, until we*
> *account for all the different letters in the plaintext sample.*
>
> *Then we look at the cipher text we want to solve, and we also clas-*
> *sify its symbols. We find the most occurring symbol and change it to the*

form of the 'first' letter of the plaintext sample, the next most common symbol is changed to the form of the 'second' letter, and so on, until we account for all symbols of the cryptogram we want to solve.

But everything is relative. Al-Kindi will fall out of favor in the conservative, anti-rationalist resurgence under Caliph al-Mutawakkil in the 840s. Some will point to fellow scholars at the House of Wisdom, the Banu Musa family, supposedly jealous of the great al-Kindi, as having slandered and betrayed him. He will even be beaten and have his library temporarily confiscated. Late in his life, another political turn will bring him back into favor under Caliph al-Mutamid.

But fortune in the physical world is impermanent and terribly relative and ultimately unimportant to the philosopher-scientist al-Kindi. After suffering so many turns of fortune, he will write:

Close your eyes, look down, when villains become masters. Grasp your hands for disappointment, and sit in the corner of your house, in solitude.... The real wealth is in the heart of men, and in their soul is glory, so that riches come forth from one who owns little, while another of material wealth turns penniless.

IN THE YEAR 1017 or so, a Muslim conquering army winds down through the high passes of the Himalaya, bound for the rich and ancient Hindu cities of India. And though most of the Muslims have their minds focused on wealth and pleasure and booty, one in their midst, one Abu Raihan al-Biruni, is looking for a different kind of treasure.

He is there as a kind of prisoner. If there were a better place to be and a better conqueror to serve—or even a place to be free—then he might be gone. But no matter. Though he does not have his freedom, he has been given moments and opportunities like this one. And he will make the most of them.

He drinks in the grandeur of mountains reaching up to sky, above the sweet vale of Kashmir, the highest peaks on Earth soaring snowcapped up into blue heaven, into swelling clouds of storm. He sees how the mountains and sky make a wall and roof over a colossal garden, the forests and glades and flowering fields at the top of the world.

Water pours from the snows and the skies, giving verdure, life, scent, and softness. This is the grandiose doorstep for the treasure house of India, a continent and a civilization reaching back to the beginning of mankind.

Al-Biruni sees the upthrust wall of mountains stretching east and west, range upon range, off into ever fainter silhouettes, each one higher and more distant than those in the foreground. He sees the rivers spreading from their glacial birthplaces, tumbling downward through chasms and canyons, gathering water, and gathering force.

He sees these great rivers pouring out of the mountain source land into the hot plains, now becoming wider and slower, the vast plains and deltas of their outwash where live tens of millions of men and women, tilling the flat soil and providing food and sustenance for one of the oldest civilizations on Earth.

What scientific physical process, short of the hand of God, has produced this landscape? What has caused the upthrust of northern mountains? What has caused the hot and spreading riverine plains to the south? And how has it shaped the Indian mind and life?

Al-Biruni was born in Khiva in a region of Persia, which will one day be known as Uzbekistan. Like many in his time, he is trying both to survive and to give expression to the titanic urge for discovery and understanding welling up inside. This journey into India sets the stage for new insights.

On a mountaintop far from the sea, al-Biruni finds seashells, bleached and broken and calcified, but apparently brought there by no man's hand. How did these shells come to be situated on this mountaintop?

Then he sees the ancient and vibrant and puzzling land of India and its people, its many religions and traditions, the juxtaposition of phenomenal wealth and shocking destitution. He recognizes that his planet and its ruling race are dazzling and strange, all at once, and where better to study them than in India?

Though al-Biruni will serve so many masters and dynasties in his 75 years that he has trouble remembering them all, it is these campaigns into India beginning in 1017 in the employ of Sultan Mahmud of Ghazna that will affect him the most.

Ironic that the patron of these priceless Indian expeditions is a cruel and abusive ruler. On bad days, Sultan Mahmud mercilessly torments al-Biruni, who has been brought along on these trips as royal tutor and advisor. Mahmud employs al-Biruni, both for his scientific wisdom and most likely for his astrological knowledge.

In his heart of hearts, al-Biruni doesn't believe in astrology. In his eyes it is not a science, it is a mystic cult. He is a fierce believer, like al-Kindi and al-Haytham, in empirical science. Theory, no matter how compelling, must stand up to observation and testing.

Like so many Muslim thinkers lost to history, from a time without intellectual divisions, al-Biruni is a master mathematician and astronomer, ranking with al-Kindi and the astronomers of the House of Wisdom. He is also one of the best medical and pharmacological experimenters, carrying on a correspondence with that giant of Muslim medicine, ibn Sina.

And he is also one of the best Muslim historians and cultural observers of all time. He will deeply immerse himself in Hindu philosophy and religion, and in exchange, he will teach Hindu scholars about the wisdom of the Muslim and Greek thinkers. But in the breadth of his hunger and his aspirations, he is also a pioneer geographer and geologist. Oh, but astrology keeps him fed. His rich and powerful clients love it and believe in it and will pay for it. So he gives them what they want.

For now he is the employee-prisoner of Mahmud of the great and mighty Ghaznivid Empire. Mahmud's capital city, Ghazni, lies in what will become known later as Afghanistan. One day, in a thousand years, Ghazni will be nothing more than desolate ruins crumbling into dirt in a country riddled by war. But in the time of al-Biruni, Mahmud, and his Ghaznivid dynasty, Ghazni will exert considerable power. Those in much bigger and richer centers of power will be at their mercy as his armies reach far into modern-day Pakistan and India.

But, al-Biruni concludes, it is all ebb and flow: his life, the rise and fall of dynasties, the shaping of the Earth. In one of his journeys, he will trace the sacred river Ganges from its glacial source down to its outflow into the Bay of Bengal. And he will come to an important discovery. He will note that the size of the river sediment particles is directly related to the speed of the river's current. This means that upstream and closer to the headwaters, where the river tumbles down faster, the sediment is bigger, from rocks and pebbles to big grains of sand, and so, upstream the outwash is less fertile. But downstream, closer to the ocean where the river slows, the tiny particulates will settle out, creating the dark and rich mud of the valley fields, of the deltas where rice and other nourishment are best grown.

He will show how erosion shapes the land, from the broad formations of Earth to the rounded stones tumbled into smoothness by the water running from mountains to sea.

On one of these trips he will stumble upon the Indian theory that says the tides of the ocean are related to the phases of the moon. That one will fascinate him, though he will not yet be able to explain why this is so. From his discovery of the seashells high atop the mountains, he will voice the theory that the Ganges Valley was once under the ocean.

Then he will turn his attention to the infinity of substances he finds in and below the ground. His work on gems, written late in life, under the employ of another Ghaznivid sultan, will focus on precious stones and metals. He will catalog and analyze one hundred gems and metals, looking at their value, how they are made or refined, their hardness to the touch, and color to the eye. His mineral density measurements will be the most accurate for about 700 years, until European advances will catch up.

He will explain how artesian wells and natural springs yield water, through a theory called the hydrostatic communication of vessels. He will postulate that the Earth spins on its axis, and he will compute latitude and longitude for hundreds of cities.

Showing his intellectual resemblance to al-Haytham, who is also fascinated by the properties of light and vision, and whom he will apparently never meet, Al-Biruni will investigate the negative spaces created by the absence of light. Subsequently he will name one of his 100-plus works *Shadows*. Just as al-Haytham will be entranced by light, al-Biruni will be drawn to the mathematical and chronological aspects of darkness. He will even calculate Muslim times of prayer from angles of shadows. In *Shadows* he will also introduce a new way of finding a point in three-dimensional space.

Mercifully, in his final years, when his health and vision are slipping away, he will be in the employ of a generous ruler, who lets him live in comfort and security, content to have the presence of this great thinker at the end of his days.

Unlike many of his medieval counterparts, he will never be translated into Latin, nor be given a Latin name. His name will be unknown to

Europeans until the 20th century, when historian George Sarton refers to him as "the master of those who know."

THE SOUTHEAST OF ANATOLIA, walled by lower mountains to the south and the massif of Ararat to the east, is forever a place of shifting political borders. Empires, emirs, and caliphs have called it their own, though it has never belonged to anyone for long.

Byzantines, Turks, Persians, and Arabs have come and gone. The Byzantines and the Abbasids, the Syrians and the Persians all consider it theirs, at some point. Just beneath their line of sight, over time, the shadow kingdom of Kurdistan floats there, wanting to be born but never quite able to break free.

The unofficial capital of this land is Diyarbakir, a haunting place of thick stone and masonry walls keeping out the dry and rocky Anatolian steppe, of quiet interior gardens watered by streams, of stolid mosques topped by Seljuk minarets, and of caravansaries to shelter those riding the Silk Road east and west. No onion domes are here; this is a slightly different aesthetic, a place where the need is greater for fortification than for a temple of beauty. Would this Diyarbakir seem to be a center of genius?

The world will know the answer one day. When the Seljuks of Omar Khayyám's time fade from absolute power to a desperate competition with a dozen players, Diyarbakir floats free for a time. And then when one of the Seljuk generals from Malik Shah's disintegrated army, expelled from Jerusalem by crusaders in 1098, looks for a place to settle, he chooses this city as a base.

This jobless general's name is Artuk, and his short-lived dynasty of Turks will be called the Artuqids. In their employ will be a family of talented craftsmen and designers, looked to for new ways to measure time, to guard and regulate and move precious water, to wash things, and to make life easier. Not a family of mathematicians or scholars, this family likes to build things, and tinker.

In the 12th century, the family gives birth to a boy, and he is the best of his people. As a child he apprentices to his father and his uncles in the Artuqid workshops, learning the tools, absorbing how to eyeball and estimate, becoming familiar with all sorts of little clever devices and implements that when combined with others become much more than the sum of their parts.

His name is al-Jazari, and but for lost history, he would be as well known to the world as Leonardo da Vinci.

Looking into these little things and their components fitted into contraptions in the palace workshops, he sees an intelligence independent of man, an intelligence certainly inferior to humans in its range and flexibility, its lack of creativity and self-awareness. But this intelligence is more durable than humans' in its sheer muscularity, in its ability to follow and hold to a formula, day after day, year after year, when the human mind would long ago have shriveled from stupefaction. He sees that metal tubes and bowls and pipes, wood buckets and struts and frames, leather straps and belts, when combined in a certain way, can hold knowledge.

Sometime between childhood and mature adulthood, a spark goes off in al-Jazari's head, and he perceives this element of mechanical intelligence to hold all sorts of promise and application. And when the spark goes into full flame, out will come not so much theories and formulas as designs and prototypes, real things doing real tasks, and often with a piece of intelligence so that it does not need a human mind to direct it, only to keep it repaired and to turn it on or off.

The irony of many Muslim inventors and craftsmen is that they will not be faithful about writing things down, or about precisely recording the critical specifications and measurements of their devices and inventions. For other inventors and tinkerers, the inventions themselves will be the only record of their existence. There will be no diagrams or blueprints for those who follow behind. Al-Jazari is different. He will use his fierce eye and intuition, plus trial and error, to build his inventions. And he will record them.

Al-Jazari will manage to leave at least one book behind, and it will be called *The Book of Knowledge of Ingenious Mechanical Devices,* published around 1206. It will be complete with diagrams and blueprints. This book will only be translated into English in the 20th century, but bits and pieces of it will seep out from Diyarbakir, possibly making it into Europe via the crusaders in the Levant, or the Muslims in Sicily and Spain.

This is not a literary work like the books of the philosophers or mathematicians and astronomers. This is a book of illustrations and designs— designs of things that will one day be taken for granted, hidden away in compressor rooms and machine shops and utility closets. But these designs are so important to making life civilized that when they first appear, they will be seen as quasi-divine marvels. Maybe to some, they will bear hints of the satanic.

Al-Jazari invents the lowly crankshaft, hardly thought of by most humans today, but essential to so many machines enabling modern life. He designs a most ingenious pump for the movement of water, independent of water wheels and water buffalo, spinning in lustrous wonder. Copper pipes, finely meshing gears, crankshafts, intake valves, and outports do their job. This pump will fascinate engineers and thinkers for centuries.

His giant water pump, with pistons and paddles and camshaft, will be capable of using the flow of the river to drive the pump's action, forcing water up through pipes and out to the city streets or the farmers' fields.

A third of his water pumps uses a unique design, elegant enough to be considered a piece of fine technology, in line with astrolabes and telescopes. His incredibly elaborate "elephant clock," about four-by-six feet, uses a complicated set of gravity-driven triggers, gears, and water flow to sound the hours by a chirping bird atop the elephant. Another of his portable water clocks, shaped like a scribe sitting on a table, marks the time by using the scribe's pen as the hour hand.

This kind of technology will start to show up in Europe very quickly. Nevertheless, historians will debate whether its development is parallel and coincidental, or derivative of al-Jazari. The answer will not be clear. And to many, as machines become part of the European and world landscape, the answer will not matter. What was once an exquisite skill and artistry will become a mainstream everyday profession. But the spirit of al-Jazari will live in every gear and crankshaft.

AS THE MONGOLS POUR WEST into the Muslim lands, in their arsenal of wondrous horrors is something never before seen in these parts—screaming tubes of fire—as opposed to flaming arrows, which have been around almost as long as arrows. These new devices take off from the ground in a shrieking burst of smoke and flame, and soar arcing across the sky to bring terror and destruction onto the enemy.

These are the first rockets. No one knows the name of their inventor, though he or she was in ancient China and did this work to honor the

Chinese gods at festival time. So Chinese rockets were born as religious decoration and entertainment, until someone realized they could also be used in war. In time, the pre-Mongol Chinese had come to depend on them more and more to hold off the Mongols, until they were finally overwhelmed, and the enemy absorbed this new weapon into its arsenal.

A Mongol rocket runs on a solid fuel of gunpowder, tightly packed to make the first engine. Depending on the rocket's size, the impact of its explosion can be heard a dozen miles away, and it scorches and devastates the ground for yards nearby.

In 1241 on the outskirts of Budapest, Mongol rockets crash down on the trembling Hungarian defenders. Far to the south, the doomed inhabitants of Baghdad watch the Mongol rockets rain down on them in 1258, harbingers of their coming slaughter and extermination.

But just as happened after the defeat of Abd al-Rahman al-Gafiqi when Charles Martel had the stirrups stripped off the fallen Muslim knights at Tours in 732, some of these Mongol assaults will leave things behind for clever men to recover and study and assimilate.

The gunpowder in the engines is not unknown to the Muslim chemists. They have been formulating variations of gunpowder for centuries and watching the powder ignite. Now they see a new use for the fiery powder, other than causing scorched eyebrows and bad lungs.

A 13th-century Syrian named al-Rammah quickly absorbs the Mongol method of mixing saltpeter, charcoal, and sulphur in rocketry and writes a text that will be marveled over, though not just for reasons of pure science. In this time of invading hordes and borders that collapse overnight, many rulers and warlords are interested in this new device for protection.

Al-Rammah will not only take a hard scientific look at packed gunpowder, he will diagram and describe a jet-powered "egg" with a kind of warhead to be launched on the water's surface against enemy ships. Later analysts will conclude this to be the first torpedo, and the text will swiftly make its way into Europe.

Another application of gunpowder is to hurl bullets and cannonballs, and though there is some evidence of cannon-like weapons in China, they have a more definitive appearance in the Muslim world, and often in conflicts with the European Christians. There are accounts of cannons being used by the Muslims in the Crusades.

Only eight years before the fall of Baghdad, in 1250, some accounts of the Seventh Christian Crusade tell of Muslims using rockets against the European Army of French King Louis IX in the battle of al-Mansura.

The long period of the Crusades between the 11th and the end of the 13th centuries will result in the final victory of the Muslims.

Cannons are used by the Spanish Muslims against the Christians in their various losing battles of the Catholic reconquest in the 13th century. The Christian winners will take the Muslim weapons and make them their own.

Ottoman Turks will absorb both cannons and rockets from the Mongols and Arabs, and they will use both in their winning siege of Constantinople in 1453 and their assaults on Austria and Hungary in the 16th and 17th centuries.

With the fall of Constantinople and the birth of Istanbul, it is the Turks who will fulfill the long-dead dream of the Abbasids and erase Byzantium from the map. By 1453, on the eve of the battle for Constantinople, the Byzantine Empire that once ruled Anatolia, the Levant, and the Middle East has dwindled to the old capital and its western environs, plus several small territories in Greece and on the Anatolian coast. Though the last Byzantines resist valiantly, they are radically outnumbered, about 10,000 men to the 100,000 or more under the Ottoman flag. Their pleas for help to Pope Nicholas V bring nothing in return; the kings of Europe have no stomach for a fight with the Turks. Spain is caught up in its final reconquest, France and England are exhausted from the Hundred-Years' War.

All sorts of omens are seen to mark the end of Byzantium. They include a lunar eclipse and a strange red light seen dancing on the dome of the Hagia Sophia and out beyond the Turkish invaders, symbolizing to some Christians the departure of the holy spirit from the ancient church. Imagine the thrill in the hearts of the Turks and the gloom in the hearts of the Europeans, as the ancient dream of al-Mamun and all the caliphs and sultans since to absorb the beating heart of Byzantium finally occurs, lit up by the symphony of cannon fire and rockets' glare. Six hundred years in the making, a victory does not go to the Arabs or the Seljuks. Final victory over Byzantium comes to the descendants of Osman, the patriarch of the Ottoman Turks.

No matter that this millennial struggle for Constantinople has lost much of its original meaning and significance, or that Constantinople has been on its deathbed for centuries, or that its grandeur and glory rest so far back in time that it is like Greek mythology. No matter that the attacking Muslims have so long been at the gates, been so long threatening, that they are more like unpleasant longtime neighbors than aliens pouring out of the desert.

No matter that the end of the Muslim golden ages is now nearer. The sons of Osman do not even think of that, do not look on the deepening shadows of historical mid-afternoon racing toward sunset, the sunset of a vision, of a way of life. They brighten the shadows with the glare of rockets on the Byzantine towers and cover the whispers of doubt with the explosion of cannon fire.

Through the returning crusaders, the advancing Turks, and the retreating Muslims in Spain, these wickedly wondrous new weapons will filter up into France and Italy and England and Germany, one day to provide the firepower and enforcement of the Age of Imperialism beginning about 1860. But even when centuries later the European conquerors are well on their way to engulfing much of the world, these weapons from the siege of Baghdad and Constantinople will sometimes rise up to haunt them with echoes of lost history.

One final haunting is the British-Indian battle at the fortress of Srirangapatnam in Mysore, South India in 1799. At this point the Indians are succumbing to the invading British, but under Muslim ruler Tipu Sultan, they are still fighting. One tactic, put in place by the sultan's father Hyder Ali, is a formidable rocket force. Each Indian battalion has 200 rocketeers in place, armed with ample supplies of rockets capable of traveling a thousand yards and tipped with lethal warheads, including gunpowder charges, pointed tips, and even a kind of whirling blade that shreds everything on point of impact like a meat grinder. Though by now Europe has rockets, none of them have the range and lethality of these rockets.

During the battle, thousands of Indian missiles slam into the British forces, considerably slowing down their advance. Finally, when the fortress falls, the British capture several hundred loaded rockets and rocket launchers and thousands of unarmed ones. Some of these are packed up and shipped back to Britain for study. They come to the attention of one William Congreve, an armaments expert in the service of the king. He swiftly sets about incorporating the Indian design into the British forces.

And then, only 14 years later, when the infant United States is under attack from the same British Empire, the so-called Congreve rockets fashioned after the Indian rockets are fired at the uncooperative Americans, in particular from ships in the Chesapeake Bay against one Fort McHenry, protecting the American city of Baltimore.

An American prisoner of the British will watch throughout the night as his captors launch volley upon volley of Congreve rockets at the American fortification. The next morning, when he sees the tattered American flag still flying above the fort, he will be inspired to write a patriotic song called the "Star Spangled Banner."

Most Americans know about Francis Scott Key and their national anthem. But because of lost history, they do not know that those rockets inspiring the song were born in faraway China, brought west by the Mongols for events like the attack on Baghdad, then transformed by the Muslims into more versatile weapons of war, and shot into the European mind through the Crusades, through the reconquest of Spain, through the Turkish attack on the gates of Vienna, and through the final Muslim-Indian resistance against the British.

Nor do they know that one day, distant descendants of those rockets and rocketeers will animate renewed bloodlettings in the 21st century in the so-called clash of civilizations, tiresomely like the battles of lost history, and in many of the same places: Baghdad, Israel, Afghanistan.

It is one irony of lost history that its blade cuts both ways.

IT IS THE YEAR 1630, and a Turkish scientist stands high atop the Galata Tower overlooking the Bosporus. This 282-year-old tower was built by the Genoese to secure their hold on Constantinople. A crowd of observers stands below; others are in boats on the Bosporus; even more optimists are on the Asiatic side in Üsküdar.

It is 755 years after ibn Firnas stood on the cliffs above Cordoba and made his life-changing flight. The Turk's name is Ahmet Çelebi, and he is from one of those families steeped in science and language, in ideas and machines. Like ibn Firnas, he has always been fascinated with flight; he has read accounts of the Andalusian, and he has looked at Leonardo da Vinci's designs for flying machines; and he has watched eagles soaring in the air. He has built a pair of artificial wings and an artificial tail.

He knows the fear that ibn Firnas felt. At least, he thinks, if I fall, my fall will be into the water. Though from high enough and falling fast enough, water can feel like granite. Ahmet Çelebi is not an old man. He is in his late twenties, strong and in good health. Aside from the advance of science, he also has that advantage over the ancient Spanish flier.

Now or never. He jumps off the tower and the wind catches him and he soars out, gliding from Europe toward Asia. He sees his friends in the boats, the ships heading to the Black Sea and the Mediterranean, warships and trading ships, the towers of Topkapi Palace, and the minarets of the Süleymaniye Mosque, and the dozens of other mosques in this capital of the Ottoman Empire. This is the empire that has recaptured all of the old Abbasid caliphate.

He soars from Europe to Asia, flying about two miles. And coming down, he is ready for the landing that ibn Firnas fumbled. He settles slowly and uninjured to the ground of Asian Turkey. His spectators cheer, and the news is carried back to Sultan Murat IV, and someone decrees that Çelebi be given the title of *Hezarfen,* meaning "a thousand sciences."

The sultan is so impressed that he gives Hezarfen one thousand gold pieces, and at his young age the brave flier seems destined for greater things. So it seems a reversal of destiny when only a short time later Çelebi is inexplicably branded as blasphemous for his deeds by religious leaders and driven into exile in Tunisia. There he will die at the age of 31.

But that is not the last flight for the Turks. Two years after Çelebi's feat, a family member named Lagari Hasan Çelebi will fashion a jet-powered flying machine consisting of a wire cage with rockets mounted onto it. To commemorate a royal birthday, he will launch himself out in night's darkness over the Sea of Marmara, and will roar out across the water separating two continents. According to some accounts, he makes a soft landing in the waters of the Bosporus and is rewarded by the sultan with a military position in the Ottoman army.

6

HEALERS AND HOSPITALS

And when I am sick, then he restores me to health.
QUR'AN (XXVI:80)

CORDOBA, 2007—Cordoba in the Spanish province of Andalusia sits astride the Guadalquivir River, that ancient river whose name is descended from the Arabic, *al-wadi al-kabir*, meaning "The Great River." Once reputed to be one of the largest cities in the world, Cordoba is now a manageable town of 350,000. The city is quiet and prosperous and mercifully free of the war and conflicts that plague so much of the world. From this snapshot of the present, it would seem that Cordoba is a provincial city—not a capital and not a center. Like most of Europe, it would seem to always have been a very pretty and peaceful place.

From above and far away, it would also seem that nothing of more importance has happened here than in dozens of other similar scenic and richly textured places along the greater Mediterranean in Europe.

Its old Roman and Arab and medieval core is crossed by streets with seemingly incongruous names like Calle Damasco and Avenida al-Nasir. There is a bridge from Roman times, a royal castle built in Mudejar style called the Alcazar, and a roseate and earthen-hued Catholic cathedral built on the structure of a place of worship of another, long-proscribed religion. All this is surrounded by a more conventional city of modern Spain, with utilitarian and nondescript suburbs of the kind that now surround most cities in Europe.

On the edge of the old city is a hospital attached to Queen Sofia University. Large and modernist, though generally undistinguished in architectural style, it is prosperous and ever growing, and glutted with car traffic as are most hospitals in the 21st century. From above and afar it could seem to have been located anywhere, as much in Kansas City or Singapore as in Cordoba. It seems not to be connected to the landscape or history of where it is, except by its name.

It is named for the living Queen of Spain, a Greek-born royal related by blood to all the relatives of the late Queen Victoria of England. Her husband King Juan Carlos has brought Spain out of a suffocating period of military dictatorship. The royal couple are almost universally loved and respected.

In the university hospital, Dr. Patricia Gonzales de Medina is delivering her fourth baby of the day. She is quite tired, because she has come off six straight days of work covering for her partner who has gone to a conference in Mexico. She has had to postpone her own vacation twice, and she wonders why at her age she is working so hard.

It reminds her of her years of medical study at Stanford University and her internship at a hospital in Palo Alto. With the energy of youth she had worked 60 hours straight once and regularly gone on 48-hour stints, living on coffee and cigarettes when those things were not politically incorrect. She had loved that wicked pace for a time because she loved medicine, and she felt honored to have been admitted to one of the best medical schools in the world. Though she, like most Spaniards, had a continuing coolness to American culture quite different from other Europeans, she knew the state of medical research. And the Americans, like them or not, were the leaders. She wanted to be associated with that.

But the coolness had always remained with her. She knew she would not stay in America after she had completed her training. She would go back either to her native Spain or to Latin America, perhaps Buenos Aires or Montevideo.

California had been tolerable because of the sun and the climate, and it had echoes, fading by the year, of her homeland. The Spanish facades of the Stanford campus, the arches, the red tile roofs, had made her feel slightly at home. The place names were all Spanish, and they gave her comfort even though hardly anyone spoke Spanish anymore.

What a day this has been. Each birth has been more difficult and demanding than the previous one. This last one, with the baby in an odd breech position and the mother appearing out of nowhere with a strange blood condition, not Patricia's patient but assigned to her by the lottery of timing, has given everyone a scare. The mother's condition has forced Patricia to avoid the easier Caesarian delivery and use forceps to work the baby into place. Patricia has always seen forceps as a last resort. She wishes there were something better. But there isn't.

Patricia is taking a break up on the fourth floor lounge, drinking a coffee and looking out into the sunset. She has another four hours on duty. She's well overdue to go home and have a good glass of wine, though the apartment will be quiet as it has been since her divorce. Her husband Rodrigo went off with someone else, a woman from his sales organization. She and Rodrigo did not have children. Something always told her not to try.

Now her life is work and a few hours of rest and vacations. A native of Madrid, she took this position in Cordoba because she'd had enough of the capital. And this was a better position, with more responsibility.

But something is missing. She knows it's not Rodrigo. She was glad to have him gone. And it's not a leisurely life. She really enjoys her work. Cordoba has hardly mattered to her. She could care less about the old sites that draw the tourists, the museums and the narrow little streets with their Mudejar architecture.

Out on the western horizon, silhouetted by the sun, she thinks she can see those ruins. It's an old fallen royal city, Medina Azahara, built by a caliph a thousand years ago. The site is quite disappointing for tourists because so much of it has fallen down or been carried away; it's not nearly as well preserved as the old mosque downtown. The remnants are ravaged and collapsed by time, much like Pompeii, which she saw once. A developer is building houses right up to the ruins. Nowadays young couples like to have their weddings catered out in the remaining arches.

People at first assumed there was some connection between her and the ruins because they shared a name. Pure coincidence, she has always said. The Medinas are *buen católico* and the name is as common as Garcia. The implication of the name has never gone any further. She doesn't get into lineage. Unlike many Spaniards, the Medinas were not interested in family lineage. Should she have stayed in America, married an American boy, had kids? Is that why Rodrigo left her? No kids?

And it is at this moment that one of her nurses comes in to tell her that the mother of the baby she just delivered with forceps has not survived.

Not because of the forceps; as the mother was being wheeled into intensive care, without warning she went into shock and cardiac arrest. In five minutes she was gone.

Although Patricia has lost mothers and babies, today she can't take it. This hardened professional obstetrician feels as if she is going to break down. Looking off into the ruins, she is utterly despondent. What has she lost? Is it her childhood? Her dreams? She can't stand at this window any longer. She runs to the stairwell and leaves through one of the emergency exits. Outside, sobbing with current and ancient loss, she wonders how she will be able to go back inside to finish her shift.

BAGHDAD, A.D. 865—Many muezzins are calling at dawn from mosques at every point of the compass. The caliphal city is slowly awakening to the silhouette of minaret and dome against brightening sky, to the growing thunder of horses and camels on pontoon bridges and dusty roads pouring into city gates. Thousands of men and women are on the move. Laughter from unseen courtyards resounds; secret whispers are muffled in lush and grandiose gardens and plazas; arguments are heard from the shuttered windows of the great houses, where the rich and brilliant celebrate, debate, tell stories.

An ocean of shouts and noise echoes from the backstreets where the workers, the fishermen, the stevedores and camel drivers, the hucksters and magicians, the undertakers and sweepers and washerwomen live and sleep.

About 230 years after the death of the Prophet, the quickening rush to the great Muslim cities is coursing fast, a current of hundreds of thousands pulled away from former lives on deserts or fields or from older, smaller places now falling out of fashion, all of them impelled toward the light of excitement and change.

The rise of the cities is driven in part by a prophecy that calls for a society fair and humane; a prophecy that elevates the quest for knowledge and learning; a prophecy dignifying commerce, just as the Prophet was a man of commerce; a vision of a society clean and healthy just as the Prophet recommended.

And what does this new culture of urbanity mean to the Muslims? To the thinkers and artists and inventors it means patronage and income; it means libraries; it means centers of learning and discussion; it means debates and arguments, the interaction of many minds trying through agreement and dispute to find the universal answers. It means places of taste and sophistication, and palaces of the imagination where the ideas of many can be accumulated and aggregated. It means centers where men can attempt to rise above the level of struggling to find enough food, water, and shelter to stay alive and have energy and time left over to consider the great questions.

To the rulers the cities mean memorials and stone testimonials, civic architecture in mosques and palaces that will outlive them and inspire and embody their ideals and their visions. The cities mean court societies where the best and brightest will be nearby and at hand, making life richer and more interesting.

To the families of commerce, cities mean meeting places, points of intersection where buyer and seller connect, large groupings of people who must be clothed and fed and entertained.

To the women, these cities mean a better chance of survival for their children, the possibility of a future brighter than the past, clean and plentiful food and water. The cities offer beautiful clothes and jewels and coloring for the lips and eyes and hair. The cities give them some freedom and anonymity.

And to the administrators of these places, cities mean assessing taxes and spending them on water and building materials and roads, on markets and schools and mosques. And cities mean the need for public health. Because these clusters of millions of people at the nerve centers of states with millions more cannot function if cities are also centers of contagion and infection, of squalor and misery. The society is only as healthy as its individual members, whether caliph or water carrier.

Against this backdrop in about 865, a slender sixtyish, gray-bearded teaching doctor employed by the Abbasids pauses at midday in his courtyard near Baghdad's House of Wisdom to take a quiet lunch with one of his prize students, a Persian boy with an unusually prominent head. The boy has been sent from Ray to obtain the best of learning from many masters. Together they look at a vial of yellowish liquid taken from a cadaver.

"Do you think Galen is right about the humors?" this student asks his teacher, and the teacher does not answer. First, because few people if any have ever seriously questioned Galen's theories. And second, because it shows that his young student is thinking for himself. "Maybe you and I should start work on a book about Galen," says the teacher, and the student's big face lights up. "But I warn you: Many people will be upset to hear questioning of the master."

The teacher is from an old Jewish family of Merv known as the Sahls who have converted to Islam, and his name is Ali ibn Sahl Rabban al-Tabari. Al-Tabari has been trained in the Persian and Greek methods based largely on a Greek thinker and medical doctor from Pergamon in Anatolia, named Galen, 600 years ago.

The Persian boy is Zakaria al-Razi, of a family possibly also converted from Judaism to Islam.

Long-dead Galen is showing them the way to medical wisdom. For the Byzantines and the Muslims and the Europeans some 1,300 years after his death, Galen is to medicine as Ptolemy is to the planets and Aristotle to reason. With very little medical science to draw on, Galen had created a comprehensive body of knowledge and information, some of it very prescient, much of it dead wrong, that nonetheless provided the first unified attempt to understand the connections between the organs within the body, and nutrition, environment, disease, injury, pharmacology, and surgery. And Galen had not only gathered theoretical knowledge; he had been checking out his ideas first-hand, dissecting live pigs to see how the organs were functioning before they expired. He had cut a pig's spine to show how paralysis sets in; he had tied off urinary ducts to show that urine comes from the kidneys; he had looked at live beating hearts, heaving lungs spurting blood, and clusters of nerves.

Galen had also conducted surgery on live humans, including one heart-stopping technique for removing cataracts. He would insert a needle into the eyeball just behind the lens and either dislodge or extract the cataract, an operation where a slip of the hand or a sneeze could leave his patient blind, or worse.

Flourishing in the fertile time of imperial Rome of the second century A.D. and of Marcus Aurelius, Galen was not constrained by later Christian concepts of sin and sacrilege. He had given himself permission to find out how organisms work. And he had been the primary conveyor of the much older thoughts of another Greek physician, Hippocrates, from the fourth century B.C.

To the early Muslims like al-Tabari, Galen is deemed religiously acceptable because he said that all organic life and functions spring from a single source: nature. For the Muslim theologians this is close enough to their monotheistic belief that all life springs from God.

But now in the ninth century, Galen for the first time has serious competition. Some of it comes from the waning light of the Byzantines. But increasingly, the medical innovators are Muslims like al-Tabari. Unlike the Europeans of the time, the Muslims do not feel as constrained by superstition or anti-intellectualism, or by some Christian Stoic-inspired beliefs that the miseries of physical life must be endured so as to cleanse the soul for heaven. The Muslims are not so wedded to the idea that the body is a place of corruption and sin. Their Prophet had several times repeated divine guidance on medical matters that revealed a very matter-of-fact and modern outlook. So the Muslims will pick up where Galen left off.

"Galen's humors are really Hippocrates's humors," says al-Tabari, and the young al-Razi nods. "The body is composed of a balance between the four elements present on Earth—fire, Earth, water, and air—they are manifested in the body as yellow bile, black bile, blood, and phlegm."

"What if there is more at work in the body than the humors?" ventures al-Tabari, following the line of the question offered by his young student. "Take this vial. There are many substances that we cannot yet even isolate. Hippocrates was doing his best, but that was more than a thousand years ago."

After lunch, they go back to their study of the organs of the body. In that moment, al-Tabari is pleased to have this bright boy at his side and pleased to think that maybe destiny will make them collaborators over many coming decades. But that is not to be. In just a few years the teacher will be dead, while his student will travel home to Ray and then back to Baghdad to head up two great teaching hospitals.

And while al-Tabari will pass on into the footnotes of history, the odd-looking boy al-Razi will grow to become the first great Muslim doctor, whose work will be translated into Latin and who will bring to Europeans medical innovations of Galen and Hippocrates and the Muslim world.

While al-Tabari will be largely forgotten, al-Razi will be remembered by his Latin name of Rhazes. And for the Europeans a hundred years later, Rhazes, along with ibn Sina, another Persian, will be the greatest of all Muslim physicians.

Al-Razi will author some two hundred major manuscripts on nearly every known aspect of medicine, as well as on philosophy, alchemy, and metaphysics. He will be the first physician to clinically and scientifically describe the scourge of smallpox and the less dire disease of measles, and to show that they are separate afflictions. In his book *Kitab al-Jadari wa'l Hasbah,* or *The Book of Smallpox and Measles,* he writes:

> *The eruption of smallpox is preceded by a continued fever, pain in the back, itching in the nose and nightmares during sleep. These are the more acute symptoms of its approach together with a noticeable pain in the back accompanied by fever and an itching felt by the patient all over his body. A swelling of the face appears, which comes and goes, and one notices an overall inflammatory color noticeable as a strong redness on both cheeks and around both eyes. One experiences a heaviness of the whole body and great restlessness, which expresses itself as a lot of stretching and yawning. There is a pain in the throat and chest and one finds it difficult to breath and cough. Additional symptoms are: dryness of breath, thick spittle, hoarseness of the voice, pain and heaviness of the head, restlessness, nausea and anxiety. (Note the difference: restlessness, nausea and anxiety occur more frequently with 'measles' than with smallpox. At the other hand, pain in the back is more apparent with smallpox than with measles). Altogether one experiences heat over the whole body, one has an inflamed colon and one shows an overall shining redness, with a very pronounced redness of the gums.*

In the vision of al-Razi, disease has specific, scientifically based physical causes. It is not a punishment visited on men by God.

He will reject superstition and primitive dogma that is not based in observable physical reality. And this fierce rationalism will lead him to undertake the project first mentioned by his old teacher al-Tabari—to critically analyze some of the bedrock lessons of Galen in his *Shukuk 'ala alinosor,* or *Doubts about Galen:*

> *I prayed to God to direct and lead me to the truth in writing this book. It grieves me to oppose and criticize the man, Galen, from whose sea of knowledge I have drawn much. Indeed, he is the Master and I am the disciple. Although this reverence and appreciation will and should not prevent me from doubting, as I did, what is erroneous in his theories.*

I imagine and feel deeply in my heart that Galen has chosen me to undertake this task, and if he were alive, he would have congratulated me on what I am doing. I say this because Galen's aim was to seek and find the truth and bring light out of darkness. I wish indeed he were alive to read what I have published.

Some 1,200 years in the future, a debate will arise over whether al-Razi was deeply questioning the assumptions of Galen and his theory of humors. More skeptical scholars will say that although al-Razi does attack certain elements of Galen's thought, he will accept the overall structure of it, including the humors, and that Galen's theory will stand until the European Renaissance. But others will see in al-Razi's writings a deeper and prescient rejection of certain basic premises of Galen. In *Doubts about Galen*, al-Razi explicitly questions whether the theory of humors can explain why giving a patient a hot drink causes his body temperature to rise much higher than the liquid itself; al-Razi holds that such a reaction would imply that there are certain other regulatory processes at work in the body that the humors do not address.

Al-Razi will also undertake chemical experiments that suggest that there are other characteristics of physical matter than Galen's fire, water, earth, and air. Al-Razi will specify inflammability, saltiness, oiliness, and sulfurousness as other qualities of matter.

Out of the flood of his works will also come conclusions about allergic asthma and the origin of hay fever, the theory that fever is the body's natural defense mechanism, the first hints of a mind-body disease connection, and his belief that individuals are responsible for their health through their behavior and diet.

He will sympathize with the doctor who must treat the patient who refuses to take responsibility for his lifestyle. He will invent the pharmaceutical mortar, spatula, and vials; mercurial ointments; and treatments for common ailments such as constipation, headache, colds, coughs, and even depression. His depression treatments will include the use of poppies for their euphoric narcotic effect.

He will fiercely attack medical charlatans who have no scientific basis to their diagnosis or treatments. He will urge doctors to commit themselves to a lifetime of continuing study of medical advances, lest they fall behind. Al-Razi will begin testing mercury-based cures on monkeys before he takes them to humans. During the years of his experimentation, including a continuing foray into alchemy, he will burn his eyes and over time will succumb to growing blindness. He will fatalistically dismiss the possibility of treating grave diseases like advanced cancer and leprosy, saying that doctors can only do so much.

He will write the first medical manual for the general public. In his teaching days, he will gather about him several rings of students. Throwing out questions to the first ring, he will move to the next ring, if the first cannot answer right.

Though he has the favor and support of caliphs and lesser rulers, he does not ignore the poor, and in fact, he gives them free treatments. This generous practice will cause some to allege that he is wealthy from dabbling in alchemy, charging that he has found a way to transform base metals into gold. He will reply that he has done no such thing and has come to believe that it is not possible.

Late in life he will write in *Al-Syriat al-Falsafia,* or *The Philosophical Approach:*

> *I have written so far around 200 books and articles on different aspects of science, philosophy, theology, and (hekmat) [wisdom].... I never entered the service of any king as a military man or a man of office, and if I ever did have a conversation with a king, it never went beyond my medical responsibility and advice.... Those who have seen me know, that I did not [go] into excess with eating, drinking or acting the wrong way. As to my interest in science, people know perfectly well and must have witnessed how I have devoted all my life to science since my youth. My patience and diligence in the pursuit of science has been such that on one special issue specifically I have written 20,000 pages [in small print], moreover I spent fifteen years of my life—night and day—writing the big collection entitled Al-Hawi [The Virtuous Life]. It was during this time that I lost my eyesight, my hand became paralyzed, with the result that I am now deprived of reading and writing. Nonetheless, I've never given up, but kept on reading and writing with the help of others. I could make concessions with my opponents and admit some shortcomings, but I am most curious what they have to say about my scientific achievement. If*

Persian 11th-century physician ibn Sina was considered the most influential philosopher-scientist of his time. His books were widely translated in both East and West.

they consider my approach incorrect, they could present their views and state their points clearly, so that I may study them, and if I determined their views to be right, I would admit it. However, if I disagreed, I would discuss the matter to prove my standpoint. If this is not the case, and they merely disagree with my approach and way of life, I would appreciate they only use my written knowledge and stop interfering with my behaviour.

The Renaissance giant Andreas Vesalius—famous for his anatomical studies that will set medicine on a new path—will write his doctoral thesis commenting on and reformulating the medical ideas of al-Razi. Later in his life, Vesalius harshly critiques Arabic medicine in his attempt to overthrow the old medical system. But it is interesting to note the importance of al-Razi in 16th-century Paris, where Vesalius will study medicine and dip into the Arabic medical tradition. In those days, it will be common for European doctors to write commentaries on Arabic medical texts, though not necessarily to agree with them.

Within a hundred years, this accomplished mind and life, rarely equaled in many centuries of time, will be matched and possibly even surpassed. The successor to al-Razi will be ibn Sina, known as the Prince of Physicians, and he will be revered by Europeans for 400 years as the greatest medical thinker of all time.

SO MANY YEARS, so many battles, thinks the weary man. Could we not just be blessed with a few years of peace, a decent bed to sleep in, and an ample supply of good wine? This rotgut out on the battlefield kills more men than arrows.

Battles require total focus on the present, on the enemy, on tactics, on staying alive, and on killing the foe. Watching the scenery and sensing the approach of combat, most other men would be distracted from reflection. Not ibn Sina, the man whom Europeans will soon know as Avicenna. He goes back to his task at hand.

Out on the wastes of Persia in the year 1020, bouncing along on horseback in the imperial party, ibn Sina gladly wills himself to momentarily forget quite where they are going and whom they are going to fight. Sometimes he even has to remind himself for whom he is working.

As he rides along, he is dictating to a young scribe one of nearly 300 works on medicine and philosophy that he will complete in his lifetime. This presenter of ideas is nearer the end of his life than the beginning. He has made a career of dictating timeless works while going into or out of battle. His job requires that he be there to treat the casualties, from the emir on down.

Looking over at his young scribe, ibn Sina remembers when he was a child prodigy and all of life stretched before him. Every door seemed open. He had memorized the Qur'an by age 10, started the study of medicine at 13, and began treating patients at 16. While still a teenager, he had saved the life of the Samanid ruler Nuh ibn Mansur and been rewarded with access to the royal library at Bukhara. Having the library was almost better than having a job, which the emir also offered, and ibn Sina, in the impetuousness of youth, turned down. How he loved being at large in the racks and racks of manuscripts, with the soft rustle of pages, the smell of leather and paper and ink, all that knowledge, all that possibility.

He could have spent his whole life there, rustling through the royal papers, treating rich patients, and teaching worshipful medical students. He could have put in his required time in court, laughing at the emir's awful jokes, guzzling his wonderful free wine, winking at the parade of female dancers and entertainers, regularly checking on the emir's state of health, helping him with his hangovers, his depression, his occasional bouts of venereal disease contracted from an improper liaison.

By night in those teenage years ibn Sina had read Aristotle's *Metaphysics* at least 40 times, reading and rereading until his brain was hurting, and yet it made no sense. Just as he did with the Qur'an, he memorized Aristotle's work word for word.

What did that Greek really mean? Ibn Sina had no answer until one day, down in the market, he saw a wretched man selling a little book by al-Farabi for 3 dirhams. It was al-Farabi's commentary on Aristotle. And in that little book he found the key to understanding Aristotle, and so he thanked God.

"Thank you for letting me live a life of peace and scholarship," he had prayed to God during those few years of peace so long ago. It was a life of contemplating beauty on the palace grounds, smelling the roses and poppies in spring, seeing the eyes of a woman glance at him from within the recesses of her veil, those eyes, glistening with the promise of the universe. And the sweetest wines in Persia. And the library.... He would have fallen on his knees in thankfulness to have those early years last a lifetime. And then in 999 everything started to fall apart.

A clique of Turks had plotted and overthrown his Samanid patrons, and his father had died. Worse than that, the Turks had burned the magnificent royal library. All those manuscripts, all that knowledge and wisdom, burned like rubbish. How could men be so stupid? What is the point of life, without ideas?

And then began ibn Sina's years of hiding, masquerading, running, begging, pleading, wearing hoods and turbans, paying thugs and traitors, and skipping town in the middle of the night. He was trying to recapture the old life, even if just a steady job, with some peace and comfort, and a decent library, and a glass of good wine.

The abusive Sultan Mahmud of Ghazni had offered him a job, but rather than suffer possible imprisonment, as would al-Biruni, ibn Sina declined. Another vizier at Urgench offered him a tiny stipend, but it wasn't enough to eat decently. A third ruler at Dailam, a fellow scholar and poet, was rumored to be a generous patron of thinkers, but by the time ibn Sina got there the emir had been killed by his own soldiers. Finally, a friend in Gorgan, on the Caspian Sea, bought him a small house where he taught students for a time.

But was this the proper culmination for a great mind, sitting in a little house out in the Persian back of beyond, teaching the sons of mediocre small-town social climbers about logic, astronomy, and medicine? His eye would wander out onto the expanse of the Caspian Sea and he would think, "bigger things are beyond the other shore."

Ibn Sina yearned for something grander, a life more like the kind he'd had as a teenager in the royal Samanid library. From Gorgan he'd gone looking for royal patronage in Ray and then Hamadan. For one brief interval the emir in Hamadan had made ibn Sina a vizier. Could it be? Was his time of troubles over? But this prodigy, who was always intellectually miles ahead of everyone else in the room, in the palace, in the city, too often let his tongue say what he was thinking. In the debates at court, he was withering, overpowering, and almost always right. And no matter how brilliant in affairs of the mind, ibn Sina was not as gifted in areas of politics, diplomacy, and tact. Those who opposed him, he called idiots, not seeing them as people of differing opinions who had a right to them and had to be won over diplomatically.

Insults and threats of violence were hurled both ways and not forgotten. And so, very quickly after finding the job that could have been the culmination of his dreams, this genius vizier alienated too many around him. The military officers, who understood hardly anything of what he was saying, knew enough to know they were being mocked and undercut. They mutinied over his arrogance, and the emir felt compelled to throw ibn Sina into jail. When the emir fell ill, he let the great healer out. Ibn Sina successfully treated the emir, and ibn Sina was briefly rehabilitated. But he had had enough of small minds in provincial places. He began secretly corresponding with the rulers in Isfahan, angling for better patronage in that grander city. When the emir in Hamadan found out that his doctor-vizier was looking elsewhere, he flew into a rage, and ibn Sina was forced to flee at night and in disguise toward Isfahan. He barely made it there alive.

At Isfahan, ibn Sina spends the last dozen years of his life. The city is gloriously beautiful, cultured, and rich. It has intellectual salons and well-stocked taverns and wondrous avenues and parks. It has beautiful women. It is as sophisticated or even more so than Bukhara.

It doesn't matter that the job as court physician also requires that ibn Sina accompany the emir in battle, and the battles are nonstop. It is a price he is willing to pay. He senses this is his last chance to find a home and life even partway fitting his vast mind and ambitions.

In all those nearly 30 years of disruption ibn Sina has come to a momentous decision. If he wants to unlock the knowledge of the human body and of life, he will have to do it on the fly. He will have to improve his powers of concentration. He will have to live in two worlds, the world of physical survival and the world of the mind.

Although ibn Sina writes several hundred works on everything from mathematics to astronomy to mineralogy, including *De Mineralibus,* or *Book of Minerals*—the translation of his work on geology and mineralogy is misattributed to Aristotle until modern times—his greatest contribution is in medicine. His two most important works are the *Canon of Medicine* and *The Book of Healing*, and they are widely translated and discussed not only in the Muslim world but also in medieval Europe. Together with al-Razi's work, the *Canon* probably does more to develop European medicine and thought than any other single work or event.

In the *Canon of Medicine* ibn Sina writes:

Medicine considers the human body as to the means by which it is cured and by which it is driven away from health. The knowledge of anything, since all things have causes, is not acquired or complete unless it is known by its causes. Therefore in medicine we ought to know the causes of sickness and health. And because health and sickness and their causes are sometimes manifest, and sometimes hidden and not to be comprehended except by the study of symptoms, we must also study the symptoms of health and disease. Now it is established in the sciences that no knowledge is acquired save through the study of its causes and beginnings, if it has had causes and beginnings; nor completed except by knowledge of its accidents and accompanying essentials. Of these causes there are four kinds: material, efficient, formal, and final.

While these four causes originate with Aristotle, ibn Sina is the first to fit them into a logical, scientific framework for medicine. While Galen indeed uses logic and a scientific methodology, it is ibn Sina who gives medicine its formal scientific structure in his *Canon*. Ibn Sina's genius may lie in the fact that he transforms the human body into something that can be understood—like any other physical phenomena—in terms of causal chains of events that lead to various states of health, illness, and disease. And out of this outpouring of medical wisdom, what does ibn Sina bring to the world?

Aside from providing a massive compendium of much of 11th-century medical knowledge, ibn Sina will tell the world of more than 700 drugs. He will talk about diseases that are spread by water and in the soil. He will conclude that tuberculosis is an infectious disease, though he will be wrong about the method of transmission, thinking it is spread through the soil and not by air. He will suggest the treatment for lachrymal fistula, a swelling in the tear gland, and will invent an instrument for probing the tear duct. He will say that the only way to understand the workings of the body is to scientifically and impartially test and observe, that speculations and theories have no value until proven.

In parallel with ibn al-Haytham—who was conducting his research in Cairo at the time—but from a more detailed anatomical and medical perspective, ibn Sina will delve deeply into the various parts of the eye, including the cornea, iris, retina, aqueous humor, and optic nerve. He may enlarge on Galen's theories in describing much more esoteric and remote optical organs, such as the optic chiasma, a structure in the brain formed by the partial intersection or crossing of the optic nerve fibers on the underside of the hypothalamus. He further describes how the aorta works, noting that its three valves prevent blood from rushing back into the heart after the heart completes contracting. And he confirms that nerves are critical message paths for virtually all physical functions, in particular muscular contractions, concluding that pain is transmitted from its source via the nerves.

A long section of the *Canon* will be devoted to the subject of beauty, which is really a medical analysis of the surface features of the body that create the effect of perceived beauty, such as hair or lack of it, skin color and tone, and the effect of disease on appearance.

He will devote several volumes of the *Canon* to the subject of bone fractures and will innovate ways to treat them. And he will take the lead in describing meningitis and its complications.

He will be dedicated to the Arab Muslim concept of dietetics, in which cures are best effected by natural products and approaches. He will delve into how to anesthetize the mouth for dentistry and oral surgery. He will investigate and describe the causes of rabies, breast cancer, tumors, and of hydrocele, or the accumulation of fluid in a body cavity, often in the scrotum. He will offer information about toxins and their antidotes. He will describe a plethora of other physical and biological conditions such as ulcers, kidney disease, and facial paralysis. He will conclude that the lowly hookworm causes certain intestinal ailments.

Ibn Sina will set down empirical scientific rules for testing and rating the effectiveness of drugs in treating various conditions, rules that will be the backbone of clinical drug trials nine hundred years later. Rather than take a substance on faith, he will say that the purity of the drug is important, that it must be universally effective, that the dose must be tied to the severity of the illness, and, finally, that it must be tested on humans under strictly observed and controlled conditions.

And though he will be wrong in many ways, he will also be prescient. His adoption of the basic structure of the Greek theory of "humors" will later look dated when Leeuwenhoek in the 16th century uses his microscope to discover the "wee beasties" that are wriggling in drops of water and blood or crawling on skin and surfaces. Germs and viruses, not humors, are the cause of infection. But he will be uncannily right about some things, still valid in the 21st century.

He will eventually be proven right in his belief that tuberculosis is infectious, though the Europeans will reject his theory for about 400 years. And he will be proven right by thinkers as varied as Sigmund Freud, Carl Jung, and Norman Cousins in many of his beliefs about the mind-body connection and the emotional and intellectual sources of disease.

Though it is touched on by al-Razi, ibn Sina will bring more fully to light for his vast readership and his patients that there are some diseases that are sicknesses of the soul or the result of unhealthy patterns of thoughts. Al-Razi will call these "moral diseases." Ibn Sina will sound slightly less moralistic in his interpretation.

Though it might be presumed that this connection between mind and soul and physical health has its origins in the more holistic beliefs of traditional Asian religions such as Buddhism and Hinduism, it is as much the result of holistic Muslim views of the interconnectedness of all the physical processes within God's universe and a revision of the Greek philosophical split between mind and body, between matter and spirit or idea.

Ibn Sina will try to bring mind and body together. He will operate from the essentially Muslim belief that it is more natural for humans to be healthy than unhealthy and that disease is the result of some disturbance of the natural state. Whereas in many cases this upset might come from an unhealthy physical environment or diet, he takes the idea to its limit, that unhealthy ideas, emotions, and states of mind can also affect the body.

His theories about the mind will prove remarkably prescient, finding expression some 900 years later in modern psychology as well as science fiction. In one of his most influential philosophical treatises, ibn Sina asks his readers to carry out a thought experiment, his famous "floating man" or "flying man" argument. "Imagine," he says, "a man floating in a room with zero sensory input, no sound, no gravity, no sensation of any kind, floating in complete darkness, no sensation even of his own body because no part of his body touches any other part—say the man was created this way, would he be capable of thought? Can the human mind have thoughts without any external sensory input? If so, what would this man be thinking? Would the floating man have awareness of anything?"

Ibn Sina's famous answer is: Yes, even though the man has no awareness of his environment, or anything external to himself, he would at least be aware of his own existence. This idea is a precursor to Descartes's famous philosophical claim: "I think, therefore I am."

Ibn Sina learns to connect how the pulse rate of a patient reacts to external stimuli such as certain key words or facts. Some will claim that this insight is a 900-year-jump on Carl Jung's word-association form of psychoanalysis.

There is a story that ibn Sina is visited by a young man in the grips of a strange and undefined sickness. Sensing that it is mind- or soul-based, ibn Sina begins reciting lists of places, addresses, events, and people. Through deduction and monitoring of the patient's pulse, ibn Sina concludes that the young man is in love with a woman in a particular town. To heal him, ibn Sina prescribes that the young man go find the woman and marry her. He does and is cured.

Other Muslim healers will use variations on ibn Sina's psychic or mind therapy, sometimes verging on the scandalous. They will frighten those who think they cannot walk into walking. One will even shock a supposedly paralyzed woman into moving, by suddenly lifting her robes.

This seemingly inarguable—but hard to quantify—relationship between state of mind and state of physical health will not make it into Western medicine for a long time. Even as the Europeans begin to catch up in shaping what will become modern medicine, their focus will be on a mechanistic approach to curing disease, through the introduction of certain physical substances.

It will not be until Freud and Jung, particularly the latter, that older, more spiritual and more holistic approaches will start to reappear in Western medicine. And an American by the name of Norman Cousins, writer and editor of *The Saturday Review*, will cause an American cultural stir in the late 20th century by his stumbling upon theories of the mind's connection to disease. He will write a fascinating account of laughing himself to wellness in his 1990 book *Head First: The Biology of Hope and the Healing Power of the Human Spirit.*

Will Cousins read ibn Sina, or Avicenna? That is lost to history. But the ideas will be reborn in slightly different packaging, in a different language and context.

No matter. Ibn Sina, after all those years of no stable home and no steady job, will find a kind of peace with his patron in Isfahan. Again and again they will go into battle. And it will not be weapons that kill ibn Sina, but a terrible bout of intestinal distress, either gastroenteritis, food poisoning, or intestinal flu. A constant scourge of the warrior, the ailment will nearly take him once, and he will bring himself back. But the second time, when it reduces him to incapacitation, he will not treat himself and ask to be taken home to Hamadan to die and be buried. He will be 57 years old.

UP IN THE ROYAL ANDALUSIAN CITY of Medina Azahara, a woman is giving birth. It is the year 1005. Out through the window of the delivery room, she can see the jasper and alabaster columns, the thousand fountains, the marble terraces polished so finely that they look like pools of dark water running down the hill. Off in the distance, the outline of Cordoba glistens in the summer sun.

She is afraid this may be her last glimpse of this marvelous city, of this world of life. Her heart is pounding. She is equally afraid that her child may never leave this room alive, may never experience what she has experienced in her 20 years. She is a royal concubine to the Umayyad Caliph Hisham II. For many months she has wondered whether her child would be a male, and if so, if he would one day grow up to be caliph.

The obstetrician is hard at work. His name is al-Zahrawi, and in a hundred years he will be known to the Europeans as Albucasis, through the Latin translation of his massive medical tome, the *al-Tasrif,* or *The Method of Medicine.*

The baby needs to be turned before it can pass through the birth canal. The doctor uses a pair of forceps that have been in his medical bag for some years. He made the forceps himself. In fact, he invented the forceps about 50 years ago, when he was a young doctor just starting out.

Some accounts say that al-Zahrawi, like his predecessor al-Razi in Baghdad, will cleanse these forceps with alcohol, but other experts will dispute that. The physician has been the first to do many things. Working in parallel with and 2,500 miles from ibn Sina, this 65-year-old Andalusian-Arab doctor is the father of modern surgery.

He was born in this royal enclave only two years after its construction began in 936. That was when the Umayyad Abd al-Rahman III felt confident enough of his power, and the power of his society, to declare that he was the true Caliph of all Islam. This was a time when the Abbasids had become figureheads, and the Fatimids were building their own empire across the Middle East and North Africa.

"Will my baby live?" the desperate mother manages to ask between contractions. "Almost certainly," Doctor al-Zahrawi answers. "You have a healthy boy. But this next moment is going to be painful."

For her, the news he has just given her is enough reassurance. The baby will live. He is a boy. And though she wants to ask if she will also live, it seems not as critical now, almost impertinent. The pain is as he warned. She briefly loses consciousness, dreaming that she and her lover, the caliph, are walking together out into the air. They are going up into paradise, as their son down below is being invested as the Caliph of all Islam. But as the two of them look down on what has been created, the dry land irrigated into rich production, the city of half a million, the royal enclave with its terraced layers of opulence and elegance climbing the foot of Jebel al-Arus, the Bride's Mountain, one day to be known in Spanish as Sierra Morena, she says to her lover, "This has been paradise. How can that above be any better?"

And just as the caliph turns to look at her in shock at her impertinence, as though she has committed sacrilege, she awakens to the sound of her baby boy screaming in the Andalusian sun.

"Thank you, O healer," she cries, catching a glimpse of the squirming red legs and face contorted in an infant's cry, before she slips back into sleep. Her sleep is allowed, for the nurse and midwife clean the baby, weigh him, and take note of his reactions.

Knowing the mother is asleep, al-Zahrawi confesses to his chief nurse, "That was close." The nurse nods, because she knows, she has been with the doctor for years. She has seen him have to make the terrible choice between mother and child or to discover that the child is stillborn or deformed. Or to watch the mother slip away into death, leaving the newborn behind. That is perhaps the hardest time for him, because he feels like the addition of one at the cost of subtracting another is no net gain for mankind, for society. He considers it a failure.

This Andalusian master surgeon is also the Muslim lord of obstetrics, of dentistry, of pharmaceuticals. All these things and more are contained in his 30-volume compendium. Because of its complexity and sophistication, it will take European translators 300 years to bring it, in bits and pieces, into Latin and European tongues.

The woman is asleep, the baby is now cooing, the nurse and midwife are attending to them. Al-Zahrawi must move on.

Checking the water clock out in the courtyard, he sees that he has time to make his appointment with another of the royal household, this one a dowager suffering from breasts that for whatever reason have swelled far beyond anything that would be exciting or beautiful, to become ponderous burdens. Her back is hurting, and she is embarrassed, reduced to remaining locked away behind doors to escape the stares and whispers.

Coming to her apartment off one of the marbled terraces, al-Zahrawi exchanges pleasantries and then gets down to business. Though this woman is mortified to be exposing herself to the man who is not her husband, he has seen so many bodies that his unaffected manner relaxes her. To him, it is all in a day's work, and the human body is capable of many aberrations. His nurse administers the sedative and anesthetic. And they wait for it to take effect.

In a technique of plastic surgery that will not be replicated for 950 years, al-Zahrawi draws the clear lines of his coming incisions with a black charcoal and makes the cuts with a scalpel that he invented. He swiftly removes the excess fatty tissue, administers oral and local remedies to lessen bleeding, then swiftly sutures the incisions.

And now to the palace of a caliphal advisor who is in unbearable pain from kidney stones. With one of his male attendants instead of the nurse, al-Zahrawi has the man tied down as well as sedated. He introduces a slender silver wire with a diamond tip into the urethra, finds the stone by touch, and by mere contact with the diamond rapidly disintegrates it. The man's screams gradually fade into the realization that maybe the problem has been solved. The patient orders gold pieces to be showered on the doctor.

That is the morning; checking the time, al-Zahrawi sees he can make two more calls before he breaks for lunch. He calls on an aging servant of the caliph, to check on the performance of the man's dentures made from bone. The old servant is in and thanks the doctor profusely for the dentures, which allow him to eat an almost normal diet.

The final visit is to one of the caliphal guards, who now lies paralyzed in the garrison dormitory near the royal palace after a freak riding accident while escorting the caliph back from Seville. The horse suddenly spooked and threw his champion rider onto a stone wall protecting an irrigation ditch. Though the man has offered to be transferred out of the palace since he can no longer be of service, the caliph has ordered that he remain in Medina Azahara until a more suitable place can be arranged.

"Good morning," the once proud warrior, now wan and depressed, says to al-Zahrawi.

The doctor nods. "More importantly, how do you feel?"

The man shrugs, meaning that there has been no change or improvement. "Will I ever regain movement here?" the guard indicates his lower body with his chin.

Al-Zahrawi pauses a moment, knowing the gravity of the question and the answer. "Though nothing is impossible in creation," al-Zahrawi says, "this humble servant has never seen such an injury repair itself."

The guard is silent for a time. Tears are welling in his eyes for the hundredth time. But he cannot be seen to cry.

"I have seen two variations on this sort of paralysis," continues al-Zahrawi, sensing that the time is appropriate to talk. "One is an injury to the spine. Galen knew of this 800 years ago, when he was cutting into pigs. Cut the spinal cord and the body is paralyzed from that point down. And there is no repairing such a cut. The good news for you is that I found no such break in your spine, which was remarkable considering your fall. I checked each vertebra. I found no trauma there. What I did find was a powerful blow to this point, at the medulla oblongata, where your spinal cord passes into the brain. I've performed several investigations in my time on those who were paralyzed like you, but without spinal injury. In their cases I found that the area at the base of the brain had been severely injured, either cutting or impeding the flow from the brain to the spine. This kind of damage to brain and nerve is beyond my humble ability to suture and repair. For now it is irreparable to human hands."

Now the guard cannot conceal his sorrow, and he weeps openly. Al-Zahrawi is respectful. His nurse withdraws, so as not to embarrass this warrior.

"I had thought if anyone on Earth could save me, it would be you," the guard finally confesses.

Both of them sense that there is no one who can do better. They have seen the streams of wandering nobles and retainers, monks and nuns coming from France and Germany, England and Italy to gawk at the Muslim wonders of al-Andalus and the royal city, to stand in awed silence at the

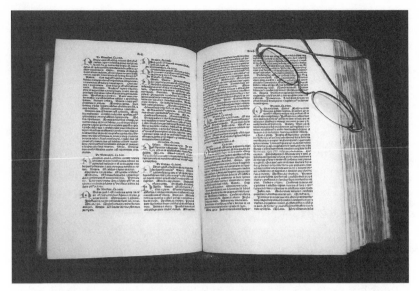

Ibn Sina's Canon of Medicine, *shown above in a Latin translation, set the standard for medicine and was in use in Europe for 700 years.*

great libraries, to see the quality of food and dress and the elevated manner of life, the comforts of a wealthy city in a humane land, to see the time accurately marked by clock and sundial.

"That any of us even make it through the birth canal, much less live a life, is a miracle," says al-Zahrawi softly. "I have spent all my years trying to extend that miracle to as many as I can." The soldier nods, for he knows it is true, this is al-Zahrawi, the greatest physician on Earth.

"This is why I have spent so much time not only studying and research-ing and experimenting, but also recording my findings," continues the doctor, now talking as much to himself as his patient. "If I write it down, at least it will be available in writing to those who come after, to improve and expand and amend. And it will not be lost. In this way, the one who comes after me may find a way to suture the medulla or even the spinal cord. But it will take the tiniest scalpel and the finest needle and suture, almost too fine to be held, too fine to be seen by old eyes like mine. Lest we make a terrible injury even worse."

He looks for a minute out at the royal city, at the vizier's procession as he makes his way from the court into the souk. Storm clouds are building in the south. They may have rain, the first rain on the valley in weeks.

"Every breath, every moment is a miracle," says al-Zahrawi, closing his bag and preparing to leave. "Even with our greatest preparations and safeguards, it can be snatched away in a second. What we must do is extend, protect the miracle, as best we can. And when we fail and have no more time, we accept what comes."

As he makes that last statement, it feels wrong to him, arrogant, presumptuous. He is ashamed of himself. He has said what cannot be said. He has never suffered as has this guard and so is in no position to be offering advice. This man will need to find his own way.

Al-Zahrawi feels as if he has failed. This physician, who has given the world its first description of hemophilia and the first documentation of the pathology of hydrocephalus, or water on the brain, feels as if it is not enough. He has been the first to give effective therapeutics for heart disease, constipation, and cosmetic issues, diet, and measurements of drug quantities. He has written in learned detail about things such as cauterizing and treating wounds, setting broken bones in both simple and compound fractures, and pulling out an imbedded arrow or other projectile. He has improvised procedures such as using animal entrails, wool, and silk to create the first sutures; widening blocked urinary tracts; and doing exploratory surgery. He has innovated surgeries such as mastectomies for breast cancer, extraction of thyroid cysts, and crushing of bladder stones. He has described how to amputate limbs without killing the amputee. He has also been a superb dental surgeon, even doing some work that precedes modern orthodontia.

He has been the first to record and promote a particular delivery position that will not be named after him, but is known instead as "Walcher's position" after a 19th-century German doctor. Al-Zahrawi has also drawn sketches of more than 200 medical instruments, many of which he personally designed, and which, with modifications, will be in use a thousand years later. Four of his inventions include obstetrical forceps, instruments to examine the inner ear and the urethra, and one to remove foreign bodies from the throat.

It is not enough for this man nearing the end of his career. Weary and sad at his own failings, al-Zahrawi goes out into the midday sun of Medina Azahara, the spray of the fountains fed from mountain water almost like a mockery of the physical suffering he so often sees. This city, these foundations, only two years older than he is, seem so permanent while human lives seem so fleeting and fragile. He assumes these fountains will long outlive him and all his patients; they will spray and give beauty long after this entire generation has become dust.

And in less than ten years, even that assumption will be proven wrong, though he cannot know it at that moment. A political succession struggle will find Berber mercenaries letting their rough war-horses drink from these very fountains and drop their manure on the marble terraces. In 1010 Umayyad rule will falter, the stability and grandeur of more than 250 years will be shaken.

Spurred by the instability, this royal city will see the mob of Cordoba pour out across the valley and up the royal terraces, demanding their share of the royal booty that the foreign invaders and mercenaries are taking, the tableware and the damasks and the carpets, the curtains and chunks of marble like dark mirrors, the horses and the food and the wine of the grape. Members of the caliphal household will scatter, trying to save themselves, never to return.

Some of the world's greatest libraries will burn here. Eight years from now, al-Zahrawi, by now in his seventies, will live to see the great libraries he watched being assembled over his lifetime going up in flames. And with that, the tragedy of human existence will fall full force on him, to see this city of kings, like a beloved sibling that made all possible, dying before his eyes. And it will be too much, and al-Zahrawi will soon follow into death.

Aside from stories and word of mouth, no record will remain of his life or his loves, whether he had wives or had children, what he looked like, how he spent his free time if, indeed, he had any. There will be virtually no record of his friends or his properties, just as this magnificent caliphal city will slip beneath the sliding earth and mud of the Sierra Morena until only a few stones extend above the soil, concealing marbles and foundations, concealing a great portion of human history and many lives of greatness.

All that will remain of this man is his single handwritten collection of *The Method of Medicine*, hidden here and spirited there, kept as a private treasure of a lost time, until one day a hundred years later an Italian monk happens upon it and thinks that it would be of value to the Christians in the north.

THE TURBANED DOCTOR, named ibn Zuhr, en route to see the Almoravid emir in Seville in 1120 sees an emaciated man sitting by the side of the road with a water jug. The man's belly is swollen, and he is obviously in distress.

But the healer is late and he continues on to his appointment. The next day, passing the same poor man in the same declining state, he stops. "Man, are you sick?" he calls. The man nods. "What have you been eating?"

"Only a few crusts of bread and the water from this jug."

"Bread won't hurt you," says the doctor. "It must be this water. Where are you getting it?"

"From the well in the town."

"The well is clean. It must be this jug. Break this jug and find a new one."

"O healer, I cannot. This is my only jug."

"And that is your only stomach there bulging out. It is easier to find a new jug than a new stomach."

One of the sick man's companions takes up a stone and smashes the jug, even as the sick man protests. A dead frog flows out with the foul water.

"See, man," says the doctor. "That frog would have taken you with him. I'm giving you a coin to go buy a new jug."

The next time the doctor passes, the man's stomach has shrunken, he has gained weight, and his color has come back. He sings the praises of the good doctor.

For those on the losing side of history, defeat can seem like the end. But in defeat and death there can often be a rebirth and a renewal, and in the case of Umayyad Andalus, the death of one consciousness and society will be followed by a new one.

After the death of al-Zahrawi and the Umayyads, the Umayyad vision of a wise and rich al-Andalus controlling all of Iberia under the mantle of Islam will be gone forever. But in place of that lost vision will come the Almoravids in 1090 and then the Almohads in 1145, taking ownership of the great Muslim cities.

And in the employ of these new rulers, a hundred years after the death of al-Zahrawi, will be a most accomplished family of healers, both men and women, with the most famous being one ibn Zuhr, known by the Latin name as Avenzoar.

Ibn Zuhr saves the man by the side of the road. He is also the first Muslim scientist who limits his work solely to medicine. He graduates from the medical university at Cordoba, and he will spend much of his life in Seville. In his 70 years he will be medical physician to the Almoravids, then find himself imprisoned by them. When he is freed again, he will be working in the service of the Almohads.

Although autopsies are considered disrespectful, ibn Zuhr is rumored to have dissected cadavers to add to the knowledge of anatomy described by the Persian physicians and al-Zahrawi. He will write about ways to avoid developing kidney stones through diet and lifestyle, so as to avoid the painful and difficult repair in future years. He will continue al-Razi's practice of testing new remedies on animals. He may be the first to comprehensively describe parasites and the diseases they cause. He will also formalize the practice of tracheotomies, allowing patients in danger of suffocation caused by throat blockage to survive.

Ibn Zuhr will develop his tracheotomy technique on goats before he tests it on humans. He will perform autopsies on sheep who have apparently died of ulcerating diseases of the lungs. As befitting a graduate of a formal medical school, he will be a strong supporter of a rigorous, supervised training program for future doctors that is not unlike today's internship system.

Just as importantly, ibn Zuhr, this man of the 12th century, will see to it that two of his women relatives, his daughter and granddaughter, go into medicine. Though they are largely limited to obstetrics, they will begin a tradition that will be common in even the most gender-segregated Muslim societies until modern times. While women will be excluded from politics in many countries, they will be accepted as medical doctors.

Ibn Zuhr will write as much as his predecessors, and he will describe in graphic detail in his *Kitab al-Taysir,* or *Book of Simplification Concerning Therapeutics and Diet,* how he manages the most critical illnesses and injuries, including the following passage on belly wounds:

> *Wounds can occur in the belly because of a piece of iron, or a sharp stick, that pierce through both the skin of the belly and the hypochondrium, and the intestine comes out. When this happens, someone dexterous*

enough must return it to its place. If it is affected by earth, dirt or saw-
dust, it is necessary to wash it with tepid water and to return it to its
place with care. If a part of it is torn and becomes black, the solution
is to cut off the part of it which is torn and corrupted and to return it
to the belly and seam it with a silk thread. A skillful and responsible
person must make the repair, as this is only learned by practice, not by
science. Over the suture something is put that helps promote scar tissue.
At the same time, it is necessary because of the wound to moderate food,
as much as possible, in order to reduce the flux of humors. If the flux of
blood is not excessive, a little blood-letting in the medial arm vein is not
bad to him. This is a general means in all kind of wounds for reducing
the flux of humors. It is possible that some portion of the bowels comes
out. If bowels come out uninjured, without a great or a small injury,
except their issue to the outside, you must hurry to return the bowels to
their place with care in order to avoid inflammation. And if the bowels
cannot be returned the same way they came out, because the bowels are
swollen due to slowness of action, then you must pour tepid water in the
surface of the fissure, so that it may be pleasant for the man, pouring it
softly on the inflamed part until the swelling disappears. After this has
disappeared, you must reduce it softly. The tearing of the skin and the
peritoneum are seamed with a silk thread, with great care. Make the
patient stay calm, not raise his voice, not move, and not stuff himself
with food or drink. Nourish him with something in little quantity but
very nutritive.

Ibn Zuhr and his family will flourish under the Almoravids and Almohads, despite an occasional imprisonment or flight into exile. The risk of depending on powerful patrons means one's fate is entwined with one's master's fate. Five generations of this family will be healers.

But even as they flourish, one Jewish family will decide that al-Andalus, now fracturing into city-states where the tradition of Muslim-Jewish collaboration is not as strong, may not be the best place to be. The Almohads in particular, together with some of their Christian allies, will persecute the Jews of Cordoba, sending chills through this other family. They will move on to Cairo, no longer under the rule of the Fatimids but under the control of the General Saladin.

IN THE YEAR 1199, Musa bin Maimun, or Maimonides, astronomer, philosopher, and physician, is sitting on a carpet while his royal patient reclines on an imperial bed of silk pillows and sips an effervescent drink, droning on and on about what he would like.

"To put it directly, Abu Musa," says the sultan, "what I need is one of your potions to give me more male prowess. To be able to go five or even six times a night. So that I might please my female companions all the more."

The doctor-philosopher ruminates for a moment on how far they have all fallen, since the time of the lordly rule of Saladin. Now his chief patient and employer is Saladin's nephew al-Malik al-Afdal, and he is a far cry from his uncle. This young man is as devoted to conquering women, bottles of wine, and gambling companions as his noble uncle was to trying to bind up the fractured Muslim armies, to find some accommodation with the hotheaded crusaders, and when that was not possible, to defeat them in battle, and when victorious, to be magnanimous.

And now, after all he has been through to pay his bills and feed his family, Maimonides is reduced to a form of royal pimpery.

"My sultan," ventures the 70-year-old Jew in his native Arabic, his first tongue since his birth in Cordoba so long ago. "Might it not be more prudent to accept the limits of nature and give yourself a few hours of sleep at night? Our powers of cohabitation are best granted by God, not by juice in a bottle."

The young playboy glowers at his doctor.

"You are just envious because you are an old man," says the sultan. "You've forgotten the pleasures of the night."

Musa bin Maimun pauses a moment, then laughs. "O my sultan," he says. "Though my physical powers are only a shadow of yours, I very much remember, and still occasionally know, the pleasures of the flesh. God has seen fit to bless me only with a single wife, and that is plenty for me. Otherwise I could not have the strength to do my work. In your case, the nation depends on you and your good health; trying to service a group of women runs a risk."

"I want to run the risk," says the sultan. "Get me a potion."

"As you wish, my sultan," says Maimonides, bowing and taking his leave.

As he trudges out of the caliphal palace, he is wondering which of his concoctions will work best with this profligate fool. He certainly has a few in the medicine chest. In fact, this young man has inspired him to write an entire book about the influence of health on sexuality, and he has included his knowledge of aphrodisiacs.

On the other hand, he remembers that his predecessors, men like al-Razi and ibn Sina, have written about the mental connection to disease, diseases of immorality, the interconnection of lifestyle to health, and preventive medicine. He has nursed the sultan through all sorts of self-inflicted ailments, depression, exhaustion, venereal disease, and pneumonia. If he did not need to support so many children and nephews and old aunts, Maimonides would quit this job, telling the sultan that ultimately it is the patient who heals himself, not the doctor and his potions.

But Maimonides feels as if he were supporting half the Jews in Egypt, so he has no such freedom. It has been this way since his old father died and his mother and brothers were on the verge of starvation. Those sweet years of reading and study came to a swift end, and though he continued writing about philosophy, he paid the bills by being a doctor.

And his reward had been to be the chief physician to Saladin's grand vizier al-Fadil, who ran the court and the nation while Saladin was off fighting the Christians. That was no easy job, but at least it dealt with more serious issues. He had felt that he was making a difference.

Musa bin Maimun described his typical workday in those years—a day with a schedule not unlike those doctors and interns would struggle with 800 years later—in a letter to Rabbi Samuel ibn Timmon:

> I'm obliged to visit him [the caliph] every day, early in the morning, and when he or any of his children or concubines are indisposed, I cannot leave Cairo but must stay during most of the day in the palace. It also frequently happens that one or two of the officers fall sick and I must attend to their healing. Hence, as a rule, every day, early in the morning, I go to Cairo and, even if nothing unusual happens there, I do not return to Fostat until the afternoon. Then I am famished but I find the antechambers filled with people, both Jews and Gentiles, nobles and common people, judges and policemen, friends and enemies—a mixed multitude who await the time of my return. I dismount from my animal, wash my hands, go forth to my patients, and entreat them to bear with me while I partake of some light refreshment, the only meal I

eat in twenty-four hours. Then I go to attend to my patients and write prescriptions and directions for their ailments. Patients go in and out until nightfall, and sometimes, even as the Torah is my faith, until two hours and more into the night. I converse with them and prescribe for them even while lying down from sheer fatigue. When night falls, I am so exhausted that I can hardly speak.

Maimonides had done such a good job in those days that his fame had spread far and wide. He had even gotten an offer of employment from the Christian warrior Richard the Lionhearted, which he had ignored.

Maimonides had written ten volumes on medicine, health, disease, and treatments. He had written on everything from how Galen had been wrong, to describing strokes, seizures, liver disease, diabetes, sexual health, and hemorrhoids.

He described hepatitis as follows:

The signs of liver inflammation are eight in number as follows: high fever, thirst, complete anorexia, a tongue which is initially red and then turns black, biliary vomitus, initially yellow egg yolk in color which later turns dark green, pain on the right side which ascends up to the clavicle. Occasionally a mild cough may occur and a sensation of heaviness which is first felt on the right side and then spreads widely.

Maimonides will give a graphic treatment for snakebite that will survive in modified form in the mid-20th-century *Boy Scout Manual*:

When someone is bitten, immediate care should be taken to tie the spot above the wound as fast as possible to prevent the poison from spreading through the body; in the meantime, another person should make cuts with a lancet directly above the wound, suck vigorously with his mouth and spit it out. Before doing that, it is advisable to disinfect the mouth with olive oil or with spirit in oil. Take care the sucking person has no wound in his mouth or rotten teeth ... should there be no person available to do the sucking, apply cupping—glasses with or without fire; the heated ones have a much better effect because they combine the advantages of sucking and cauterizing at the same time. Then apply the great theriac. Apply some medicine to the wound that will draw the poison out of the body.

And the irony is that Maimonides will be remembered not so much for his vast medical wisdom, as for his writings as the greatest Jewish philosopher of medieval times and the spiritual godfather of Jews from Spain to the Middle East. Those celebrating his memory will most often be Jews, when throughout his life he worked with and healed as many or more Muslims and Christians.

The further irony is that in 800 years, few if any Jews will hold such high and trusted positions in Muslim society as did Musa bin Maimun, and few Muslims will remember that at one time, Jews thought of Muslim cities as places of opportunity and intellectual refuge, as had Maimonides when he and his family fled Spain.

The last irony is that Maimonides will spend his final years doing medical repair of the effects of the sultan's decadent lifestyle.

EVEN AS THE GREAT Muslim physicians live and die, more lasting memorials to their medical wisdom will rise across the cityscapes. These new structures will be virtually unknown anywhere else in the world and will not be replicated in any significant way for centuries to come. Many of them will resemble palaces, in part because some are actual palaces donated by royal patrons to make the lives of their citizens last longer, be healthier and more humane. They will be driven by the egalitarian message of the Prophet, to care for the poor, the sick, and the less fortunate.

These buildings will be called hospitals and pharmacies. They are open not so much to the wealthy, who prefer to be treated at home. They are open to anyone who can walk in the door, and if they cannot walk, they will be brought in on litters.

In the Muslim East, hospitals will be known as *bimaristan,* literally "sick places" in Persian, later shortened to *"maristan."* And rather than places where people go to die, they will be places where people go to be treated and to recover from a variety of ailments and injuries, including mental illness.

The pharmacies, while they will be limited by the technology of the day, will dispense remedies that more often than not have some positive effect on the patients. Because they are partly the result of experimentation and observation rather than folk medicine or superstition or magic, they will be years ahead of their counterparts in Europe.

The first known Muslim hospital will be a clinic in Damascus, built at the Umayyad caliph's order sometime between 705 and 715, and largely dedicated to segregating lepers from the general population.

Decades later, in the late eighth century, Haroun al-Rashid will invite a physician from Gundishapur in Persia to open the first *bimaristan* in Baghdad. In the ninth century, al-Razi will head up the new Audidi hospital in Baghdad. To find the best place to put the new hospital, he will hang raw meat at different places in the city and then recommend putting the hospital where he sees the slowest rate of decay. Once built, the new hospital will have two dozen doctors, including surgeons, eye specialists, and physiologists. By the 12th century, this hospital will be described by visitors as looking "like a great castle."

By the year 1000, five major hospitals will have been built in Abbasid Baghdad. These hospitals will serve multiple purposes, not unlike modern hospitals containing surgery centers, outpatient clinics, psychiatric wards, convalescent centers, and even nursing homes. And quite often they are free to those in need.

In Egypt, the 13th-century al-Mansuri hospital will have 8,000 beds and an annual revenue of one million dirhams, and it will be distinguished by a policy of treating any patient who arrives, rich or poor. Men and women will be segregated. Separate chapels will give services for Muslims and Christians. Al-Mansuri will also have lecture halls, an in-house pharmacy, and separate wards for surgery, fevers, and eye ailments. The grant establishing the hospital reads:

> *The hospital shall keep all patients, men and women until they are completely recovered. All costs are to be borne by the hospital whether the people come from afar or near, whether they are residents or foreigners, strong or weak, low or high, rich or poor, employed or unemployed, blind or sighted, physically or mentally ill, learned or illiterate. There are no conditions of consideration and payment; none is objected to or even indirectly hinted at for non-payment. The entire service is through the magnificence of Allah, the generous one.*

Cairo will later add two other major hospitals, Damascus as many as five. Mecca and Medina in Arabia and the major cities of North Africa will have many more. Al-Andalus will come to the concept fairly late, building one in Granada at the very end of the 14th century. Ottoman Turkey and Mughal India will also have multiple major healing centers.

One medical historian will one day write of Muslim advances in treatment of the mentally ill:

> ... at Fez, Morocco, an asylum for the mentally ill had been built early in the 8th century, and insane asylums were built by the Arabs also in Baghdad in 705 A.D., in Cairo in 800 A.D., and in Damascus and Aleppo in 1270 A.D. In addition to baths, drugs, and kind and benevolent treatment given to the mentally ill, musico-therapy and occupational therapy were also employed. These therapies were highly developed. Special choirs and live music bands were brought daily to entertain the patients by providing singing and musical performances and comic performers as well.

There are other revolutionary innovations. Pharmacies—dispensing drugs that address symptoms and make people feel better—loom large. The profession is called *saydalah* in Arabic. Pharmacies spread from Baghdad to other Muslim cities within 50 years of the first opening in the capital at Haroun al-Rashid's hospital. Later royally endowed hospitals have their own dispensaries, which distribute syrups, ointments, powders, and other products that have been made in large in-house labs. All this is overseen by government inspectors, who look at accuracy of measurements and drug purity. Their job is to prevent the use of out-of-date drugs and to protect the public from error or incompetence.

Why are the flagship Muslim medical institutions so advanced relative to Christian Europe? Although the Muslim world then and now is not entirely free of superstition, Muslim society in the golden ages will more often offer medicines that work, as proven in medical trials and observation. Public expectation will quickly follow society's technological capability. Additionally, the medical profession itself will become well defined and have more of its basis in real science. While many Christian monasteries in Europe will offer hospices that give comfort to the sick and dying, they will not have the resources or technology to treat disease.

But the sophisticated Muslim medical climate will lead to much more than useful drugs and hospitals and psychiatric wards. It will lead to the rise of healers like ibn al-Nafis, perhaps one of the greatest cardiologists of the pre-modern era. Ibn al-Nafis is born in 1213 in a small town near Damascus, but after studying medicine there, he spends most of his working life in Cairo as the first head of al-Mansuri hospital and dean of its school of medicine. And there he makes his earthshaking discovery around 1284: the true anatomy and functioning of the heart and understanding of how blood flows through it to the lungs, where it "mixes with air."

Until al-Nafis, the standard explanation of heart mechanics has been Galen's. Galen wrote that blood moved from the right ventricle to the left through a series of pores or passageways between the two sides. No matter that no one had ever found such pores.

Al-Nafis upends all that when he takes a hard look at heart-lung blood circulation, observed through many surgeries and possibly dissection.

In his *Commentary on the Canon of Anatomy of Avicenna* he writes:

The blood from the right chamber of the heart must arrive at the left chamber, but there is no direct pathway between them. The thick septum of the heart is not perforated and does not have visible pores as some people thought or invisible pores as Galen thought. The blood from the right chamber must flow through the vena arteriosa (pulmonary artery) to the lungs, spread through its substance, be mingled with air, pass through the arteria venosa (Pulmonary vein) to reach the left chamber of the heart.

Al-Nafis's discovery is about as important to modern medicine as al-Khwarizmi's zero is to modern math. Al-Nafis is also the first to map the network of vessels supplying blood to the heart. Yet lost history means that his monumental work remains largely unknown outside the Arabic world, until some of it is translated by Andrea Alpago of Belluno, Italy, in 1547, and in a separate translation project in Spain only five years later.

Suspiciously, the Alpago translation appears about 60 years before the sudden breakthroughs in understanding of the heart and circulation by William Harvey, English court physician to James I and Charles I, who studies at the University of Padua. Oddly, Alpago's known translations of ibn-Nafis' work do not contain references to blood moving from the heart to the lung. It is an omission odd enough to make one think that Alpago deliberately leaves out that passage for fear of being repudiated by the medical authorities in Italy. But it is possible that Alpago confides al-Nafis's discoveries to close associates he can trust.

It is in Padua that Harvey would probably have been exposed to the work of his Arab predecessor. Harvey begins to expound his ideas around 1628, some 350 years after ibn al-Nafis made his own discoveries. It is important to note though that Harvey demonstrates the *full* circulation of the blood through the whole body, not just the *pulmonary* circulation of blood from heart to lungs as described by ibn al-Nafis.

And one tragedy of lost history is that by the time al-Nafis's work is translated, Renaissance Europe is no longer so in awe of the Muslim discoveries, and so he never receives a Latin name or much recognition. The days of European reverence for Avicenna, Rhazes, and Albucasis are long gone, buried by centuries. As Europe now awakens and the Muslim world falls into shadow, it seems fitting that Europe is seen as the real center, the new Athens, the new Rome.

THOUGH THE GREAT Muslim physicians and other thinkers have faded from the European mind by the late Renaissance, they will have achieved their fame in medieval Europe via a small group of determined Catholic and Jewish translators who are lucky enough to be able to read, write, and travel. These pioneering translators serve the same purpose in medieval Europe as the translators at al-Mamun's House of Wisdom in Baghdad centuries before, but the process of transmission into Europe is much slower. Knowledge remains the property of the Church, and few are deemed worthy of being allowed into the secret sanctums of the ecclesiastical libraries.

Despite all these impediments, Muslim medical, mathematical, and other knowledge continues its long seepage north, most often through taifa Spain, the porous, multicultural, intellectual capital of Europe until the 15th century. Cities like Toledo, Barcelona, Leon, and Segovia are like beacons drawing the curious to their intellectual lights. Similar transmission happens in southern French cities once touched by the Muslims, including Marseilles, Narbonne, and Toulouse. Sicily and southern Italy—Salerno,

St. Benedict monastery of Monte Cassini, and Palermo and Syracuse—are other transfer points.

One early medieval Catholic high official to appreciate the importance of Muslim advances in mathematics and the sciences is Sylvester II, the first French pope, who dies in 1003. Before his death, he has the Church replace the cumbersome Roman numeral system with the much more efficient Arabic-Indic numerals, as well as adopt Muslim astronomical and mathematical methods. Since most of Europe remains illiterate and in grinding feudal poverty, however, these innovations will only be felt at the higher echelons of church thinkers and will not generally be in use until the middle of the 15th century.

In 1065 Constantine the African, from Tunisia, brings Muslim manuscripts to Salerno, to Europe's first medical school. There the monk and scholar translates the Arabic medical texts into Latin.

A century later, in the 1100s, Robert of Chester in England will do several influential translations of al-Khwarizmi into Latin from Arabic, including his treatise on algebra known in Latin as *Liber algebrae et almucabala,* or *The Compendius Book on Calculation by Completion and Balancing,* and al-Khwarizmi's masterwork on algorithms, known in Latin as *Algoritmi del numero Indorum,* or *Al-Khwarizimi on the Hindu Art of Reckoning.* Robert, who works in the middle 12th century, has a strong interest in things Arabic and leaves England to spend almost a decade in taifa Spain, primarily in culturally mixed Segovia. The Catholic ruler there, Ferdinand I, is intrigued by the advances of the Arabs and encourages his work.

Gerard of Cremona is a 12th-century Italian who immigrates to Spain for the express purpose of learning Arabic and translating Muslim knowledge into Latin. He settles in Toledo, only wrested from Muslim control in 1085; by Gerard's time it is under the rule of a French Archbishop named Raymond, who is infatuated with Muslim intellectual advances. Under the patronage of Raymond, Gerard is believed to have translated more than 70 works from various disciplines, including mathematics and medicine. He is credited with creating the translations that will later be the foundation of work by Roger Bacon, Albertus Magnus, Thomas Aquinas, and Copernicus. One John of Seville, a Jewish scholar, is his understudy and continues his work in that city.

Abelard of Bath in England, sometimes called Adelard, joined the other translators. He is rumored to have masqueraded as a Muslim in early 12th-century Spain to get around the concern of at least one local Spanish Muslim ruler that Christian translators would be "stealing" the accumulated wisdom and knowledge of the Muslims, to appropriate the information and call it their own and to turn it against non-Christians. Valid or not, Abelard takes the safe route. While he translates numerous mathematical works of the Arabs and Greeks from Arabic, the Europeans will best remember him for getting his hands on Arabic translations of the great Euclid. Other lesser-known translators include Plato of Tivoli, Hermann of Carinthia, Rudolf of Bruges, Michael Scot, Philip of Tripoli, William of Lunis, and in Spain, Dominicus Gondisalvi, and Hugh of Santalla. Spanish Jewish translators of Arabic will include Petrus Alphonsi, Abraham ben Ezra, John of Seville, and Savasorda. Thus the Europeans will assimilate from their Muslim predecessors a rich, multicultural fusion of scientific thought. Even purely Greek works are now understood through the lens of centuries of Islamic thought, cultivated in regions as diverse as Iraq, Spain, Iran, and Egypt.

These "cultural bridges" will enable the intellectual work of the next generation of European mathematical and scientific thinkers. Albertus Magnus, a 13th-century Dominican monk-scholar, is deeply indebted to Gerard for translations from Arabic into Latin of Aristotle and the great Persian thinker ibn Sina. Albertus Magnus is in turn the teacher of St. Thomas Aquinas, who will take the deep philosophical musings of the Muslims and Greeks and put them in a new context for Christianity.

Roger Bacon is a 13th-century Franciscan monk in England, a contemporary and coequal of Albertus, who takes the handwritten translations of the Catholic Arabists and puts them to work in multiple fields of mathematics, chemistry, astronomy, and optics. He is particularly affected by the genius of ibn al-Haytham.

The actual method of translation depends on the translator, but it is never an easy task. Many attempt word-for-word translations from the difficult Arabic into Latin, sometimes improvising by taking an unknown Arab word and creating a Latinized equivalent sound. Rarely are these translators schooled in the disciplines they are translating, and so they either guess, or call in experts to help them resolve critical words and phrases. Sometimes they use intermediaries, trilingual Spanish-Jewish scholars versed in Arabic, Latin, and vernacular Spanish. The Jews take the manuscript from Arabic into Spanish, and then recite the words aloud so the final translators can render them into Latin.

In another telling move, the translators Latinize the very names of the Muslim thinkers. Though this is done to help Europeans with the unfamiliar sounds and difficult pronunciations of the Arabic names, over time it blurs the identity of these Muslim thinkers, making them somehow Latin and Western.

And in this way will Muslim medicine, like Muslim mathematics and science and thought, be absorbed into Europe. And it will not be done in a neat compartmentalized way, because neither the Muslim thinkers nor the European recipients will be working in that way. Muslim medicine will be the twin of Muslim mathematics and science, and the first cousin of Muslim music and art, philosophy and law.

7

VISION, VOICE, CITADEL

For them will be Paradise of [everlasting Gardens]; wherein rivers
flow underneath them, therein they will be adorned with bracelets
of gold, and they will wear green garments of fine and thick silk.
They will recline therein on raised thrones.

QUR'AN (XVIII:31)

MASHHAD, IRAN, 2007—Mashhad sits in its orange noon haze, the city dust and exhaust and noise rolling across the valley of the Kashaf River. The city rests in the heart of old Khorasan, where men and women have traded and raised crops for 5,000 years, now overlaid with the noise and effluent of more than two million people mixing with the muezzins, the traffic, and the bustle of commerce.

This is now the second largest city in Iran, second only to Tehran. Aside from being a center of business, Mashhad is also a place of universities and the holy Imam Reza shrine. The shrine holds the tomb of an imam revered by Shiites, believed to have been assassinated on orders of Caliph al-Mamun in Baghdad. It is a place of Shiite pilgrimage; many locals joke that the rich make their hajj to Mecca, the poor go to Mashhad.

It is also a place of refuge for Afghans fleeing the Soviet invasion or later the Taliban. Many have been here for decades, and a new generation of expatriate Afghans has grown up, holding onto its Afghan heritage but moving to an Iranian rhythm.

In the library at Firdausi University, named after Iran's revered poet of the 13th century, a second-generation Afghan refugee woman named Leila has been reading several different translations of *The Thousand and One Nights*. She is captivated by the character of Scheherazade, and though she consciously accepts that the bulk of documentary proof concludes that the narrator as described in the most famous versions of the stories did not exist, or was a composite, still on an emotional level Leila wants there to have been such a woman, with such courage and brilliance, who defined a narrative that shaped so many literary offsprings.

Growing up in Iran, which has been more empowering of women than was her Afghan homeland, she has come to believe, though she cannot prove, that Scheherazade was by no accident depicted as a woman poet. For she believes that women are more naturally poetic than men and by their natures more given to the sensitivity and observation skills that yield the best poetry. She feels that it is not that men cannot write poetry as moving; it is just that they are not as naturally inclined to the poetic awareness.

She also likes to hold to the ideal of a woman who stakes her life every day on her storytelling skills. Leila has not risked her life in the ten years or so that she has been a serious poet, but it was not easy to persevere. She is a mother of two young children, and though her husband, who is a professor of engineering at the university, has really worked to pick up the slack, there are only so many hours in the day. And she knows she has gotten a few dirty looks and insults from several of the men in the Afghan community. So she has found her support and comfort in the companionship of other refugee Afghan women writers, and the Iranian women who have joined them.

In a few weeks she will be reading at a national gathering of Afghan exile writers in Tehran. It is a big moment for her, though it is still uncertain whether her husband will be able to find a babysitter and a substitute teacher for some of his classes, or whether she will have to take the children with her on the long bus ride to Tehran. It is a small price to pay, much less than what Scheherazade risked. And it is less than what Leila would risk, were she still in Afghanistan, yet trying to stay true to her poetic ideals.

Until recently, she has told herself that she would never have become the woman that she is, had she grown up in Afghanistan. She might never have gotten an education, might never have learned about poetry, and might never have had permission to become a poet herself.

Now she is not so sure. Though she has never been there, the memories handed down and the ways of her lost homeland are so intense that she feels she knows Afghanistan. She also reads whatever news she can find on the various websites and whatever new information is passed around among her friends.

At times she feels almost guilty at her good fortune in having had parents who were lucky enough to get out during the worst times of the civil war.

Mashhad has always been her home. Until recently, she never wanted to go back to the other place, the home of her parents in Balkh, the ancient Silk Road city that was also the birthplace of Rumi, the 13th-century Sufi poet, who has become so famous in the West in recent years. Even now, in the city's reduced circumstances, would there be something in the stones and air and landscape of Balkh that could have nurtured her voice?

Sitting in the library this warm noonday, watching other students read or write at tables or snooze on the divans, she wonders if she has lost as much as she has gained by being an expatriate. Should she be like Scheherazade would have been, fighting for women on the front lines in Afghanistan?

Her thoughts are interrupted. One of the librarians who knows her taps her on the shoulder.

"That new critical commentary that you had us order has been lost in a recent shipment."

"Lost?" Leila whispers, disappointed. The book had been written by a group in Paris and translated into Farsi. She has been waiting for the treatment for more than a year.

"It was shipped from Tehran more than a month ago. We've got a trace on it."

"Won't they find it?"

The librarian shrugs.

"Can't you reorder?"

"Not for six months. We've got an entire new list to order."

Leila sighs in disappointment. For some irrational reason she believes that book might have given more evidence to her quest for the lost Scheherazade. Now she will have to wait longer—who knows how long?

The afternoon winds on. She can't read or think. Mid-afternoon prayer comes and goes in the far distance; the students wander in and out, though not in any quantity. The children need to be picked up, she remembers. She has wasted hours in her self-pity.

The uncertainty about her choices and her destiny, and what in this moment she sees as her selfishness come down on her so hard that she slams her notebook shut, stands up abruptly and marches away into the bright afternoon of Mashhad. She walks among the various student groups singing of plot and betrayal, of part-time jobs and grant opportunities, and discount airfares to Tehran and the Caspian Sea and hometowns at vacation time.

What has she risked, by following this path? What has she lost?

JERUSALEM, A.D. 691—An ancient gold dome is shimmering in a holy city at the intersection of the three faiths of Abraham, a gold hemisphere atop an eight-sided base of blue-and-white tile. Beneath the gold dome lies a rock, the foundation of the world for the Jews and the place where Isaac was bound up by his father, Abraham, in preparation for God's test of his faith. For the Muslims it is the place where the Prophet ascended into heaven with the angel Gabriel.

The Dome of the Rock is the first and longest-lasting architectural vision of the Umayyads, ordered to be built by Caliph Abd al-Malik in 691, nearly 60 years after the Prophet's death. The octagonal structure is supported by a double row of pillars and columns. In partial obeisance to traditional belief that the Prophet forbade representations of most living things, the interior is decorated with floral designs, and the walls are covered with colored and gilded stucco.

The golden dome will catch the sun's rays and add to the awe-inspiring feeling of Jerusalem, the old holy city of the Jews and Christians and now as holy to the Muslims. Unlike many Muslim edifices, it will survive for more than 1,300 years. Caliph Abd al-Malik will place an inscription noting his patronage of the project.

Even as this symmetrical and harmonious structure survives, some people will try to steal its history. Only 150 years later, the Abbasid Caliph al-Mamun will remove Abd al-Malik's name from the inscription and insert his own; because he does not change the completion date, scholars will see through his theft. Later Muslim caliphs and sultans will renovate, revise, and repair the structure right into the 19th century.

Though it is the oldest surviving building of sacred Muslim architecture, its history and meaning will not be lost, perhaps because of its importance to two other faiths as well. This architectural success in defeating time will not be repeated in Baghdad, when the center of the empire has fallen.

Even as al-Mamun counterfeits his name to the Dome of the Rock, hardly anything of his beloved Baghdad will remain. The alabaster palaces will not withstand the onslaught of Genghis Khan's grandson or the grinding torture of centuries.

Other places of legend and history will fare better. But even for those cities, the tragedy of leaving your memory and your love in stone is that in time the memory will lose much of its meaning, the love will have no more life than stone. When admiring the pyramids, for example, later visitors will wonder how and why these monuments were created. A magnificent ruined city on a hill from one thousand years ago created in a context that is long lost, which was once filled with the now-vanished color and movement of life, will leave observers in the future to only guess at the meaning.

One partly surviving love story in stone lies in ruins out on the edge of Cordoba on the Sierra Morena. Scorned when the Umayyads fall to the Almoravids, the forgotten royal city on a hill will gradually crumble, columns and stones tipping over or being carried off for newer building projects, such as the Alcazar of Seville and the monastery of San Jeronimo. Marble columns will be stolen to adorn new palaces or to be carved into religious icons; fountains will fill with the dust and waste of centuries, finally overrun with earth driven down by erosion.

This place will even lose its name. One day, Medina Azahara, the City of Zahara, will be known only as Cordoba Vieja, Old Cordoba. Will anyone even remember the meaning of the forgotten name, Medina Azahara?

One man knows the meaning of the name. In lost history, he stands on the mountain with his most beloved wife, Zahara. She has olive skin and brown eyes, and he knows and has told her she is just as smart as he is, that she more than any mortal captures the power of love, which can be greater than the power of the sword.

In his most private moments, he has had to castigate himself for his love of this woman. Not only is she his favorite wife, she has been his intellectual and political help mate, his ultimate confidante as he has made his late-night decisions about tomorrow's appointments and policy. And even though he has given her this special role, he has been further enamored because she has not abused it. Often she has told him it is none of her business, but he has insisted, knowing that her advice comes from a place of humility and understanding.

Zahara further sweetens his life because she loves poetry, and she loves music, and she brings him pleasure by night when his days are given over to administration and politics, to warfare and patronage. Such things to the exclusion of others can destroy a man's soul. Though so many would give their lives to stand where he now stands, having possessed this ultimate power, he knows how deadening it can be.

He has told her that it is only in their balance, of him controlling the physical world and her controlling the spiritual, that he can live, that al-Andalus can live. And she is content to be his muse, to channel grace and gentleness into the hardness of war and power. She likes that bargain. She loves being the sultana of the night to his caliph of the day.

And though he knows in his daylight mind of power that he must create a new city where he and his court will be removed from the ever more unruly and numerous factions and mobs of Cordoba, though he knows that it is his destiny to create a city that will be the envy and marvel of Europe, where foreign ambassadors will see it floating in the sky for hours before they finally draw up to its gates, and though he knows it must be true to the aesthetic of the Umayyads and their love of the Prophet, he also knows that his royal city must possess the love of Zahara.

He is the Caliph Abd al-Rahman III, who after 250 years of his dynasty's rule in al-Andalus feels powerful enough to declare that he, not one of the duplicitous Abbasids of Baghdad, is the true Caliph of all Islam. And befitting this newly claimed role as ruler of much of the world, he must have a city as beautiful and grand as the world he rules.

More than that, he must find a way to inject the city's stones and fountains, its palaces and mosques, its terraces and fountains, with the love of Zahara.

How to bring love and music and the intelligence of a woman into buildings, into streets, into palaces and fountains? It will take the best architects and stonemasons and marble cutters and sculptors and engineers. It will take a ruler who feels in absolute control of his people. It will take fully one third of the entire national treasury 40 years to fund this stone poem of love and power.

The city will be more than a mile long and more than half a mile wide. It will have three vast terraces sloping down to the Wadi al-Quivir. The royal city will have its own aviary and zoo, four massive fishponds, and 300 baths in the palace alone. It will take 400 dwellings to house just the palace retainers; to arm them, the compound will have its own armory.

The wonders of its interior—which will be open only to the courtiers and the senior commanders and financiers and thinkers of the Umayyad caliphate, and to the foreign emissaries who come to bow and pay tribute—will include a vast conference room decorated with crystals so as to create an indoor rainbow when struck by sunlight. Another room will have a bowl of quicksilver at the center, which will send interior sunbeams streaking across the walls when illuminated from outside.

And as the caliph and then his son continue this vast project, which sucks up oceans of money, they will turn to the Jewish financier Hasdai ibn Shaprut, who will enable the caliphs to indulge their obsession. Hasdai's power, which rests at the intersection of love and money, will extend to every aspect of the caliphate. Though he is a Jew and will never have the formal title, all will know him as the Jewish grand vizier of the last Umayyads, attaining the ultimate sweet equipoise of Andalusian Muslim and Jew at the zenith of their Andalusian codependency, entwined in destiny to create a work of art only attainable by kings and sultans.

As the Egyptian Coptic historian al-Makin will write in the 13th century in his ambitious histories of the world based on an account by ibn Hayyan, a courtier of the Andalusian caliph:

> *During the reign of 'Abdu'r-Rahman III six thousand blocks of stone, great and small, cut into various shapes, and either polished or smoothed, were used every day exclusive of the uncut stones used for paving and the like. The number of beasts of burden daily employed to convey the materials of construction was fourteen hundred, some say more, besides four hundred camels belonging to the Sultan, and one thousand mules hired for the occasion at the rate of three mithqals a month, making the total expense of hiring amount to three thousand mithqals monthly. In the building eleven hundred burdens of lime and gypsum were used every third day.*
>
> *The number of columns, great and small, supporters or supported, employed in the building amounted to four thousand; others exceed that number by three hundred and sixteen. Of these some came from Rome, nineteen from the country of the Franks, one hundred and forty were*

presented by the Emperor of Constantinople, one thousand and thirteen, mostly of green and rose colored marble, were brought from Carthage, Tunis, Sfax, and other places in Africa; the remainder were extracted from and quarried in his Andalusian dominions, as for instance the white marble from Tarragons and Almeria, the streaked marble from Raya, and so forth....

Ibn Haiyan goes on to say that the wonders of Azahara:

...included two fountains, with their basins, so extraordinary in their shape, and so valuable for their exquisite workmanship.... The smaller one, above all, appears to have been a real wonder of art.... When the Khalif received it he ordered it to be placed in the dormitory of the eastern hall called Al-Munis, and he fixed on it twelve figures made of red gold, and set with pearls and other precious stones. The figures, which were all made in the arsenal of Cordoba, represented various animals; as for instance one was the likeness of a lion, having on one side an antelope, and on the other a crocodile; opposite to these stood an eagle and a dragon; and on the two wings of the group a pigeon, a falcon, a peacock, a hen, a cock, a kite, and a vulture. They moreover were all ornamented with jewels, and the water poured out from their mouths....

And though the Medina Azahara is built to last an eternity, to last as long as stone can last, this exorbitant work will be one of the things that brings its own ruin. The city will live only 65 more years, which is but the blink of an eye in the chronicles of lost history. Single rulers, minor dynasties long forgotten will survive much longer. Ugly places not imbued at all with love or grace, only with the utilitarian purposes of survival, will outlive it ten times.

The first to attack Medina Azahara will be mercenaries from North Africa sent up by the Almoravids to bring down the Umayyads. But right on their heels will come a mob of the taxpayers of al-Andalus who have helped fund this project for two generations, the furious and downtrodden citizens and rivals of Cordoba, who will sack and burn the compound of their rulers in 1010 and try to reclaim the riches for themselves.

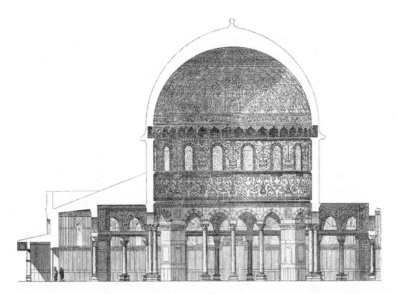

Completed in 691, Abd al-Malik's mosque in Jerusalem, or Dome of the Rock, shown in a 19th-century engraving, is the oldest surviving Muslim sacred architecture.

And this palace will be scorned and nearly forgotten for 950 years. When scholars and archaeologists finally begin to push back the veil of ruin and erosion, they will find so little of value there that they will argue among themselves whether the shimmering marble terraces and interior rainbows really existed.

They will find no whispering olive groves, no jasper or alabaster, no diamonds nor rubies nor pearls inlaid in geometric walls. They will find no bronze griffins, no lions or horses pouring mountain water into an ocean of marble fountains. They will find no shade of cypresses and palm trees, they will find no paradisiacal gardens forming living carpets, no myrtle or rosemary, no oleanders or tuberoses, no lilies or roses.

They will even question whether Princess Zahara existed or whether the city was named after something or someone else, now lost to history.

GRANADA, SPAIN, 1492—It is a clear January day, the air chilly but dry, the inclined sun glinting off the red tile roofs and the dun colored hills and ridges ringed by distant sea. A new year has just begun, a new world is being born. But to some of those present, it is the end of a world.

A Muslim king whose forebears had been sultans and emirs looks down from his terrace at the crowd gathering below. He can see the assembling royal party of the Catholic king and queen and their retainers and guards and armies in scarlet and blue, the latest leaders of a force that has been coming at him and his ancestors out of the north as long as anyone can remember, a group which is now victorious.

He has only a few more moments up here in the city of his birth. His Nasrid dynasty—the last Muslim dynasty in Spain, successors to the long fallen Umayyads, Almoravids, and Almohads—is deeply connected to these fountains, these gardens, these pavilions on the hillside. He imagines his forebears are watching him, weeping with him to see this sight.

Their fortress of paradise has fallen forever. Al-Andalus will only live another few moments. It is the sad destiny of this small man to give back the last bit of all that Tariq ibn Ziyad and Abd al-Rahman had taken more than 700 years ago in their improbable conquests.

Fighting the tide of history, the Nasrids, reduced to their small enclave in a southern corner of Spain, had prolonged the life of this Muslim dream longer than would have seemed possible. Nearly 500 years after the fall of the royal enclave at Cordoba to the Catholics, the Spanish Muslims still have kept this precious and magical place.

Granada, the last Muslim taifa, has been the holdout. To preserve this remnant of their dream, for the last 250 years the Muslim kings of Granada have been vassals of the Catholic kings of Castile, paying them tribute, even helping them put down Muslim uprisings. And this is the repayment.

The last Muslim king, Muhammad XII, the man the Christians know as Boabdil, is waiting to go down to the Catholic victors and give them this final prize. He hangs back a moment. This is the last time he will see his city in the sky.

He looks out at this skyborne retreat where his family has lived for generations, the pavilions with their tan and sandstone and cream-colored walls, nearly every surface adorned with Arabic inscriptions, whether from the Qur'an or poetry commemorating the last victory of the Nasrids at Algeciras, so long ago, all these words carved in the looping calligraphy of the Arabs so that they give texture and depth to surfaces that would otherwise be flat and cold. He sees the architecture that will be imitated for another

500 years in Spain, in New Spain, and all around the Mediterranean, those curious and richly crafted stalactites, called *muqarnas,* hanging down from the ceilings, each one inscribed with its own unique designs. He sees those columns topped by semicircular and slotted arches, those gardens, those patios, and those walkways. In one courtyard, a fountain is ringed with lions; in another lies a long reflecting pool.

What was the vision that had driven the creation of this place? While Baghdad had been the center of the world, while Medina Azahara had been a declaration of a new world empire and a love that surpassed everything else, this place—called in Arabic the al-Hamra, the Alhambra, the Red Palace of the Nasrids—was a last retreat, a place to look inward and upward to preserve the memory of all that had gone before, a way to somehow float above the Earth and avoid the hard and inescapable reality on the ground, that the Muslim dream in al-Andalus was finite in time and would end someday.

Every one of these rooms and chambers opened out into air and space so that this king and his wives and ancestors could feel as if they were floating out in the air. As a boy, Prince Muhammad had imagined he was flying just like ibn Firnas, but without risking his life. He could have the best of the world and the sky in his dreams. How could he have ever dealt with the declining truth on the ground, when he was born and lived in the air?

And now his time has come. He must go down to those who have decided that this historical oddity has outlived its time; that this rival religion that has been around for seven centuries must go away; that this Semitic language that has penetrated into the Latinate tongue so much that a good third of it is unintelligible to the Romance speakers farther north, and this Eastern way of life, just do not belong here anymore. He and his family and his people are being evicted.

It is time. A letter written by an eyewitness to the bishop of Leon describes the scene:

> *With the royal banners and the cross of Christ plainly visible on the red walls of the Alhambra ... the Moorish king with about eighty or a hundred on horseback very well dressed went forth to kiss the hand of their Highnesses. Whom they received with much love and courtesy and there they handed over to him his son, who had been a hostage from*

the time of his capture, and as they stood there, there came about four hundred captives, of this who were in the enclosure, with the cross and a solemn procession singing the Te Deum Laudamus, and their highnesses dismounted to adore the Cross to the accompaniment of the tears and reverential devotion of the crowd, not least of the Cardinal and Master of Santiago and the Duke of Cadiz and all the other grandees and gentlemen and people who stood there, and there was no one who did not weep abundantly with pleasure giving thanks to Our Lord for what they saw, for they could not keep back the tears; and the Moorish King and the Moors who were with him for their part could not disguise the sadness and pain they felt for the joy of the Christians, and certainly with much reason on account of their loss, for Granada is the most distinguished and chief thing in the world.

In that crowd another man is watching, a man whose family might have been Jewish once but is no longer, a man of the new world coming—in fact, the man who will discover the New World. His name is Christopher Columbus, and he writes in his diary:

After your Highnesses ended the war of the Moors who reigned in Europe, and finished the war of the great city of Granada, where this present year [1492] on the 2nd January I saw the royal banners of Your Highnesses planted by force of arms on the towers of the Alhambra, which is the fortress of the said city, I saw the Moorish king issue from the gates of the said city, and kiss the royal hands of Your Highnesses.

And then it is done, and the last Moorish king is riding away, first to a temporary safe haven on the coast of Spain and then on to North Africa, where so many Spanish Jews and Muslims have gone in retreat of the Christians.

But from a high point on the road he must look back one last time, to see the Alhambra floating there against the sky. He sighs, and then he cries to have lost all this, to be the one to surrender the last piece of the dream. His mother, who has never been good at times like this, turns to him and hisses: "You do well to weep like a woman for what you could not defend as a man." And he is thinking, "Was it cowardice to want this life too much? We had paradise here. What good would our dying have done?"

His city on the hill will lie vacant for some time, its lower quarters falling victim to construction projects of different objectives, until one day only the topmost chambers and fountains and pools will remain. For too long the old Alhambra, superior in symmetry and grace to anything that will rise in these parts for centuries, will be a symbol of a history that no one wants to remember or acknowledge. It will be a symbol of what has been deliberately and unnecessarily lost. No one will remember the purpose of those vast salons carved with calligraphy in stone. Few people will even remember the name of the place.

But one day, a generation will come again and marvel, "Who created this place? And why?" And there will be few who can answer them. The only answer will be in that chill dry air blowing across Andalusia, a sound like a sigh.

SAMARKAND, UZBEKISTAN, 1417–1660—On the Silk Road, at the opposite end of the Muslim world from al-Andalus, out in that windy and borderless place, stands a trio of gargantuan bluish monoliths each cut in the heart by identical peaked arches, looking somehow as if they are not of this world. From above and afar, they resemble in some ways the prehistoric holy places, the ancient observatories such as England's Stonehenge and Guatemala's Tikal.

Up close, the three monoliths face each other across a square. They expand into works of art, scientific tablets, statements of absolute earthly and heavenly power. They expand to become three seemingly identical doorways fit for three giant jinn, or genies, yet inlaid with the most exquisite stone and tile.

This unearthly place is called Registan, meaning sandy place, in the city of Samarkand. In 1370 Tamerlane made this ancient city—going back to 700 B.C.—the capital of his empire. He laid the foundations for what would come to be perhaps the most magnificent and powerful place of monumental architecture in Central Asia.

Timur had come out of nowhere and terrorized the world after the Mongol Khans were gone, when it had seemed that all could breathe safely again. On the square he would behead his victims and put their heads on stakes in the bloody sand, where royal proclamations were heralded by blasts on long copper horns called *dzhurki,* and where the city market once thrived. This is the heart of Samarkand.

In the 15th century Timur's grandson, Ulugh Beg, decreed in the imperial tradition of his grandfather that at Registan the first of the three structures be built by his architect, Kavomiddin Sherozi. Laboring for him who had absolute power over life and death, Sherozi put his own personal fear and awe into this extraterrestrial portal. Though it looked like a colossal doorway into heaven, attached to it was the complex of an imperial madrassa, a religious school.

To anyone standing before even a single vast arch, framed on either side by minarets that look like giant pillars holding up the sky, gazing into the cosmic bluish facades of time and space, one of these structures would seem to be enough to dwarf mankind and communicate the grandeur and power of heaven and the mind. But then, over the next two centuries, two more such structures would be built, so that a triangle of three nearly identical gateways with madrassas would be created, two facing one another, the third rising across the courtyard out into the vastness.

Standing out there in the expanse, at the convergence of the three arches, visitors wonder about this piece of the Muslim vision. It is about as far from the Medina Azahara and the Alhambra as can be, yet these structures belong to the same universe. Like the Spanish counterparts, the Registan buildings show the intricacy of the diagonal and circular and geometric patterns of blue and turquoise and gold and yellow tiles, a microcosm of the universe itself, with mathematical and astronomical theories, a map of the stars and planets in tile, the representation of atomic and chemical reaction. Registan is a representation of cold and intimidating intellect and absolute power, as opposed to the warm sentimentality and nostalgia of the designs of the Alhambra and Medina Azahara. But all three represent the stone memories of all that has gone before and will never return, by using many of the same forms.

Looking closer at the Registan buildings, the interior arches of the Tilla Kari madrassa support tiers of muqarnas, those manmade stalactites hanging down, which could have been inspired by those at the Alhambra 3,000 miles west. The buildings serve not only as a place for training and housing students, but also as a grand mosque. Long after Timur and his heirs are swept away, these monuments still stand. The reaction they provoke, now as then, more than anything is awe.

So the long-dead sons of Timur have perhaps done better than any-one in capturing feeling in stone. While the nostalgia and love built into Andalusian architecture can only be fully understood by recovering lost history, in Samarkand the awesome symbolic power of the Timurids is as alive as it was some 600 years ago.

ISFAHAN, PERSIA, 1592—There is an ambitious politician and leader in 16th- and 17th-century Persia. His name is Shah Abbas, and through the convergence of several things—his seizure of the throne by over-throwing his father, plus a flow of wealth through the Silk Road trade and the quiet support of the British in trying to undermine the Ottoman Turks and other European colonial powers—he sets about to restore Persia to the explicit centrality it held long before the arrival of Islam.

He knows that Persia—which was once one of the centers of the world and has been the intellectual and financial and artistic powerhouse for Baghdad and the Central Asians and the Mughals—has not had its just share of overt power and recognition because of disunity.

And so he sets about bringing all the pieces of Persia back together again. He is victorious against the Turks, pushing them ever farther back. He is victorious against the Georgians in the west and the Portuguese sea-farers. And the riches of the Euro-Asian trade flow into his coffers.

In time he chooses to make Isfahan his imperial capital. Though it is already a lavish and beautiful city dating back to the time of the Seljuks, he will make it grander. He will create a city as grand for its time as Persepolis was for the ancient Persians.

With his patronage, his architects and planners and artists will proceed to execute a vast symphony in stone, for even in those times, the disciplines of music and mathematics and architecture are still seen as reflections in different media of the same source codes of God's creation. These creators will decide that just as music is based on a system of notes, so shall archi-tectural creation be based on eight essential elements: garden, platform, porch, gateway, dome, minaret, chamber, and arch.

And using these elements, not only will Abbas and his planners enrich the already sumptuous tapestry of Isfahan with new mosques and palaces and public spaces. They will weave it all into perhaps the most monu-mental city not only in the Muslim world, but in the world at large, a

*The Taj Mahal, built in the 17th century by Sah Jahan as a monument to lost love,
is the epitome of Mughal architecture.*

16th-century Muslim forerunner to Bernini's 17th-century colonnaded St. Peter's Square in Rome, L'Enfant's 18th-century Washington, and Hausmann's 19th-century Paris.

Shah Abbas's new city will be arranged around a vast square known as Shah or Imam Square, at 95,600 square yards twice as large as Red Square in Moscow. In its imperial days it will be used as a royal polo field. Among its gems will be the Sheikh Lotfollah Mosque created by architect Muhammad Reza ibn Ustad Hosein Banna Isfahani. Facing the two-mile-long expanse of the rectangular square will be a blue tiled gateway flanked by the tan-colored arcades of noble palaces, offices, and apartments.

Of the Sheikh Lotfollah Mosque, Robert Byron will write:

> *I have never encountered splendor of this kind before. Other interiors came into my mind as I stood there, to compare it with: Versailles, or the porcelain room at Schönbrunn, or the Doge's Palace, or St. Peter's. All are rich, but none so rich.*

Another construction will be the Ali Qapu, or Sublime Gate palace, rich in naturalistic wall paintings by court painter Reza Abbasi and his pupils. Reza will use the designs of flowers, birds, and other animals, long-standing symbols and subjects from high Persian Muslim art and designs seen in countless manuscripts and chronicles. But this will be no bound volume. This will be the story of Persian imagination in tile and stone and gold.

A third masterpiece will be the Shah or Imam Mosque, its grandiose blue facade and minarets rising opposite the Sheikh Lotfollah Mosque.

Though they are uniquely Persian, all these buildings will echo the two geographic extremes of Islam, both of fallen al-Andalus and faraway Registan. Like Registan, the monumental buildings of Isfahan will have that dazzling turquoise and blue tile exterior, and the intricacies of design mirroring the complexity of the universe. And like the Alhambra, many of these buildings will have the downward hanging muqarnas, carved with inscriptions. The cavernous interiors will attempt the impossible, to capture the infinity of space in a glorious man-made enclosure.

The stone and tile symphony of Isfahan is so huge and so intricate that it will be hard to fix the eye on any single gem in its creation. Isfahan and Imam Square have to be taken as a whole, one of the most dazzling architectural and artistic constructs of human history. And though the sculptured domes and brilliance of decoration will suggest the Orient, the layout of the square and the design of the flanking arcades and palaces and townhouses will be adapted in Western Europe, for imperial architecture in France, England, and Austria.

The lavish court at Isfahan will have its own version of excess. Even as the mosques and minarets rise higher throughout Persia and the artistic representations of the grandeur of heaven grow more ornate and layered, deep in the palaces, in the townhouses, out in the shadow of the gardens, the pleasures of the senses will be at their peak, in ways that can only happen in times of absolute power and infinite wealth.

Isfahan and its artistic and political and sensual glory will be the product of a particular moment in time that will never come again. The unique confluence of the vision and power of Shah Abbas, with the wealth generated by the overland trade between Europe and Asia, will soon come to an end. Shah Abbas will pass on, followed by squabbling successors.

Europeans will soon shift their trade from land to sea, using ships to circle Africa and head for India and China and the East Indies. The Silk Road and the riches of cities like Isfahan will be struck a deathblow. The effect will be like someone turning off a tap.

But facing the end of his time, Shah Abbas will look out on his square and think: "Gaze, mortals, on the enduring grandeur of Isfahan and know the artistic and creative power of the Persian people, when their minds are unleashed, and when they are guided by an enlightened vision."

Today the buildings on the square are preserved in their splendor as a UNESCO World Heritage site.

AGRA, INDIA, 1631—There is a Mughal ruler of India known as Shahbuddin Mohammed Shah Jahan, and he has several wives, but the one closest to his heart is Mumtaz. They are married when they are still children, barely teenagers, so they live most of their lives together.

Mumtaz bears Jahan 14 children. Unlike many royal wives, she travels with him into battle. She is by his side almost all the time. She is with him so much that he loses a sense of them as separate people. His love is beyond an awareness of love, a vital coexistence. They are two parts of the same body.

Aside from having such a love, this Shah of India is most fortunate. He controls a country that is an empire and a world unto itself. India's wealth in the 17th century is probably greater than that of any other nation on earth, including those growing imperial powers of Europe, who covet its riches.

And this country, though it is ruled by Muslims, incorporates so many peoples, religions, and languages that you could say that the Muslim part of India is only a very rich veneer on an equally rich and old work of creation.

The imams of the mosques speak in Arabic and write in the Arabic script. The Mughals, originally from Central Asia, have adopted the forms and style of the Persians. And to complete the circle, they have conquered old Hindu India.

The predecessors of this Shah of India include patriarch Babur from Uzbekistan, who founded the Mughal empire, and Jahan's grandfather Akbar the Great, one day to be judged the greatest Indian ruler of all time, whether the judges be Muslim, Hindu, or others.

Shah Jahan does not have the vision of Akbar, nor the military prowess of Babur, but he will be known for splendid architecture. He builds the Red Fort of Delhi, the red sandstone fortress that for a time defines the nature of Mughal design. He builds palaces and gardens. But his greatest homage will be inspired by love.

In 1631, when he goes into battle, Mumtaz, pregnant with their 14th child, comes along. Not that it is advisable. But she doesn't even consider not making the journey with her warrior husband. She has done it so many times that she will do it again. And during the campaign, Mumtaz gives Jahan another child, a girl named Shahzadi Gauhara Begum. And all should be well. But in the terrible spinning of time and destiny, Mumtaz leaves the world of the living.

And for the ruler of the richest empire on Earth, who lives with a power and opulence that only a few dozen people in many thousands of years have known, it is as though his heart and lungs have been torn out. Mumtaz is his alter ego. A life without Mumtaz is not a life. And for a long time, this man cannot think or breathe, and it is as though his heart has stopped.

He prays that he be taken with her, down into the black whirlpool of death. He cannot even remember his name, or his other wives and children, or his role as Shah of all India, his armies, his palaces, his wagonloads of emeralds and gold and rubies, his tens of thousands of elephants, his hundreds of millions of subjects, their prayers and blessings and testimonials and tributes, none of it even exists. He wants to die.

But though his spirit and his heart are gone, his body goes on. The imams, the spiritualists, the friends, and the courtiers can do nothing to help. How can they help? Can they bring back Mumtaz?

Court historian Abd al-Hamid Lahawri writes that Shah Jahan's grief "crumbled his mountain-like endurance," and that his beard turned white overnight and he did not make a public appearance for one full week.

The 17th-century French traveler François Bernier also reported that Shah Jahan had been so in love with his beautiful wife that 'he was constant to her during life, and at death was so affected as nearly to follow her to her grave.'

And from this pit of despair, Shah Jahan fixes upon the only thing that will help correct this terrible betrayal by time and destiny and allow him to stay in this world. He vows to create a memorial to his departed love that will stop everyone who gazes upon it, causing them to gasp and lose their breath and fall to their knees to behold the memorial to a love as big as India, to a woman who was the other half of him, to two lives that stopped when hers stopped.

The orders will go forth, summoning the architects and the engineers and the financiers and the calligraphers. They are told that they must build the greatest monument ever built as befits the greatest love ever known, or they need not apply.

And they come, by the dozens, by the hundreds and thousands, ultimately 20,000 men in number, from all over India, from Persia, from Ottoman Turkey. Rumor has it that Europeans also respond.

While most of the millions of Mughal official court documents will one day be destroyed, historians will conclude that the final team will include the master architect Ustad Ahmad Lahori and possibly Shah Jahan himself. There is speculation that the shah draws the plans, making alterations and fine-tuned submissions from several court architects.

All this grief and commotion result in a plan to defeat death by bringing heavenly beauty and power down to the riverbanks of the Jamuna in Agra, to create in stone a poem of love and adoration tinged with the terrible grief of death and separation.

Legions of elephants will thunder across the land. They will bring tons of translucent white marble from Rajasthan; they will bring wagonloads of jasper from Punjab to create the black lettering of the Qur'an on the white marble background; they will bring jade and crystal from China to create decoration and lighting. They will bring turquoise from Tibet and lapis lazuli from Afghanistan. They will bring sapphire from Sri Lanka and carnelian from Arabia. To inlay the marble, they will bring 28 different types of precious stone.

Thanks to the labors of the Shah's financiers, this project begins and, according to some accounts, takes 22 years to complete. It will cost an estimated $500 million dollars.

This memorial is called the Taj Mahal.

On its elevated square marble base will rise the white marble mausoleum of love, marked at each of its four corners by white marble minarets. The structure will be surmounted by a white marble dome, topped by an Islamic crescent moon pointed upward in such a way that when seen with the full ornament, it also suggests to some the symbol of the Hindu God Shiva.

And five years after completion of this project in 1653, Shah Jahan, never having regained his former self, will be overthrown by his son Aurangzeb, who will bring the imperial focus back to things on Earth. His father Jahan will spend his final years under house arrest, gazing out through his window at the temple of love. When he dies, his son will have the good grace to place his father's body next to the long-departed Mumtaz so that they are together again.

Jahan had intended to build an exact replica, down to the last Qur'anic letter, on the other side of the river in black marble for himself, to reflect his grief and loss endured for all the years after Mumtaz's death. It will not matter. The two lovers will be united under the marble, Mumtaz at the very center beneath the apex of the dome, Jahan at her side and slightly off center.

And then this place will fall on hard times. As the Mughals lose power, the looters will come. When the British invade and occupy, Britons and their Indian conscripts will pry the precious stones from the walls. Later a British viceroy will order a restoration.

And then the stories will grow, like whispers in the shimmering palatial gardens and reflecting pools. Rumors claim that Jahan had not really built the Taj Mahal, that it had been a Hindu site.

Beyond the perimeter of the park, hotels will rise, and visitors holding hands will wonder if their love equals this one, frozen in stone.

MECCA, ARABIA, 600—There is a love song that begins very early in Islam. This song then ring out across much of the world, spawning new musical instruments, creating entire new forms of music and influencing other forms, but spreading so wide and deep and for so long that many will debate their original source and influence.

This music derives from the many songs of rich and older cultures that are engulfed and absorbed by the Muslims—Byzantine and Roman and Greek and folk Arabic, Jewish, Persian, Indian, Berber, Balkan, and Mongol. This song can be about many things, so the best term that can be ascribed to it is the "song of civilizations." And though it will branch off into many expressions, this song will probably have its greatest and broadest impact by evolving into a song of earthly love, a song about the attachment to a lover, faithful or treacherous, present or absent, attainable or forever removed, sacred or profane.

Within the song of civilizations, always resonating in the background is another song of love for God. Many of the thinkers who also plumb the stars and spin out the numbers of the source code of the universe will extend those theories and studies to music, which they see as a branch of philosophy and directly related to mathematics. Many of the giants of Muslim mathematics, philosophy, and even medicine will also add complexity and formal structure to the song of civilizations. The scholars al-Kindi, ibn Sina, and ibn Rushd will delve deeply into musical theory and will begin to use a form of musical notation based on letters of the alphabet. Ziryab, the ninth-century Baghdad musician driven by jealousy to the Umayyad court in Cordoba, will create the world's first music conservatory there, even as he cooks, designs clothes, and creates new hair styles.

Another high theorist of music is ibn al-Farabi, a ninth-century Persian who gravitates to a court in Syria. Al-Farabi will write five treatises on music, including the following observation to his theories:

> *The man and the animal, under the impulsion of their instincts, emit sounds that express their emotions, as they can be the one of joy or fear. The human voice expresses greater variety—sadness, tenderness, rage. These sounds, in the diversity of their notes, cause in the person that listens to them, such shades of feelings or passions, raising to him, controlling to him or tranquilizing to him.*

Al-Farabi will write about pitch and diatonic tuning—staying within a key or scale—and microtones or neutral intervals.

Theologian-philosopher al-Ghazali, the 12th-century thinker who will begin to lead a final retreat from rationalist Islam into a more heartfelt and mystical orientation, will see a direct linkage between mystical faith and mystical music. He writes:

> *It is not possible to enter the human heart without passing by the antechamber of the ears. The musical, measured subjects emphasize what there is in the heart and reveal their beauties and defects.*

These theories will over time be translated and gradually make their way northward to Europe from al-Andalus and Sicily, brought by the crusaders or by other means of transfer, though often with a time lag of centuries.

According to historian H.G. Farmer, one key transmission from Muslims to Europeans is Arab-Muslim musical notation. He states that although few European music historians will consider that the notation "do re mi fa so la ti" started other than in 11th-century Italy, compelling evidence exists that Italians were simply using earlier Arabic notation from the ninth and tenth centuries. In his book *Historical Facts for the Arabian Musical Influence,* he gives the following comparison of the Italian and Arabic notations:

Arabic alphabet:	Mi	Fa	Sad	La	Sin	Dal	Ra
Italian notes:	Mi	Fa	Sol	La	Si	Do	Re

Another musical form will find its roots in seventh-century Arabian poetry. One of the greatest early poets of Mecca, 'Umar ibn Abi Rabi'ah al-Makhzumi, will contribute to a poetic form called the *ghazel,* literally a love poem. He will write poems about his affairs with noble women pilgrims visiting Mecca.

Something gallant will also begin to evolve in the laboratory of early Arab poetry: the idea of courtly love. The Arabian poet seen as the forefather of later European chivalric love is Jamil, a seventh-century poet of the city of Medina. He writes about lovers who become martyrs to their love, dying for the highest emotion in earthly life.

One of the last eighth-century Umayyad rulers in Damascus, al-Walid ibn Yazid, will write amusing love poems and odes about drinking.

In medieval al-Andalus and Sicily, the Muslim poetic and musical forms will begin to spin off in several directions that will echo around the world. An Andalusian musical form called *al-muwashahat*—strophic songs with a refrain—will spread throughout the Arab world and spawn a hybrid form called *zajal,* an early type of troubadour song, which will also resound north of the Pyrenees. Ninth-century Muslim wandering poet-singers will sing of chaste love for a woman. Whether this woman is an earthly symbol of the divine, or divine in her own right, is forgotten.

In the 13th century, Christian King Alfonso the Wise of Castile and Leon will sponsor the creation of more than 400 sacred Christian songs, a good 300 of which are in form and content replications of the Muslim muwashahat.

Other Christians north of Spain will start to sing similar song-poems several centuries later, initially devoted to the Virgin Mary, but eventually dedicated to any deserving fair lady. These singers will be known as troubadours in France and *trovatori* in Italy, their names possibly derived from the Arabic word *tarab,* meaning "ecstasy," as in the ecstasy of love. The concept of singing a poem to a loved one will explode into European culture, generating a new genre of music, the love song, which will prove eternal. With it will come a new awareness of the value of women and the concept of chivalry and honor will begin to lay the seeds for a more humane and enlightened European society.

Some of this musical transmission will come from travelers on both sides of the Pyrenees, among them Charlemagne, according to some sources, who spends seven full years in Spain during his military campaigns.

Other music historians will argue that the many Muslim women taken prisoner in various military campaigns in northern Spain and transported to Christian Europe will also serve as musical messengers. These hundreds of women, captured in the fall of places like Balbastro and trained since childhood in the musical forms of the Andalusian home and street, will be taken all over France and also to Italy by Pope Alexander II's armies.

According to 21st-century music historian Dr. Rabah Saoud, not only Muslim musical theory and forms will go north, but from the eighth and ninth centuries musical instruments also will spread into northern Christian Spain, France, and Italy by Muslim minstrels and entertainers. The Muslim *'ud* will spawn the European lute and later the guitar and mandolin. The Arabic *ghaita* will evolve into the Scottish bagpipe and Spanish and Portuguese *gaita*. The Muslim *qanum* will give birth to the English harp and the German zither. The Persian *kamancha* and Arab *rabab* will morph into the fiddle. The Muslim *zurna,* a woodwind instrument, will lead to the oboe. The Persian *santur,* an early form of the hammered dulcimer, will give rise to European keyboard instruments.

And even as the Muslim musical contribution echoes through Europe, it will keep evolving in Spain. The song of love and civilizations will be transformed but not erased by the Catholic reconquest and fall of Granada. Many Spanish Muslims, faced with expulsion, conversion, or death, will disappear into the shadows of their suddenly unfriendly homeland. Some will join the gypsies, who are given a certain freedom to wander and remain apart. And these hybrid gypsy-Moors will create a form of music called flamenco, which 20th-century Cuban novelist Gabriel Cabrera Infante will say is a derivative of an Arabic term, *fellah mengu,* which means "country vagabonds."

And the Western Muslim musical form with the stamp of the long-dead Ziryab will not be confined to Spain, Portugal, and Europe. It will accompany the Spanish conquistadors and colonists as they head west to the Americas, spawning genres such as the samba of Brazil, the *jarabe* of Mexico, *la cueca* of Chile, *el gato* of Argentina and Uruguay, and *la guajira* of Cuba.

Musicologists will even claim to find echoes of the Muslim song of divine love in the American blues, created by slaves and their descendants, whose forebears had been Muslims in Africa.

KONYA, ANATOLIA, 1228—A unique Persian poet saint who hears a different kind of music, named Jalal ad-Din al-Rumi, will be born in the year 1207 in what is now Afghanistan. When he is still a child, the family will flee west ahead of the Mongol advance, to settle in the Seljuk realm of Anatolia in an old city of palaces and minarets, known as Konya.

Rumi will be devoutly immersed in the school of mystic poetry, an Arabian-Persian-Muslim tradition that holds that the poetic voice can, through its use of symbolism and the music of its sound, unlock doors into a higher world and free the mind and soul so as to better know the divine.

As a Sufi mystic, Rumi will have devotees who in his time consider him to be a living saint. And these devotees will not only be those of his particular sect but other Muslims and Christians and Jews. In fact, he will write and preach that all religions are one, whatever their name and coloration:

> *In the adorations and benedictions of righteous men*
> *The praises of all the prophets are kneaded together.*
> *All their praises are mingled into one stream,*
> *All the vessels are emptied into one ewer.*
> *Because He that is praised is, in fact, only One.*
> *In this respect all religions are only one religion.*
> *Because all praises are directed toward God's Light,*
> *These various forms and figures are borrowed from it.*

Rumi will teach at a madrassa in Konya that becomes a place of reverence and pilgrimage, where his unique brand of ecstatic philosophy and interfaith tolerance become enshrined. The inscription above the entrance gate will read:

Come, come, whoever you are.
Wanderer, idolater, worshipper of fire,
Come even though you have broken
Your vows a thousand times,
Come, and come yet again.
Ours is not a caravan of despair.

The followers of Rumi will be expected not only to conduct the mystic search for the divine, but to work at useful crafts such as leatherworking and weaving and to involve themselves in the community by helping the poor and infirm through donations of food and other necessities.

His habit of spinning around a pillar in his home when in the grips of religious and romantic ecstasy will become enshrined in the Mawlawiyah order, known as the Whirling Dervishes, that endures for 800 years. He and his followers believe that in the controlled rhythm of the whirl, one can more easily detach from the formulaic and mechanistic thinking of everyday life and free up the mind and self for a more direct approach to God. Rumi will preach that anyone can have a direct relationship with the divine and that no intermediary is required.

Like the other Persian poet Omar Khayyám, Rumi has a habit of writing about God in romantic and sensual language that will be misinterpreted by some to be literal romantic poetry. And Rumi will give some fuel to the fire when he forms an intense friendship bordering on obsession with a wandering street preacher named Shams ad-Din Tabrizi. He and Shams will withdraw into Rumi's quarters for long periods of time to partake in dialogue, mystifying some and scandalizing others. Eventually Shams will disappear, probably murdered by a group led by one of Rumi's sons, jealous of his power over their leader. Rumi will mourn the loss for years, finally coming to the realization that his beloved mystic partner Shams is really only a reflection of Rumi's self.

Why should I seek? I am the same as He.
His essence speaks through me.
I have been looking for myself!

Myth holds that before he dies, Shams will appear in Damascus and meet Francis of Assisi, then a young Italian nobleman sent off to the Crusades. Through this intermediary from Rumi, Francis will begin to glimpse a vision of mystical life, of charity, and of gentle communion with the world.

And while Rumi's fame will reverberate in his time far beyond his immediate environs, and his poetic voice will have deep impact on later Persian and Turkish literature, this poet will achieve a new fame 700 years later in the non-Muslim world, in Europe and the Americas. In the mid-20th century, Westerners will discover this long-lost poet saint, and it is said that by the 21st century in the United States, Rumi is the best-selling poet in a society that does not often recognize poets.

We are all powerless by Love's game.
How can you expect us
To behave and act modest?
How can you expect us
To stay at home, like good little boys?
How can you expect us
To enjoy being chained like mad men?
Oh, my Beloved, you will find us every night,
On your street,
With our eyes glued to your window,
Waiting for a glimpse of your radiant face.

THERE ARE ALSO OTHER memorable tales that spread across the Muslim world and then beyond, sometimes in parallel and sometimes in combination with the songs. They are written both in poetry and prose.

The Arabs and Persians and Indians will place poetry at the center of much public discussion. Poetry will fill the future role of journalism, policy debate, and entertainment. The Indians will hold large poetry competitions, gatherings of thousands of people who spend days and nights in competitive public recitations.

Arabic poetry born on the sandy plains of Arabia and used to entertain in intertribal poetry tournaments will blossom into odes, called *qasidas,* extolling at length the virtue of a lover or the triumph of a desert raid. They will commemorate major tribal and political gatherings with recitations from their most prized poets. Poetry will have the ability to make an Arab poet rich or dead, depending on his patrons and enemies, on what he writes and how well he writes it.

But the classical poetry of the Arabs will be immensely difficult to translate well for several reasons. First, the Arabic language will be heavily given to symbolism, with words and letters and sounds having both a literal meaning and also a hidden, mystical meaning that cannot be rendered into other languages without extensive footnotes and appendices. That kind of encumbrance will limit its transmission. The second obstacle will be its rigid rhyming structure, which will work in the original, but in other languages will sound stilted and contorted, the severe dictates of rhyme undermining its music.

These stories and poems, written more for the educated class of the caliphate, will not penetrate deeply into mass culture. For one thing, many Muslims will have trouble understanding the classical Arabic. And parallel popular stories will arise to entertain and educate the public.

But there are also the stories of life high and low, both from the Arabs and then from all the peoples who are engulfed in the religion and the civilization. There are poems and tales of love and lust and warfare, the fables and moral teaching stories, the accounts of lives great and small, the royal tributes and political diatribes, the lessons of wisdom, the reportage of history and travel. These stories will come from India and Persia and Africa, from Central Asia and Iberia and Byzantium.

There is one set of popular stories in Arabic that, though scorned or ignored by the court because of its hodgepodge mix of literary and vernacular language and themes, will resonate deeply with the people. These stories will be inspired by a collection attributed to the pre-Islamic Persian princess Afsana, a daughter of Shah Ataxerxes II. The collection is called *Hazar Afsana*—A Thousand Tales.

Sometime in the tenth century, a Baghdad editor named al-Jahshiyari will combine these stories with tales from local storytellers. This collection of stories will begin to circulate through Egypt and Syria and is called *Alf Laylah wa Laylah,* literally the *Book of the Thousand Nights and One Night.*

What is unique about these stories is that they are framed in a larger story, that of an Indo-Persian king named Shahryar and his desperate wife Scheherazade. The frame story is that if Scheherazade does not keep her royal husband entertained with a fresh story every night, he will kill her. So to stay alive she keeps him hooked, and weaves stories about Aladdin, Ali Baba, Haroun al-Rashid's court, and Sinbad the sailor.

It will so happen that Christian Crusaders, sent to recapture the Holy Land in the 11th and 12th centuries, will hear some of these stories. Though they are well versed in the Christian Bible, and a few may even have heard tell of the European epics and sagas such as *Chanson de Roland* or *King Arthur* or *Beowulf* or the *Nibelungenlied,* or the *Edda,* something about these Arab stories will strike a chord, and their echo will go back to Europe when the surviving warriors return home.

The Italian writer Giovanni Boccaccio will hear these stories, and they will influence his own coming work, a collection of a hundred amusing tales called the *Decameron.* The English writer Geoffrey Chaucer will create his own version, entitled the *Canterbury Tales.*

The 13th-century Italian poet Dante Aligheri will not need to be a crusader to hear the Muslim stories, poems, and songs. He will spend a time in Sicily, with its hybrid Muslim-Christian culture, and he will hear

In 1615 Shah Abbas I of Persia restored power to the Persian Empire, ruling a realm that extended from the Tigris to the Indus Rivers.

not only popular stories, he will be exposed to the Qur'an and the scientific writings of the great thinkers of Baghdad's House of Wisdom, as well as to later Muslim thinkers.

And 16th-century Spanish writer Miguel de Cervantes will not only spring from a land just decades out of the Moorish period, he will spend many years in North Africa, and he will have a good understanding of Arabic. His *Don Quixote de la Mancha* with its aspects of chivalry will be a product of his Andalusian heritage.

English playwright Christopher Marlowe will choose one of the great Muslim Central Asian conquerors, Timur, as the title character in two of his plays entitled *Tamburlaine.*

And another 16th-century writer of comedies and tragedies, William Shakespeare, will choose as perhaps his most compelling tragic hero, one Othello the Moor, who will be brought down by false slanders from the tongue of Iago.

Finally, in the 18th century, a Frenchman named Antoine Galland will translate for the first time into French, or any other European tongue, a significant portion of the tales of *The Thousand and One Nights,* and their publication will touch off a sudden and enduring fad of Orientalism that will result in art by Jean-Auguste-Dominique Ingres and Eugène Delacroix, followed later by works of Henri Matisse, Auguste Renoir, and their cohorts, who travel to Algeria and become enamored of Arabic decorative art and Arab women. This Orientalist fad will trigger mosque-like structures being built on the grounds of great estates in Germany, and a new interest in Muslim culture on the part of writers like Goethe, Lord Byron, and Voltaire. Tchaikovsky will insert Oriental music and moves into his ballets. Scheherazade will inspire Rimsky-Korsakov's music in the 19th century.

And into the 21st century, these once ignored Indo-Persian-Arabic vernacular stories of love, lust, magic, and betrayal will continue to inspire books and films. They are repeated so often that they almost become cliché, but the tales of *The Thousand and One Nights* will continue to draw audiences all over the world.

Despite the constant threat of death, the narrator of these tales will meet a happy ending, as the anonymous author of the stories concludes on the 1,001st night of Scheherazade's storytelling:

Now during this time Scheherazade had borne the King three boy children, so when she had made an end of the story, she rose to her feet and kissing ground before him, said,

'O King of the Time and unique one of the Age and the Tide, I am thine handmaid, and these thousand nights and a night have I entertained thee with stories of folk gone before and admonitory instances of the men of yore. May I then make bold to crave a boon of thy Highness?'

He replied, 'Ask, O Scheherazade, and it shall be granted to thee.'

Whereupon she cried out to the nurses and the eunuchs, saying, 'Bring me my children.' So they brought them to her in haste, and they were three boy children, one walking, one crawling, and one suckling. She took them, and setting them before the King, again kissed the ground and said: 'O King of the Age, these are thy children, and I crave that thou release me from the doom of death, as a dole to these infants. For an thou kill me, they will become motherless and will find none among women to rear them as they should he reared.'

When the King heard this, he wept, and straining the boys to his bosom, said: 'By Allah, O Scheherazade, I pardoned thee before the coming of these children, for that I found thee chaste, pure, ingenuous, and pious! Allah bless thee and thy father and thy mother and thy root and thy branch! I take the Almighty to witness against me that I exempt thee from aught that can harm thee.' So she kissed his hands and feet and rejoiced with exceeding joy, saying, 'The Lord make thy life long and increase thee in dignity and majesty!'

8

ENLIGHTENED LEADERSHIP

O David! Surely We have made you a ruler in the land; so judge between
men with justice and do not follow desire, lest it should lead you astray
from the path of God.
QUR'AN (XXXVIII:26)

WASHINGTON, D.C., 2007—Rubbing his eyes and looking out
his office window in the Longworth House Office Building, the U.S. congressman is weary and perplexed. Only a few months ago he barely won—
by 611 votes out of 230,000 cast—the toughest political race of his life.
Now he is wondering if he would have been better off in defeat, because
the issues and choices are giving him no relief.

The country and his district are terribly polarized on everything: war
and peace, the economy, health care, immigration, and terrorism. And for
every good argument on one side, there is an equally persuasive one on the
other. His opponent nearly defeated him by attacking him for being too
indecisive. And the challenger had a point.

Consider the congressman's visitors that very morning: He had been
first visited by a delegation concerned about port security. The large,
well-connected group demanded a personal hearing, and he had no
choice but to grant it. They represented some of the largest businesses in
his district.

They claimed that not enough was being done. They claimed that the
country was at war now and that the enemy, though diffuse, was serious
and deadly and had to be confronted. The country was still vulnerable to
chemical, biological, and nuclear weapons coming in unmarked containers. What was being done?

He nodded and said at the end of the meeting that he would give their concerns and ideas serious thought, and he would ask the Department of Homeland Security for a full status report. They responded that if he didn't come up with some answers fast, they'd hold him personally accountable in the 2008 elections.

As if that weren't enough, a group of Muslim constituents had followed them; the two groups had eyed each other in the waiting room and out in the hall. Once inside, these Muslims had their own complaints. They were deeply concerned about congressional and executive decisions on dealing with detainees in the war on terrorism. They claimed the President and the Congress were violating the Constitution and the tradition of American law and justice. They claimed that assorted relatives and friends had been snatched up by mistake and taken away and either released after torture and abuse or had never been heard from again. They had given him letters and affidavits and petitions.

And they had requested that the congressman use his powers to introduce legislation to have a sculpture of the Prophet Muhammad removed from a frieze in the United States Supreme Court. They said that the sculpture violated a tradition of not depicting the Prophet in art.

The congressman was privately puzzled, because it seemed to him an honor to have the Prophet of Islam in the chamber of the U.S. Supreme Court, shown alongside 17 other great lawgivers of history including Moses and Hammurabi. But he said that he would think about the matter, seek out other opinions, and try to come to the right decision that represented the rights of all.

And just outside his office are the daily mountains of mail and the clogged email box that his staff sorts through, looking for patterns of constituent opinion on immigration reform, pharmaceutical imports, gay marriage, stem-cell research, the war in Iraq, the budget deficit, domestic surveillance and wiretapping, tax cuts, education policy, the minimum wage, foreign policy, drug abuse, welfare reform, job creation, tobacco sales to minors, and so on. He can easily spend all day attempting to sort out policies on just one or two of these issues—but he is being asked to work on all of them.

And there is the mountain of requests from special interests, from the lobbyists and the trade associations, from the corporations, from the citizens groups on the right and the left, the special pleadings, the favors, the lost Social Security checks, the appointments to West Point, and the invitations to chicken dinners, parades, and Rotary Clubs.

He lets his mind go free. Maybe it is time for a break. Maybe his opponent was right. Maybe losing the last election would have been a good thing. He has been in Congress for ten years. His dream of becoming a senator or more has evaporated long ago. He has to raise too much money every two years just to win reelection to the House. This life has taken its personal toll: one divorce, one child fighting alcoholism, and now his own health. Suddenly he is a diabetic, puffing on a treadmill in the House gym, and trying to lose weight.

To clear his head, he decides to take a walk at lunchtime. He is nondescript enough in appearance that few people know who he is. No fan club lines up outside his door, only the lobbyists, the staffers wanting a minute, and maybe a few constituents from back home. He slips out a side door.

How can you be a good leader in this world, in this system? Is it even possible? Or is the only realistic goal of a leader to avoid terrible mistakes and keep things on an even keel?

It is summer, the air heavy, building toward an afternoon downpour. He walks past the construction of the new Visitors' Center on the Capitol's east side to the Supreme Court. Looking up at the white granite and marble all around him, the image is of ancient Greece and Rome. Wasn't that what shaped this American vision of government and leadership more than any other? Pericles, Plato, Socrates, Caesar, and Marcus Aurelius—weren't they the classical forefathers of American democracy, and later transmuted through the Renaissance and the Enlightenment to the ideals of Washington and Jefferson and Lincoln? Isn't that the historical narrative, the political tradition?

What would they have done, confronted with these issues, the special interests? What would they have done?

Curious, he slips across the street to the Supreme Court, wanting to check out this frieze. He had no idea that the Prophet of Islam was anywhere on Capitol Hill.

His congressional pass lets him in the front door, and he is able to go into the courtroom, silent now but for a small tour group and a cleaning crew. The frieze is there. After some puzzlement, the congressman finds the

Prophet, holding a Qur'an and a sword, gazing down on the room where the highest law in the American land is articulated.

And for a second the congressman wonders, is there anything of Muslim government and politics and leadership in this country of the European Enlightenment? Or has it all been lost to history?

THE ANSWER LIES IN ANCIENT STORY and song, in an unattributed ideal, in people who have almost become myth.

The enlightened Muslim leadership of the early empire enables the rise of the various golden ages. This vision of leadership, however compromised by unavoidable human ego, institutional failings, bad luck, and corruption, manages for more than eight centuries to inspire a climate of invention and intellectual ferment that will be unique and will help shape a future vision of modern leadership in Europe and other non-Muslim countries.

One result will be the intellectual achievements just described in this book in mathematics, science, medicine, and art. Other results of this leadership ideal will be innovations like proto-modern libraries and universities, an ethos of social fairness and justice, advanced public health, and tolerance of diversity in faith, nationality, and ethnicity.

This enlightened attitude will also be seen in episodes of democratic behavior, consensus building, conflict resolution, and responsiveness to public opinion.

Yet as in all human systems and endeavors, there are also powerful counterforces—the forces of self, ambition, narrowness, ignorance, prejudice, and misunderstanding. Sometimes those counterforces triumph. But the enlightened ideal, strong and often dominant in the period from the 7th to the 15th century, will always be there even if lost to history or deep in the background.

Although articulated in the Qur'an and by the actions of the Prophet, a search of ancient documents suggests that the first Muslim leaders trying to bring this vision of leadership into practical application are the early caliphs, in particular Abu Bakr, the first successor to Muhammad, and Ali, the cousin and son-in-law of the Prophet.

Abu Bakr's example of leadership is preserved not so much in eloquent statements, though his first sermon upon being chosen caliph is clear in its simplicity (see Chapter 1, pages 12-13). His vision is better preserved in his actions, recorded in multiple accounts from Muslim and non-Muslim sources. These sources show that Abu Bakr does not seek the office and resists until it seems he is the compromise candidate who can best bridge the tribal and personal rivalries beginning to arise in the young Muslim community.

Moreover he is a man of committed personal modesty and simplicity. His modus operandi once in office is to try to divine what the Prophet would have done, not to hatch any plans or strategies of his own. As the Arab empire continues to grow in wealth and power, from the time he assumes the role of caliph, he lives in the same modest residence and has only one slave working in his home.

He is credited with being the first man in Islam to free his slaves in accord with his religious beliefs, the first Muslim to build a mosque after the Prophet Muhammad, and is said to have spent his life savings of 40,000 dirhams to promote the rise of Islam. Additionally he is averse to sampling or diverting the wealth that he could reap from the streams of tax and booty flowing into the treasury.

English historian Edward Gibbon writes in his *History of the Saracens*:

When Abu Bakr assumed the office of the caliph, he enjoined on his daughter Ayesha to take a strict account of his patrimony. That it might be evident whether he were enriched or impoverished by three pieces of gold only, but on the Friday of each week, he distributed the residue of his own and the public money first to the most worthy and then to the most indigent of the Muslims. The remains of his wealth, a coarse garment and five pieces of gold were delivered to his successor, who lamented with a modest sigh of his own inability to equal such an admirable model.

Put simply, the leadership legacy of Abu Bakr would seem to be in creating a model of humility, compromise, incorruptibility, and a dedication to charity and public welfare. These values will provide an enduring ideal of leadership in the Muslim world and beyond, an ideal often contrary to the baser instincts of men, but one that will continue to draw adherents to political Islam in the 21st century.

The fourth caliph, Ali, will do a better job of articulating his ideas of leadership, and many of his statements will live on.

Ali is one of the first Muslim leaders to set down in writing a detailed template for enlightened leadership, elements of which would later surface in the Umayyad and Abbasid caliphates, in Fatimid and Sunni Egypt, in Seljuk Persia and Anatolia, in the Delhi sultanate and Mughal India, and in the Ottoman Empire.

Evidence is included in a lengthy letter on leadership, which Caliph Ali sends to his loyal follower, Maalik al-Ashtar, appointing him as the new Muslim governor of Egypt:

Let it be known to you, Maalik, that I am sending you as a governor to a country, which has seen many regimes before this. Some of them were benign, sympathetic and good, while others were tyrannical, oppressive and cruel. People will judge your regime as critically as you have studied the activities of other regimes and they will criticize you in the same way as you have censured or approved other rulers....

Remember, Maalik, that amongst your subjects there are two kinds of people: those who have the same religion as you have, they are brothers to you; and those who have religions other than that of yours, they are human beings like you.... Let your mercy and compassion come to their rescue and help in the same way and to the same extent that you expect Allah to show mercy and forgiveness to you....

Never say to yourself, 'I am their Lord, their ruler and all in all over them and that I must be obeyed submissively and humbly,' because such a thought will unbalance your mind, will make you vain and arrogant, will weaken your faith in religion and will make you seek support of any power other than that of Allah....

You must always appreciate and adopt a policy, which is neither too severe nor too lenient; a policy which is based upon equity will be largely appreciated. Remember that the displeasure of common men, the have-nots and the depressed persons more overbalances than the approval of important persons, while the displeasure of a few big people will be excused by the Lord if the general public and the masses of your subjects are happy with you....

You must know, Maalik, that the people over whom you rule are divided into classes and grades, and the prosperity and welfare of each class of the society individually and collectively are so interdependent upon the well-being of the other classes that the whole set-up represents a closely woven net and reciprocal aspect. One class cannot exist

*peacefully, cannot live happily and cannot work without the support
and good wishes of the other....*

*Remember, Maalik.... The thing which should most gladden the
heart of a ruler is the fact that his State is being ruled on the principles
of equity and justice and that his subjects love him. And your subjects
will only love you when they have no grievance against you. Their sincerity and loyalty will be proved if they gather around you to support
your government, when they accept your authority without considering
it an unbearable burden on their heads and when they do not secretly
wish your rule to come to an end. So let them have as many justifiable
hopes in you as they can and fulfill as many as you reasonably can.
Speak well of those who deserve your praise. Appreciate the good deeds
done by them and let these good actions be known publicly.*

SUCCESSION STRUGGLES in the early caliphate will do more
than create the great schism in Islam between Sunni and Shiite. The contest will bring to a temporary close their progressive models of leadership
and consensus-based experiment in selecting the caliph.

The first four caliphs—Abu Bakr, Umar, Uthman, and Ali—have been
chosen by a process somewhere between acclamation and election, though
it could be said that the followers of Ali are more loyal to a hereditary
model of leadership and that is part of the reason they split into this faction.
This early arrangement, partly grounded in the teachings and examples set
by the Prophet, coupled with political improvisation after his death, will
only last 29 years. The memory of that brief taste of Muslim consultation
and consensus will endure for 1,400 years, having impact on the eventual
development of a form of 20th-century Islamic democracy.

But as in all parts of the world until perhaps the 18th century in Europe,
Byzantium, China, the Mongol states, and the Americas, the outward
Muslim political model will be more like a military-theocratic rule, blended
with dynastic succession. And even that will be muddied when dominant
military powers like the Seljuks wield real control under the nominal leadership of the Abbasids.

The first caliph to take power by force will be the Umayyad Muyawiya
in 661. His heirs will rule until overthrown by the Abbasids in 750. And
the Abbasids will rule until decimated by the Mongols in 1258. The

Umayyads in Spain will replicate this dynastic model, as will the Fatimids and Mamelukes in Egypt, the Seljuks in Persia and the Middle East, the Mughals in India. The last Muslim rulers to assume the title of Caliphs of Islam will be the Ottoman Turks in Istanbul.

The political leadership will resemble traditional dynastic rule, and as is the case elsewhere in the world, there will be no lack of leaders who abuse their near-absolute power. But as counterpoint, all sorts of progressive methods and policies will surface from time to time.

The Umayyads in Damascus will be very much concerned about building public infrastructure, economic prosperity, and a unified state. The usurping Abbasids in Baghdad will do everything they can to create the political, artistic, financial, and intellectual center of the world. And though they rule by force and inheritance, they will not be blind to the methods of benign and enlightened rule. In Spain, seeing the enlightened achievements of the Abbasids, the Andalusian Umayyads will try to compete on nearly every level with Baghdad.

IT IS A LATE EVENING IN BAGHDAD in the year 801, and two men dressed as desert caravan traders slip into the streets. A full moon hangs over the city, and the smells of the river come up, borne on the breezes of a hot summer night. As the two men pass, the dinners of the rich are in full swing, with guards and horsemen waiting outside closed gates. The story houses are packed with audiences low and high, howling to bawdy tales, quietly dabbing at tears to hear a scriptural story brought to life. The taverns are crowded, loud laughter and shouting pouring from within, and an occasional inebriate stumbles out onto the street.

A shouted political argument catches the attention of one of the two men, and hearing his name in the stream of words, he pauses just outside the lighted doorway but within earshot.

"I tell you, we've been given over to the Persians," shouts one barfly. "They run the court, they run the country."

"Persians are smart people," shouts his antagonist. "We need them."

"They need us more," answers the first. "The great Arab armies conquered them. We need to remind them of that."

Outside in the darkness, the first listener turns to the second and winks. The pair make their way toward the riverbanks and the central souk, the market. The first man, dressed as a commoner and with his face nearly covered, is the caliph himself, Haroun al-Rashid. The other in disguise is his childhood friend Jaffar, son of the grand vizier of the Barmakid family.

Down along the perimeters of the souk, many shopkeepers are still at their stalls lit by candle and oil lamp, selling incense and perfumes and fabrics, spices and jewelry, and little bound volumes of poetry and fable. The disguised caliph stops at one shop, where an Arab vendor with deep-set darting eyes sits among his collection of polished daggers from Syria.

"How much for that one?" the disguised Haroun al-Rashid asks, pointing to one with a black leather sheath.

"A dirham," says the vendor.

"My God, man," says the caliph. "That much?"

"Are you from around here?"

"We are from ... Medina."

The man nods slowly, not entirely convinced.

"Then you don't know," he says. "I must pay my taxes, which only go up. I must pay my protection to the police and constables. I must pay the landlord for this shop, and he keeps jacking up the rent. So one dirham is a bargain."

"Are your taxes high?"

"Ha," the vendor chokes, shaking his head. "Do you see these fancy bridges, the walls, the palaces? And the caliph is building another, full of silver and gold. What was wrong with grandfather al-Mansur's palace? Not good enough? And who gets taxed?"

The caliph is listening, as is his friend.

"And you must pay protection to the police?" the caliph asks.

"Not only the police. I mean from Lord Judge Asad on down, every little secretary and minion in the government that I ever need to go to. They are bleeding me, I tell you. Bleeding me!"

"What do you think should be done?" asks Haroun al-Rashid.

"I think his royal majesty should get off his duff and come out here with us common people. See what is being done in his name. Listen to the people. At least show his face. For all we know the country is being run by lackeys."

"What do you think of the caliph?" asks al-Rashid.

"How would I know? I've never laid eyes on him. But I hear tell he is much in love with the ladies and the bottle. Lots of wine drinking, you know." He imitates a drunk, rolling his eyes, letting his mouth hang open. All three of them laugh.

The caliph pulls out a gold dirham, one just struck a few days before, and passes it to the man. The man, surprised at its shine, bites it, holds it to the light.

"This is a nice one," he says. The two men go back out into the night.

Back at the palace in the morning, the caliph with Jaffar at his side calls in his vizier.

"Who is police constable over by the souk?"

"I will find out, my caliph."

"And get me the name of every officer in that district, from Asad on down. I'm hearing they are on the take."

"As you command."

"And the tax structure. When did we last revise it?"

"Last year, caliph. To cover the extra expenditures, the new palace, the hospital."

"I want to take another look."

And then, in the bright light of midmorning, dressed in his caliphal robes and with his royal sword on his belt, al-Rashid goes with Jaffar into the courtyard where they call for horses and guards. Mounted on his white Arabian mare, the caliph leads his procession back to the souk, coming into full daylight on Baghdad public streets for the first time in a year. Crowds in the street pull back, a few citizens shout from upper windows, and the caliph waves to them.

The caliph draws up in front of the dagger shop. The dark-eyed vendor is so stunned that he cannot get up from his stool, so he just sits there holding a cup of tea halfway to his lips.

"Is it still true that the caliph never shows his face, and you have never laid eyes on him?" calls al-Rashid. The man drops his cup and throws himself prostrate, thinking he is about to be beheaded for his impertinence. But instead of threatening him, the caliph reaches into his saddlebag and pulls out a sack of gold dirhams, a hundred times what he paid the man before, and throws it to him. The man can barely look up.

"Never be afraid to speak the truth to the caliph," says al-Rashid, laughing. Then he and his entourage continue on along the riverbanks to see how the latest bridge project is going.

It is a good ten minutes before the knife-seller can even get his breath, much less stand up and think about counting his new riches. His neighbors come over and crowd around him.

THE CHARACTER OF Haroun al-Rashid has been much romanticized in legend; he is even a central character in many later editions of the tales of *The Thousand and One Nights*. But aside from that, lost history shows that he is best remembered as the role model of a progressive Muslim ruler. Not only is he militarily strong, charismatic, and clever; he is also wise and intellectually curious. He is a patron of the arts, of scientific and mathematical research, supporting many of the translation projects that will be formalized by his son al-Mamun in the House of Wisdom. He endows the first hospital in Baghdad. He supports the research of chemist Jabir ibn Haiyan, the first major translation of Indian and Greek philosophical and scientific texts, and the collection of foreign original texts including Indian mathematical treatises that will one day inspire al-Khwarizmi.

Al-Rashid's personal interests are music, poetry, and the arts. With the vast monetary tributes he receives from vassals and opponents including the Byzantines, he lays the foundation for the golden age of Baghdad.

Writing a century and a half later, the Baghdad historian al-Masudi narrates the following anecdotes about al-Rashid in *The Book of Golden Meadows*:

One day the Caliph gave a feast in a magnificently decorated hall. During the feast he sent for the poet Abu'l Atahiyah, and commanded him to depict in verse the gorgeous scene. The poet began: 'Live, O Caliph, in the fulfillment of all thy desire, in the shelter of thy lofty palace!' 'Very good!' exclaimed Rashid. 'Let us hear the rest.'

The poet continued: 'Each morn and eve be all thy servitors swift to execute thy behests.' 'Excellent!' said the Caliph. 'Go on!' The poet replied: 'But when the death-rattle chokes thy breath thou wilt learn, alas! that all thy delights were a shadow.' Rashid burst into tears. Fadhl, the son of Yahya (al-Rashid's Vizier), seeing this, said to the poet: 'The Caliph sent for you to divert him, and you have plunged him into melancholy.' 'Let him be,' said al-Rashid, 'he saw us in a state of blindness and tried to open our eyes.'

This Prince treated learned men with great regard. Abou Moawia, one of the most learned men of his time, related that when he was sitting one day at food with the Caliph, the latter poured water on his hands after the meal, and said to him: 'Abou Moawia, do you know who has just washed your hands?' He answered: 'No.' Rashid informed him that it was himself. Abou Moawia replied: 'Prince, you doubtless act in this manner in order to do homage to learning.' 'You speak truth,' answered Rashid.

Stories about the grandeur and intellect of al-Rashid's court circulate widely in his time. Not only does he have diplomatic relations with faraway places such as China and the court of Charlemagne, he begins a lengthy long-distance dialogue with Charlemagne that has much more impact on the Franks than it does on the Arabs.

Even as they are drafting the latest messages from the caliph to the Frankish emperor, the Baghdad diplomats sniff that while their own powerful leader is also a man of learning and a poet, they wonder if Charlemagne can even read and write. The truth is not so black and white: Though Charlemagne is, indeed, illiterate, he supports scholars and hires tutors.

Their two courts even plan on a summit meeting to be held in the early ninth century, but it never happens. The next best thing is an exchange of gifts in 801, when al-Rashid sends Charlemagne tribute the likes of which have not been seen in Europe. Al-Rashid gives him an elephant named Abul Abbas, and the large animal is led through the streets of Charlemagne's capital, Aix-la-Chapelle, causing a major commotion. Elephants haven't been in Europe since Hannibal's crossing of the Alps a thousand years before.

Al-Rashid also sends Charlemagne a carved ivory horn, a tray, and a pitcher of solid gold, a chess set, a royal tent, a pair of brass candlesticks, and an intricate water clock. The clock captivates all who see it. This technical wonder generates major discussions among the European thinkers of the day: It has 12 brass balls that mark the hour by falling on a cymbal and 12 carved horsemen, who parade out of little windows.

There is little doubt that Charlemagne's exposure to such a powerful and enlightened ruler shows him an ideal of leadership that exists nowhere in Europe, except in historical accounts of Greece and Rome. Even as

Charlemagne struggles to push the Muslims deeper into Spain by sheer force of arms, he is fascinated by their technological and social advances.

A parallel model of liberal Muslim rule will be emerging almost simultaneously in al-Andalus. The example of Andalusian religious tolerance and benign populist authoritarianism will reach back to the founding Umayyad, Abd al-Rahman I. But such notions will become more explicit in 796, when the aging Umayyad Emir Hashem asks his officials to swear loyalty to his son and successor al-Hakem. He will instruct his son as follows:

> *Dispense justice without distinction between the poor and the rich, be kind and gentle to those dependent upon thee, for all alike are the creatures of God. Entrust the keeping of thy cities and provinces to loyal and experienced chieftains; chastise without pity ministers who oppress thy subjects; govern thy soldiers with moderation and firmness; remember that arms are given them to defend, not to devastate their country; and be careful always that they are regularly paid and that they may ever rely on thy promises. Strive to make thyself beloved by the people, for in their affection is the security of the state, in their fear is danger, in their hatred is certain ruin. Protect those who cultivate the fields and furnish the bread that sustains us; do not permit their harvests to be injured, or their forests to be destroyed. Act in all respects so thy subjects may bless thee and live in happiness under thy protection, and thus, in no other way, will thou obtain the renown of the most glorious prince.*

Unfortunately, al-Hakem, once in power, will waste no time in heading for the harem and the wine cellar, forgetting everything his father had taught him. He will have a fairly short and decadent life. The more responsible and progressive style of his father will return with later Andalusian rulers.

But the authoritarian model and lack of checks on imperial power, when coupled with the fabulous wealth of the caliphs and Muslim ruling classes, will always provide a temptation for weak and despotic rulers. It will be up to honorable and enlightened rulers to police themselves, rather than to laws and external bodies. Sometimes it will work, and sometimes not. Yet the ideal of fair and compassionate leadership will always be there for good leaders to follow.

The Umayyads and Abbasids will not be the only ones to espouse an ideal of good government. The Seljuk Turks who assume the political power under the weak Abbasids in the tenth century will continue the tradition. One of the exemplary political thinkers is grand vizier Nizam al-Mulk, friend of Omar Khayyám and later vizier to Sultan Malik Shah.

Nizam al-Mulk will ensure that knowledge and education are critical parts of good governance and a healthy society by creating the religious universities across the Seljuk domain in Persia and the Middle East that come to be named for him. The Nizamiya, with their atmosphere of inquiry and debate within a fairly loose religious context, will be viewed by many scholars as predecessors to modern Western universities. The Nizamiya will be there to be seen by the waves of Christian crusaders coming to the holy land beginning in the early 11th century; nothing like them yet exists in Europe, where education is still dependent on closed monastic orders.

Even the sultan will question the cost of funding so many universities, thinking the money better spent on building fortifications or hiring more troops. Al-Mulk is reported to have replied:

> *The educational fortress I have built for you will defy the ravages of time and prove unbreakable. The arrows of soldiers will not travel beyond 100 yards. The arrows of the army, which I have created, will ascend into heaven itself and render your name imperishable.*

On the theoretical level, al-Mulk will make another contribution to good leadership and government. In his years of traveling the empire and listening to the citizens and officials on behalf of the sultan, he will begin to formulate a massive tome on how to rule well. It will be called the *Siyasatnama*, or *Book of Government*, written in his native Persian. In 50 chapters, the *Siyasatnama* will set out innumerable parameters and aphorisms on good government:

> *A kingdom may last while there is irreligion, but it will not endure when there is oppression.*
> *When the king sits in a place protected by doors, gates, locks, vestibules, screens and chamberlains, self-interested and oppressive persons can keep people back and not let them go before the king.*

Tax collectors ... must be instructed ... to take only the due amount ... with civility and courtesy ... and not until the time comes.

The best of rulers is he who keeps the company of men of learning, and the worst of learned men is he who seeks the society of the king.

Knowledge is better than wealth, because you must take care of wealth but knowledge takes care of you.

EVEN AS THE INK IS DRYING on al-Mulk's treatise for good government, a millennial military struggle will take shape that will suggest to many of the faithful that maybe Malik Shah's spending priorities were right to begin with: Muslims of the 11th century need not so much education and good government as more armies and fortresses.

This struggle will be the first in three centuries of violent shocks that will upend every region from Turkey to Syria to Egypt. This contest is known as the Crusades. Seen from high above and afar, the Crusades will seem to bring to the fore the primal military-religious struggle seen at Tours in the eighth century.

For some 200 years the Crusades from the late 11th to the early 13th century, consisting of nine major Christian campaigns and several lesser ones, are often depicted as "reverse jihad" by the Christians to evict the Muslims from Jerusalem and the lands of early Christian origin. These lands have been under Muslim control since the time of the first caliphs in the seventh century. They have had four centuries of Muslim rule. Twenty generations of life, in which the three Abrahamic faiths have managed to coexist under Muslim control. Christians have been going on pilgrimages to Jerusalem all this time. Jews are present everywhere.

But times are changing. As the Seljuks, Ayyubids, and Fatimids jockey for Muslim power, and Byzantium shrivels to a tiny enclave on the Anatolian coast, the Europeans sense an opportunity.

They are emboldened by the gradual Christian reconquest of Spain. And they are enraged by the inexplicable decision of Fatimid Sultan al-Hakim to destroy the Church of the Holy Sepulchre in Jerusalem. Emperor Constantine built the church in 330 to commemorate the hill of the crucifixion and the tomb of Christ's burial.

This new Christian version of holy war—which generates major debates in Rome as to how it is at all compatible with the pacifist teachings of Jesus—will finally be approved by the Western Church.

But when seen from up close and through the lens of lost history, these politico-religious struggles will be much more nuanced. They will be complicated by the fact that in 1054 the Christian Church is once and for all splitting into Roman Catholic faith in Rome and Eastern Orthodox faith in Constantinople. The Roman Catholics will want to evict not only Muslim power from the holy cities but also Orthodox Byzantine power.

The wars will be further complicated by the strange alliances that occur. The crusaders will make common cause with the Mongols against the Muslims. The Byzantines will side with their old enemies the Muslims. And the Christian Knights Templar will make common cause with the Syrian Ismailis.

To further complicate things, even as many of the crusaders win their initial battles and temporarily take back Jerusalem and other cities in Palestine and Syria, they will be forever changed by the experience. Many European warriors will settle down in the Levant and some will be granted huge estates. They will like the warmer, drier weather, and they will fall under the spell of a more refined, exotic, and comfortable lifestyle.

The earlier Crusades will be marked by Christian military inroads and victories, including the fall of Jerusalem to the Christians in 1099. With many details regrettably lost to history, this European victory in Jerusalem will be marred by an outburst of European butchery directed at just about all the inhabitants of old Jerusalem. Muslims, Jews, and even Christians, are all seen as the enemy. En route to the Middle East, the Christians will even conduct periodic persecutions of Jews along the way.

One Frankish account describes the crusader slaughter of the people of Jerusalem in 1099 this way:

> *Count Raymond and his men, who were attacking the wall on the other side ... saw the Saracens leap from the wall in front of them. Forthwith, they joyfully rushed into the city to pursue and kill the nefarious enemies, as their comrades were already doing. Some Saracens, Arabs, and Ethiopians took refuge in the tower of David, others fled to the temples of the Lord and of Solomon. A great fight took place in the court and porch of the temples, where they were unable to escape from our gladiators. Many fled to the roof of the temple of Solomon and were shot with arrows so that they fell to the ground dead. In this temple almost*

ten thousand were killed. Indeed, if you had been there you would have seen our feet colored to our ankles with the blood of the slain. But what more shall I relate? None of them were left alive; neither women nor children were spared.

Another French account is even more graphic:

On the conquest of Jerusalem by the Christians in 1099 the Saracens were massacred in the streets and in the houses. Jerusalem had no refuge for the vanquished. Some fled from death by precipitating themselves from the ramparts; others crowded for shelter into the palaces, the towers and above all, in the mosques where they could not conceal themselves from the Christians. The Crusaders, masters of the Mosque of Umar, where the Saracens defended themselves for some time, renewed their deplorable scenes, which disgraced the conquest of Titus. The infantry and the cavalry rushed pell-mell among the fugitives. Amid the most horrid tumult, nothing was heard but the groans and cries of death; the victors trod over heaps of corpses in pursuing those who vainly attempted to escape. Raymond d'Agiles who was an eye-witness, says that under the portico of the mosque, the blood was knee-deep, and reached the horses' bridles.

There was a short lull in the act of slaughter when the Crusaders assembled to offer their thanksgiving prayer for the victory they had achieved. But soon it was renewed with great ferocity. All the captives, says Michaud, whom the lassitude of carnage had at first spared, all those who had been saved in the hope of rich ransom, were butchered in cold blood. The Saracens were forced to throw themselves from the tops of towers and houses; they were burnt alive; they were dragged from their subterranean retreats, they were hauled to the public places, and immolated on piles of the dead. Neither the tears of women nor the cries of little children—not even the sight of the place where Jesus Christ forgave his executioners, could mollify the victors' passion .... The carnage lasted for a week. The few who escaped were reduced to horrible servitude.

Aside from the slaughter, the Christian reconquest will be marked by old-fashioned pillaging and raping. The Europeans will even rob rich

Christian churches. The victorious European commanders will squabble among themselves over the booty.

The deliberate European slaughter of innocents and noncombatants of all faiths in Jerusalem will number in the thousands. The event will reverberate throughout the Middle East, helping fuel a reinvigorated Muslim effort to resist; it will take them nearly a century to rebuild their power.

In the meantime, the Christians will establish their own Latin Kingdom in Jerusalem and other strongholds in Syria and Palestine. Lines will begin to blur. Enemies will gradually become uneasy neighbors.

This period of turmoil will give rise to a new Muslim leader, a deeply religious military man. He will not have the intellect of al-Rashid and al-Mamun, nor al-Hakim in Cairo or Abd al-Rahman III in Cordoba, but he will come to embody a kind of chivalric Muslim honor that will astonish and embarrass the Europeans, who will begin to whisper that their enemy is so good and decent because he has "European" blood.

His name is Saladin. And like al-Rashid, the stories about him will be enveloped in romance and legend, but his basic decency and humane rule in the face of much provocation is real and exemplary.

Saladin is a Kurd, raised and educated in Syria. His father is a military man. And they both conclude that the only way the Muslims can resist this Christian onslaught is to unite all the fighting factions of the Muslims. Saladin will be the one to pull off this feat.

He will get his chance at revenge in 1187, when after many years of struggle, he and his armies surround Jerusalem to recapture it and destroy the Christian Kingdom. And when the moment of victory comes, and the crescent and star are once again raised above the city walls, everyone, including many of his own troops, expect him to exact the brutal tit-for-tat. Heads must roll; blood must flow.

Except… as ibn al-Athir relates after the battles for Jerusalem:

When the Franks saw how violently the Muslims were attacking, how continuous and effective was the fire from the ballistas and how busily the sappers were breaching the walls, meeting no resistance, they grew desperate, and their leaders assembled to take counsel. They decided to ask for safe-conduct out of the city and to hand Jerusalem over to

Saladin. They sent a deputation of their lords and nobles to ask for terms, but when they spoke of it to Saladin he refused to grant their request. 'We shall deal with you,' he said, 'just as you dealt with the population of Jerusalem when you took it in 1099, with murder and enslavement and other such savageries.' The messengers returned empty-handed. Then Balian ibn Barzan asked for safe conduct for himself so that he might appear before Saladin to discuss developments. Consent was given, and he presented himself and once again began asking for a general amnesty in return for surrender. The Sultan still refused his requests and entreaties to show mercy. Finally, despairing of this approach, Balian said: 'Know, O Sultan that there are very many of us in this city, God alone knows how many. At the moment we are fighting half-heartedly in the hope of saving our lives, hoping to be spared by you as you have spared others; this is because of the nature of horror of death and our love for life. But if we see that death is inevitable, then by God we shall kill our children and our wives, burn our possessions, so as not to leave you with a dinar or a drachma or a single man or woman to enslave. When this is done, we shall pull down the Sanctuary of the Rock and the Masjid al-Aqsa and the other sacred places, slaughtering the Muslim prisoners we hold—5,000 of them—and killling every horse and animal we possess. Then we shall come out to fight you like men fighting for their lives, when each man, before he falls dead, kills his equal; we shall die with honour, or win a noble victory!'

Then Saladin took council with his advisors, all of whom were in favor of granting the assurances requested by the Franks, without forcing them to take extreme measures whose outcome could not be foreseen. 'Let us consider them as being already our prisoners,' they said, 'and allow them to ransom themselves on terms agreed between us.' The Sultan agreed to give the Franks assurances of safety on the understanding that each man, rich and poor alike, should pay ten dinar, children of both sexes two dinar and women five dinar. All who paid this sum within forty days should go free, and those who had not paid at the end of the time should be enslaved. Balian ibn Barzan offered 30,000 dinar as ransom for the poor, which was accepted, and the city surrendered on Friday 2 October 1187, a memorable day on which the Muslim flags were hoisted over the walls of Jerusalem.

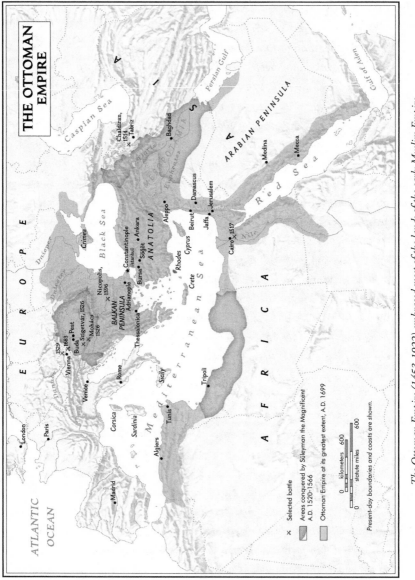

THE OTTOMAN EMPIRE

× Selected battle

Areas conquered by Süleyman the Magnificent
A.D. 1520–1566

Ottoman Empire at its greatest extent, A.D. 1699

Present-day boundaries and coasts are shown.

The Ottoman Empire (1453–1922) embraced most of the lands of the early Muslim Empire,
with the exception of Spain and Morocco, but with the addition of the Balkans.

The Grand Patriarch of the Franks left the city with the treasures from the Dome of the Rock, the Masjud al-Aqsa, the Church of the Resurrection and others, God alone knows the amount of treasure; he also took an equal quantity of money. Saladin made no difficulties, and when he was advised to sequestrate the whole lot for Islam, replied that he would not go back on his word. He took only ten dinar from him, and let him go, heavily escorted, to Tyre. . .

Once the city was taken and the infidels had left, Saladin ordered that the shrines should be restored to their original state. The Templars had built their living quarters against al-Aqsa, with store-rooms and latrines and other necessary offices, taking up part of the area of al-Aqsa. This was all restored to its former state. The Sultan ordered that the Dome of the Rock be cleansed of all pollution, and this was done.

At the moment of truth, Saladin does take Jerusalem for his own and for Islam, but he does not exact vengeance.

He allows the departing Christians—100,000 of them, to be exact—one month to depart. They must pay a departure tax. They can take their possessions with them, including those very wealthy nobles who have homes overflowing with art and jewels. These people, the descendants of those who executed the slaughter of 1099, will get nothing worse than exile.

When about 30,000 poorer Christians come up short with their departure tax and cannot pay, rumors abound. They will be enslaved, they will be killed, and they will be forced into conversion.

Saladin's advisors point out that the departing Christian Patriarch Heraclius has more than enough wealth to ransom all the remaining Christians. Why not make him pay for them? But Saladin refuses, and to pay the bill, he, his brother, and brother-in-law pay out of their own pockets. He allows Heraclius to depart with all his wealth and icons.

These acts in themselves would be notable. But a second round occurs in 1192, when the most famous of the Christian crusaders, Richard the Lionhearted, returns to try to recapture the city. Despite a valiant effort, the campaign is stalemated. And then begins perhaps the most unexpected friendship in the history of warfare. Just like al-Rashid and Charlemagne, Saladin and Richard become long-distance admirers. Though battle brings them within a few hundred yards of one another, they never actually meet. But they begin to try to outdo each other in generous and honorable acts.

When Richard falls sick at the siege of Acre in 1192, Saladin not only sends his personal physician Maimonides over to treat him, he sends ice to help him fight the fevers and certain healing fruits. When Richard's horse is killed during battle, and the English king finds himself on foot facing the entire Muslim army, the Muslims let him walk by their entire phalanx without attacking. Later, Saladin sends him two fresh mounts so he will not be at a disadvantage.

Finally Richard must abandon his crusade, based on rumors that rivals are plotting against him back home in England. The longer he stays in the holy land, the more he risks losing his throne. Saladin allows him to withdraw honorably, signaling the last serious effort to recover Jerusalem. The Crusades will sputter out a few decades later, even as the Mongols bear down on Khorasan and Baghdad.

Long after these and other chivalric gestures, the French historian René Grousset will write of Saladin:

> It is equally true that his generosity, his piety, devoid of fanaticism, that flower of liberality and courtesy, which had been the model of our old chroniclers, won him no less popularity in Frankish Syria than in the lands of Islam.

But an even greater testimonial will come from one of the finest European poets of the 13th century, writing only decades after the failed crusader struggle for Jerusalem. When his *Divine Comedy* ranks, through devoutly Christian eyes, the preeminent figures of history, Dante will distinguish between Christians and non-Christians. No pagan can rise to the highest level. Pagan Greek and Roman figures like Homer and Plato and Caesar will be placed in limbo. But Saladin will be ranked all by himself, in a special category, called "Great-Hearted Souls," by virtue of his noble gestures and policies during the Muslim rollback of crusader power in the Middle East.

EVEN AS THE CRUSADES stall and falter, a new Muslim entity is established far to the southeast. Established by Central Asian Turkic warriors sweeping into India, the Sultanate of Delhi rises in the early 13th century, lasting from 1206 to 1526. And though the sultanate will one day be eclipsed in the Muslim history of India by the Mughals, a most unusual leader of progressive bent will arise in early Muslim Delhi from 1236-1240.

Her name is Razia Sultana. When her aging father, Sultan Iltutmish, looks to the future, he thinks about royal succession. He knows his most talented son has already died in battle. He knows his other sons are incompetent at best. And then there is his daughter Razia. She is smarter than all the boys and just as good a warrior. He has often left her in charge of the court while he is off in battle; he wouldn't think of doing that with any of his sons. Though it is unorthodox, when he looks at choosing between leaving his legacy to incompetents and leaving it to Razia, he chooses her.

But after Iltutmish's death, an ambitious brother named Firuz seizes power, and Razia must concede. For seven months Firuz indulges in a binge of partying and spending while the sultanate drifts, until finally the citizens of Delhi rise up and demand that Razia be returned to the throne. Faced with open rebellion, Firuz abdicates.

Even though she has the people's support, Razia faces enemies on all sides, and there are many who disparage her womanhood. The disenfranchised Turkic nobles are just waiting for her to make a mistake, and her brothers plot in the wings. To rule, she trusts none of her family or the noble class, but instead comes to rely on an Ethiopian slave named Jalal-ud-Din Yaqut. He becomes her closest advisor, maybe more.

To consolidate her bonds with the people, Razia holds open meetings with her citizens to allow complaints and petitions to be brought directly to her. She dresses like a man, wearing either armor or a tunic and a man's headdress. She promotes commerce, builds infrastructure such as highways and wells, and plants trees to add greenery and cut wind erosion.

Then she tries to ease discrimination against her Hindu subjects. Now her enemies, all of her own religion and ethnicity, see their chance. A governor named Malik Altunia rises up and defeats Razia's army, and her Ethiopian advisor is killed. Razia is forced to marry Altunia, and together they rule under his direction. Soon one of her brothers rebels, and both Razia and her husband are killed. She is 35 years old when she dies. Her short life and career have been one cliffhanger after another.

For a time it will seem as though her rule was an aberration, never to be repeated.

And though it will be centuries before another Indian woman has her kind of political power, a strain of empowered women will begin to emerge under the Indian Muslims. More often than not these women will be royal wives and daughters, but through their access to power, they will wield indirect power. And one day, in the distant 20th century, two women will finally rule the two successor states to ancient India—Hindu Indira Gandhi in secular India and Muslim Benazir Bhutto in Muslim Pakistan. And a third woman, Sonia Gandhi, not even born in India, will be a serious presidential candidate.

Though all these women enter power by being daughters or wives of famous politicians, they will be able to hold direct power. What is there buried in the ways of India that empowers women so?

IN ABOUT 1580, the Mughal padshah, Akbar of India, sits on his throne in Agra, listening to the latest of a series of theological and doctrinal presentations. He is the first of the Mughals to be born on Indian soil, ascending to the throne when he was still a child and depending on several regents until he was old enough to rule. Confident of his military and political supremacy, the ruler wants to use his power to make India a stronger, fairer, more unified nation in this land of a hundred tongues, a thousand gods, and traditions that have been around for thousands of years.

Now 50 years old, not only does Akbar rule, he theorizes, he invents on a grand scale, he tries some of the greatest social experiments in history. He rules over 140 million people, in a time when England has about 5 million and all of Europe barely 40 million.

A group of Portuguese Jesuit priests have been invited from the coastal colony of Goa by the Muslim ruler to make their best case for Christianity. It is hot and crowded in the throne room. The sun outside is broiling. The padshah is being cooled with fans of peacock feathers. As the Portuguese drone on, whispers and gasps run through the audience.

The Jesuits make their erudite argument that leads to their inevitable conclusion in favor of Christianity, and Akbar is listening and dissecting what they say. In this same series of discussions and debates he has also heard theologians of Zoroastrianism, Sikhism, Jainism, and mainstream Hinduism.

One group has been conspicuously excluded: his own Sunni Muslim *ulema,* or religious scholars. They are livid, on the verge of declaring Akbar a heretic. In the shadows of the courtroom, some of their proxies are listening, horrified.

Akbar the Great does not care about their hissing. He considers himself a conservative, devout Muslim. His closest advisor is Abul Fazl, a Shiite historian. Between the two of them, they are thinking about religion and society with an open mind, going into areas where many have feared to tread.

In a country where most Muslims are Sunni, Shiite Abul Fazl proposes a uniquely Shiite concept of the imamate that shows echoes of Greece and Plato: a vision of a righteous Muslim realm guided by a righteous and wise philosopher-king, the imam. The Sunni scholars are upset at this potential glorification of the political ruler, thinking it heretical. What to do?

But Akbar is not afraid to be a change agent, even in matters of faith. After seven centuries of Muslim rulers imposing the *jizya,* or poll tax, on non-Muslims around the world, Akbar has done away with the tax on other religions. He has allowed the Hindus to travel freely to their shrines and has abolished the tax on their pilgrimages. And to make up the difference in revenue, rather than tax the production of poor and powerless people, he has started to apply the tax to everyone, nobles included. The nobles are stunned, but in the face of popular support for Akbar, they comply.

Akbar has done more. To knit his largely Hindu country together, he has married the daughters of almost every king and prince and sultan on the subcontinent so that he has nearly 5,000 wives of all creeds and ethnicities. His favorite wife is Amber, a Hindu princess of Rajasthan. Not only does he let her keep her faith, he allows her to practice in the Mughal palace in Agra.

Akbar has also been the first Mughal to bestow titles and nobility on non-Muslims. Fully one third of his noble appointments are Hindus. More than that, he is the first Mughal ruler to immerse himself in the various non-Muslim beliefs and practices of his people. He finds it all quite fascinating.

Sitting there that hot afternoon, listening to the Portuguese, he returns to an idea that has been simmering in his mind for months. Since religion is so often a point of social conflict, what if all these religions could be combined? Since they all seem to worship the same God and have the same general ethos of love and compassion, expressed in admittedly different ways, why focus on the differences? Why not bring them all together under the general structure of Islam? But throw in a few things like Zoroastrian worship of the sun.

I will call this religion Din-e-Ilahi, the Divine Faith, whispers Akbar to Fazl. His advisor nods.

And so the order goes forth: Din-e-Ilahi will be the new faith of the land of India. Largely based on Islam, the new religion will make nods to all those other faiths that it incorporates, and it will be enshrined in a new capital city called Fatehpur Sikri with palaces and temples to the new combined faith.

His advisor Abul Fazl will write of Akbar's entry into his new capital in 1571:

> A breeze of joy comes from Fatehpur, for my King returns from a long journey. What bliss is his advent, for from every heart thousands of rejoicings come forth. On this day of joy the great officers, the loyal servants, and others were drawn up in two sides of the way for a distance of four kos from the city. The mountain-like elephants stood there in their majesty. The Khedive of the world proceeded on his way on a heaven-like elephant, attended by the 'Avaunt' of the Divine Halo. The obedient princes moved on in their order. Many grandees proceeded in front of the mace-bearers [yesawalan]. The panoply was there in its splendour and was followed by various officers. The noise of the drums and the melodies of the magician-like musicians gave forth news of joy. Crowds of men were gathered in astonishment on the roofs and at the doors. At the end of the day he sat in the lofty hall [daulatkhana] on the throne of sovereignty. He dispensed justice by rewarding the loyal and punishing the hostile and made the increase of dominion and success a vehicle for worship and supplication.

And so from that hot afternoon, the interfaith religious proselytizing campaign goes forth to all four corners of the empire. The theory is that by combining faiths of 140 million people, conflict can be ended.

Except… the campaign founders. What exactly is one supposed to believe in Din-e-Ilahi? There is much debate and confusion about the lack of detail such as ritual and dogma.

The traditional Sunni, even though the faith is in essence an expanded Islam, find it appallingly heretical. Many of them begin to support dissident and insurgent movements. All the believers of other faiths of India just sit and listen. Akbar is a great ruler, and he has done much to bring India together and to remove the sense of Muslim overlordship. But this new religion: Could he explain it once again?

And so Din-e-Ilahi will gradually fizzle out somewhere on the vast expanse of India, already dying while Akbar is still alive. It will be a memory after his death. Records show that a grand total of 18 people actually convert to the new faith, all members of Akbar's court.

Abul Fazl will write of the dying Akbar:

What a personality he was! He was pure from every stain and endowed with all perfections. What a jewel free from every blemish and pure of every stain! Lofty prestige, a happy horoscope, an awakened fortune, complete auspiciousness, a daily-increasing dominion, mounting victoriousness, pleasant friendship, a love of pleasantry, friend-cherishing, foe-destroying, a kingdom-bestowing liberality, a might that overthrew enemies, a world-embracing majesty, a world-conquering resolution, a firmness and gravity together with the working of conspicuous miracles, lofty converse, an illuminated mind, a God-given understanding, an enlightened soul, a taste for knowledge, an expounder of mysteries, and an opener of mysteries, conquest over difficulties, etc., etc.—all these were gathered together in that sublime personality and created astonishment among the lords of insight.

The scrutineers who counted all the perfections gave him the title of the Imam of the Age, He is the spiritual and temporal lord, the unique Akbar Shah, who made the poor, lords of fortune,

That elementary mould has gone, from whose spirit the pure-hearted gathered eternal truths.

As symbol of his noble failure to unite faith, Akbar's capital city of Fatehpur Sikri will be deserted within a few years of his death. For not only is the powerful energy and visionary charisma of Akbar gone from this world. There is not enough water to sustain life in Fatehpur Sikri; it literally dries up and becomes a shrine of the forgotten.

And for some centuries conservatives will say that Akbar the Great failed at his most ambitious test. Lord of the Indian earth, he could not master the multifaceted Indian soul. For several centuries Akbar's sweeping reforms and intellectual laboratory will seem like esoteric ancient history, when India is under the English overlords, and her wealth is carried off to fund the global dominance of the British Empire.

But four centuries later, secular, democratic India will look like a modern version of the inclusive dream of Akbar, even the tolerant dream of Sultana Razia. The many faiths of India will not be united, and they will not be above conflict. But they will coexist. The minority Muslims of India will hold many leadership positions, just as the Hindus did under Akbar. And they will coexist in a secular state that respects individual faith but in public matters stand apart from all.

It is hard to be ahead of one's time. But it does not mean you are forever lost to history.

In the 15th and 16th centuries, the afternoon and night of classical Muslim history are now rushing forward, the deepening shadows, the enveloping melancholy, the glorious chronicles of the past seeming to be greater than anything that could come in the future.

The power of Damascus, Baghdad, al-Andalus, and Khorasan are long gone, never to be regained. Though the passage of time and the aging of a civilization cannot be ignored, one group of Muslims will make a valiant last effort.

These Muslims are the Ottoman Turks. Much of the world will tremble at their power. A thousand years after that first glorious engulfment of the world by the Arab armies, the Ottoman Turks will more than match their achievement. After the fall of Baghdad and Cordoba, the Turks will rebuild the entire Arab empire, lacking only al-Andalus. But they will make up for the loss of Spain by engulfing the Balkans and Romania up to the southern border of Poland. Their capital will not be Baghdad, but Istanbul, and they will forever and totally remove once proud Byzantium from the map.

Ultimately embracing three continents from their capital on the Bosporus, the Turks spring from the far distant reaches of Siberia and arrive in Turkey after a centuries-long journey of extended conquest and pillaging, beginning at the very gates of ancient China, where they were known by their Chinese name *Tu K'ue*, a name that has stayed with them all these years and miles and language shifts.

But the Turks are not only about power. Though they will be most remembered for their ability to create an empire that lasts for 600 years right up to the 20th century, at their best they will also be about religious diversity and inclusion, merit over privilege, and fairness.

It is 1492; from the docks of Istanbul—only 40 years after the fall of Constantinople to the Turks—a small foreign ship is seen coming into the harbor.

A delegation of Sultan Bayezid II stands on the docks to welcome the arrival. The delegation is headed by the grand vizier and assorted other representatives of the sultan's court. It would seem that this ship is carrying a foreign delegation, representatives of an allied or friendly or important government. Who could the visitors be?

But as the ship comes into view and the passengers on deck come into clearer definition, it is apparent that they are probably not ambassadors. These men on the ship wear skullcaps and dark beards and are dressed in a Biblical way that suggests refugees from time, ancient wise men. Their faces are sunburned but betraying a terrible melancholy, a melancholy at the thought of a loss that can never be regained.

These arrivals are refugees, and they have lost much. They have lost an entire homeland, an entire history. They have accepted the invitation of Turkish refuge.

These are the Sephardic Jews of al-Andalus, the last Jews of Granada, Cordoba, Seville, Toledo, and Madrid, once part of the heart and mind of the great tri-religious state, the last citizens of dying Sefarad, expelled by the treachery of Isabella. Rather than accept Catholic conversion or death, they have come here at the sultan's invitation to make a new home.

The Jews' new home, Istanbul, though in Turkish Muslim hands, also has tens of thousands of Orthodox Christians; in fact, it is the seat of the Orthodox Patriarchate. Istanbul has Jews from earlier migrations and holds many sects of Islam. Ottoman Turkey is one of the last incarnations of the sweet coexistence of many faiths that has flourished at times throughout the Muslim world.

Not that Turkey is the only land of Muslim tolerance. Between the 15th and 16th centuries, Jews and Christians live all over the Muslim world. Large minorities of Christians remain in Egypt, Iraq, Syria, and India. Large Jewish communities thrive in the cities of Morocco and all across North Africa in Egypt and Iran.

But in Ottoman Turkey, tolerance and coexistence are not just quiet unofficial policies. They are loud and explicit. As the sultan's edict reads, Turkish governors are not "to refuse the Jews entry or cause them difficulties, but to receive them cordially."

ONLY 60 YEARS after the arrival of the Jews in Istanbul, the Ottoman Empire is at its political and military zenith. The Turks and their bureaucracy administer more than two million square miles of earth and many millions more in adjacent vassal territories. The Turks hold an agglomeration of lands and peoples stretching from Oman and the Indian Ocean in far southwest Asia, to southern Poland and Russia in the far northeast of Europe, across all of North Africa up to Morocco. Turkish fleets periodically dominate the Mediterranean and harass the ships from the Italian city-states, and they land forces at the tip of the boot in Otranto. Turkish mapmakers contemplate the same kind of global adventures that their adversary Spain is pursuing in the Americas.

This empire is a universe unto itself. Why should it not have welcomed the dispossessed Jews of Spain? Within the Turkish dominion are Arabs and Byzantines and Greeks, Serbians and Bosnians and Croats, Poles and Ukrainians and Czechs, Slovaks and Hungarians and Austrians, Romanians and Persians and people from the Caucasus, Berbers and Azerbaijanis and Armenians, Georgians and Somalis and Ethiopians. The languages and dialects are almost too many to count.

The religions of the Turks are also plentiful, and just as in the tradition of al-Andalus and the Baghdad caliphate, Muslims, while dominant, depend in amazing degree on the partnership and support of other faiths. The elite guard of the Ottoman sultan, the janissaries and the broader *devsirme* cadre of administrative officials are all Balkan Christian boys specifically recruited for their religion. The guard forces are not allowed to marry or have families so that they will give their entire lives and energies to the sultan and the state. As a result, some Christians have risen to become grand viziers, the second highest position in this intercontinental empire, including Bosnian-Serb Mehmet Sokollu Pasha, grand vizier to Suleiman and also to his son and grandson.

Amazingly, this massive empire is not ruled by a hereditary nobility as in most other realms. This mightiest of states is run by a career meritocracy, young officials selected from schools and tests and training, elevated to become the senior officials of the empire. And in the strangest twist, most of these officials are non-Muslim.

Only the House of Osman, the lineage of the sultan, rules by birth.

And in a show of civil tolerance, the Ottoman sultan, who as protector of the holy cities of Mecca and Medina 1,500 miles to the south is also the Caliph of all Islam, and so the "shadow of God on earth," rules not through the total imposition of *sharia*. The Turks, though loyal Muslims, set up a diverse and tolerant legal system that includes sharia for Muslims, Jewish and Orthodox Christian law for those communities, and the same for other distinct religious groups, as well as a system of *canun* civil law administered by the sultan and applied in areas like business where the other legal systems do not extend.

This relative diversity and tolerance comes from many sources, in part from the Turks' nomadic origins. Accustomed to moving across the steppes of Eurasia, the pre-Muslim Turks had been used to absorbing the influences of other cultures. Some of these liberal views come from the tolerant guidance of the Prophet and thinkers like the Rightly Guided Caliphs of early Islam. This unique mix of power tempered with fairness and diversity makes the Turks great. And the very embodiment of all that is greatest about the Turks is Sultan Suleiman I, ruler from 1526 to 1566.

SULEIMAN IS ENTERING OLD AGE as he sits on his balcony in Topkapi Palace in the early fall of 1566. The air is still like summer, the sultan's bathing pool full, no fires yet lit to hold off the chill of night. Out on the Bosporus the mist of dusk has cleared away, and the reflection of the autumn moon is spread on the cold waters, a fragmented heaving spray of fragile stars.

An old man of 71, and though the mightiest ruler on Earth, he is truly alone. His beloved Ukrainian wife Hurrem has been dead since 1558, and his favorite sons have died in civil war or in illness. He has just learned that Hungary, which was an unruly region when he first ascended the throne in 1526, and which he has subdued six times since, is again making trouble. Will he, at this age and stage of isolation, have to go into battle again? He has not been on the battlefield in ten years. It seems an unfair request of a man who has already done so much for his people.

This is a ruler who is believed to embody his Biblical namesake—Solomon—because he always chooses to pursue the greater civic good over the particular desires of vested interests, trusted advisors, and sons and relatives, to the point of firing or exiling them, or worse, should he think they are subverting the greater good.

Baron de Busbecq, the Hapsburg ambassador to the court, which has given Austria its most serious challenge, meets Suleiman in 1555 and describes him at age 60:

> His expression ... is anything but smiling, and has a sternness, which though sad, is full of majesty ... he is beginning to feel the weight of the years, but his dignity of demeanour and his general physical appearance are of the ruler of so vast an empire.

In a bit of irony for the caliph of all Islam, this is a man who many believe has done more to advance the cause of Protestantism in Europe than any European ruler, primarily through his alliance with French King Francis I, who was aligned with Protestant interests, against the more powerful Catholic forces led by Charles V of Spain. Suleiman chuckles briefly at that thought. Me, a Protestant!

Aside from being wise and fair, Suleiman is a symphonic conductor of warfare, an artist of the military arts, a poet of weaponry and command. His intuitive sense of battle enables him to capture Belgrade in 1521 and the Mediterranean island of Rhodes in 1522, to defeat the Hungarians at Mohács in 1526 and be halted in Central Europe only by his failure to take Vienna, capital of Austria, after a siege from September to October 1529. In 1534 he turns more successfully against Persia, and then in campaigns against the Arab world takes almost all of North Africa and the Red Sea port of Aden. Only the Knights of Malta inflict severe defeat on both his army and fleet when he tries to take Valletta in 1565.

Suleiman is also a poet in the Arabian-Persian-Sufi tradition. In one of his couplets, Gazel No. 6, he writes:

> Throne of my lonely niche, my wealth, my love, my moonlight.
> My most sincere friend, my confidant, my very existence, my Sultana
> The most beautiful among the beautiful....

My springtime, my merry faced love, my daytime, my sweetheart, laughing leaf....
My plants, my sweet, my rose, the one only who does not distress me in this world....
My Istanbul, my Caraman, the earth of my Anatolia
My Badakhshan, my Baghdad and Khorasan
My woman of the beautiful hair, my love of the slanted brow, my love of eyes full of mischief....
I'll sing your praises always
I, lover of the tormented heart, Muhibbi of the eyes full of tears, I am happy.

But poetry for him is only a temporary refuge from the painful political decisions he must make every day. As an example, he has been forced to execute two of his own sons, Bayezid and Mustafa, who were accused of trying to overthrow him in separate rebellions. What memories to have to carry.

Some day, historians will write that this early Ottoman tradition of succession by coup or fratricide—and its successor in 1603, the *kafes* system, whereby rival male heirs are imprisoned—is perhaps the most fatal flaw, more than anything else that will bring down this empire. Having generated one of the greatest leaders of the millennium and having set up a brilliant structure to support that leader, the Turks have not found a way to institutionalize the continuation of that leadership at the highest, most important level.

For the terrible fact is that the architects of the Ottoman Empire have never dealt well with the issue of royal succession. Just as the Byzantines maim their rival heirs, the Ottomans will try equally bad alternatives. Perhaps the original intent, as befitting a state built on meritocracy, not aristocracy, is to allow a Darwinian free-for-all among the sons, with the best man winning. Perhaps it is a desire to allow the sultan extra flexibility in choosing the best successor from many sons, who might not necessarily be the eldest. But whatever the reasoning, the result is an unending competition of plotting and scheming by rival harem women, their sons, and their various supporters, resulting in periodic violent and untimely deaths of the weaker or less favored competitors. For centuries, many of the male rivals are killed or locked up in small prison-like quarters or larger rooms in Topkapi Palace, to keep them out of trouble until they are needed on the throne. This practice results in installing a number of sultans who are emotionally damaged and withdrawn, uninformed and uneducated, unable to connect to the world mentally, much less to rule half the world when summoned to power by accident, intrigue, or natural death of the sitting ruler.

Perhaps for Suleiman on that late summer night, whether or not to attack Hungary will prove an easier decision than whether or not to kill a son or brother.

On the next morning, Suleiman summons his most trusted advisors, Mehmet Sokollu Pasha, his vizier, and Abu Su'ud, his counselor for the law. They gather in the Hall of Whispers after receiving the news about Hungary to give the sultan their recommendations on how to respond.

Although it is not Suleiman's request, the visitors enter their lord's presence from the anteroom on their knees as a sign of respect and fealty, begging his mercy as they approach. It is a reenactment of the kowtowing the first Turkic warlords had received on the steppes of Mongolia a thousand years ago.

Suleiman's pallor is the first thing to strike newcomers in his presence, and though his advisors are used to it, the passage of time has carried him to such a new degree of bloodlessness, their breath is taken away for an instant that day. The gray, trimmed beard, the blue lips, the abysmal shadows under his eyes only accentuate it. And yet, even at this low physical ebb he is not an ugly man. In an ascetic way he is handsome and seems possessed of warmth. But given his advanced age and elevated station, they wonder if it is not true warmth but only a vulnerability sprung from sadness and loss—whether the loss of family or friend or of his own freedom to the burden of serving as master of the destiny of many millions, they cannot know.

He asks them to consider all options short of war and then the various ways to engage in warfare to put down the Hungarians once and for all. They know he is decisive, and his verdict from what they find will be swift and cold.

"We will complete your mission, my lord," they say. And they want to say more, for they would go to the ends of the Earth for this man, who has raised them up, and who has raised up their people. For there are few like him on Earth, wise men, merciful men, men entrusted with military power, who are blessed with personal power as well.

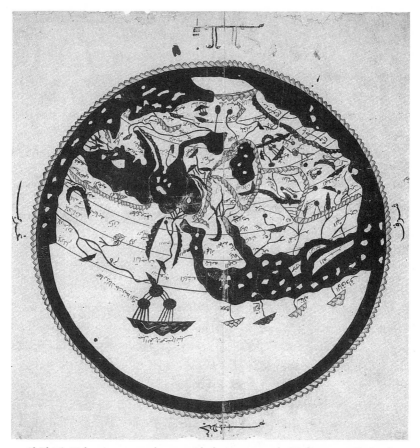

Al-Idrisi's 12th-century map, shown upside down, presents the Mediterranean Basin, the Middle East, and Asia. Such maps served Europe's sailors in the Age of Exploration.

It is not a Turk but a Venetian, Bernardo Navagero, who has said that Suleiman, provided he is given all the information, does injustice to no one; and it is another foreigner who calls the Turk "il magnifico," the magnificent one. That is why these men will do whatever Suleiman asks, and why the possibility of his death, whether by assassin's knife or old age's scythe, fills them with a fear for their people and their dominion.

IT IS NOW TWO MONTHS LATER, November 1566. Suleiman has made his decision.

In what he sees as completion of his own destiny, he has sent his armies north to do battle in Hungary, and he is now joining them there, again arrayed against the armies of Austria and Christendom in that damp and cold northland where he has led the armies so many times before. But this time he departs his imperial city a sick and melancholy wretch at the end of his life, his greatest days behind him. His departure, while grand and imposing, has an undertone of tragedy, because he must be lashed to his horse to keep him from falling off in his weakness as he passes the cheering throngs. Away he has gone nevertheless, a sick old man, to do battle in Europe.

And though his army will be strong, he will die there in his command center in Hungary.

AND THEN SULEIMAN is gone forever. And the world does not end when he is gone, though historians mark his passing as the apogee of Turkish dominion. Another sultan will bring siege to Vienna a century later; his defeat marks the final turning point for the Ottomans. But the world where children play, where spring brings life out of the lifeless twigs of winter, and where boats come in from the Bosporus with their hulls brimming with the catch of the sea, this world goes on after he has left.

The Turks have a new sultan. All he has to do is sit in his chambers, and those about him see to it that affairs run as they should. Couples are married; babies are born. The summer's heat brings the families of the peasants into the gardens Suleiman has built for their pleasure, and the domes of the mosques and the spires of the minarets rise higher and higher, testimony to the glory of Allah and his Prophet.

And the Ottoman Empire, the last caliphate of Islam, the last Muslim nation able to challenge and check the rise of Europe, will survive for another 350 years, largely intact, but gradually losing the pieces that Suleiman and his predecessors had fought so hard to weld together. While various efforts at reform and renewal are made, efforts to modernize the empire and make it competitive with the new imperialist states of Europe, the efforts are never enough to halt the slide downward. This is caused perhaps more than anything by the lack of leaders of the quality of Suleiman. Or perhaps the empire is just weighed down by the burden of administering such an agglomeration of people, all of them clamoring for freedom from foreign rule.

And so the empire gradually comes apart. Greece becomes independent in 1829, after a war of independence that excites the aristocratic and literary elite of England. Lord Byron dies in that struggle. The Russian Tsar takes the Crimea, and Iran, Armenia, and Georgia break free. Romania leaves in 1877. Bulgaria declares independence in 1908. Albania departs in 1917. Distant Yemen breaks free in 1918.

Finally only Turkey and the Arab lands remain in the sway of the failing Ottomans. It takes World War I to end that legacy, when T.E. Lawrence fights alongside Sharif Hussein bin Ali, Emir of Mecca and King of the Arabs (and great grandfather of King Hussein), to create new Arab states.

The aftershocks of the Ottoman collapse reverberate still a hundred years later.

The Balkans will often fall into outright warfare and ethnic cleansing, with bloody and probably futile efforts to undo the patchwork of multireligious and multiethnic lands that the sultans oversaw and often helped create. World War I and the Muslim-Christian clashes of Kosovo and Bosnia will be the violent undoing of what once peacefully coexisted under Ottoman power.

Future Turkey will be torn between its rich Muslim heritage and the anti-clerical revolution of Mustafa Kemal Ataturk, himself once an officer of the last sultan, later creator of the new Turkish state. An uneasy balance will prevail.

Iraq's arbitrary borders and often incompatible communities of Shia and Sunni Arab and Kurd will be drawn up by the British out of the Ottoman wreckage, as will the outlines of future Jordan, Saudi Arabia, and Israel-Palestine. Under the Ottomans, the tricultural mix of Muslims and Christians and Jews had managed to live and coexist in Lebanon, in Syria, in Palestine. But after their passing, the daily headlines will report one more clash, one more nail in the coffin of the diverse cultures that once shared those places. In that future, the preferred model will seem more like the absolutist vision of Isabella, with religions and peoples each moved to their separate territories, rather than the diverse multihued model of the early caliphs down to the Ottomans.

This is the tragedy of lost history. Despair to think of all that has been lost, even as new things are found.

Does humankind learn? Or do people simply forget and rediscover?

EPILOGUE

IN 2007 TIME HAS ACCELERATED; for many people it seems to gather momentum and never stop or rest.

For some people history is irrelevant; they believe they have passed the end of history and moved into a new, timeless world of speed and progress. They believe they can overwhelm the deep structures of history by their sheer wealth, power, and technology. Too often, they feel they do not need to honor history or can afford to be ignorant of it.

For others, the past is as recent as a moment ago, intense and powerful and permeating every aspect of their lives. They are not yet seduced by the power of the present. For them, the past can seem greater than the present and can be too often a source of anger, of resentment, of vendetta. They will not rest until they correct the real or imagined wrongs and crimes of the past.

What does the future hold, when mankind is so divided about history and time? Is there a third way to build the future, a way that acknowledges the reality of the present and the value of the past?

In 2007, the golden ages of Damascus, Baghdad, Cordoba, Cairo, Samarkand, Isfahan, Agra, and Istanbul are now a distant memory for some, unrecovered memory for most. The British conquest of India, Napoleon's forays into Egypt, assorted European colonial ventures in Africa, the Middle East, and Asia, and the disintegration of the Ottoman Empire at the end of World War I all mark the end of these exceptional cultural flowerings.

History might have taken another course. At that moment of rare equipoise between China, India, the Muslim world, and Europe in the late 15th and 16th centuries, any one of Europe's rivals could have made the same fateful decisions that Spain, Portugal, and England undertook to support voyages of exploration and conquest. The Chinese could have easily sailed the Pacific, and the Ottoman Turks might have controlled the Atlantic.

What if the colonial rivalries in the Americas and Southeast Asia had been between Europeans, Chinese, and Turks, not just among the European powers? What if the Turks and Chinese had established colonies, had had to reform their economies and societies and intellectual climates to accommodate the needs of new transoceanic empires? Would there have been a more dispersed Renaissance and Enlightenment?

This author believes it could have happened. Christianity could have become ever more locked in anti-materialism and zealotry; a few blips in royal succession could have brought the Inquisition to England; and Oliver Cromwell could have become the key patron of English political philosophy and not John Locke. In this parallel universe, the Muslim world could have led and enjoyed the benefits of the Renaissance and Enlightenment that it seeded. The Muslims could have led the Age of Discovery and Imperialism that the Christian Europeans undertook instead. This author does not believe there was any inevitability to the rise of the West.

The decline of these early inventive cultures is tragic in an historical and a human sense. Why did these societies that for centuries led the world in many areas and laid the foundation for the rise of European thought and science fall behind?

Historians and scholars will debate this question until the end of time. While there is no single answer, a number of factors contributed to the stagnation: Some were the result of sheer bad luck, some the result of cultural evolution.

The geography of Islam lies in the cradle of civilization where the earliest cultures arose in Mesopotamia, the Nile Valley, and the Indus Valley with their rich early agriculture. These same regions have turned into deserts over the millennia, providing fewer economic opportunities.

The impact on the Muslim heartland by the successive waves of Central Asian invasions, led by the Seljuks, the Mongols, and the Ottomans, gradually destroyed the centers of Muslim invention, while Central and Western

Europe were spared the devastation and disruption at the time, allowing them to continue their development even as much of the Middle East, Iran, and Turkey had to rebuild.

In the 17th century, as European nations began to colonize the Americas, they received a flood of overseas wealth that enabled them to also undertake colonial ventures in the Muslim world.

The impact of European imperialism on the Muslim world—in the Middle East, Iran, Africa, India, and Southeast Asia—proved the final blow. Colonialism sent much of that world into an economic recession that will take centuries to throw off.

Because science and development are based on the support and funding by a nation's leadership, Muslim science declined when its nations had to shift its resources to military defense after the 16th century. The rise of Europe and the decline of the Muslim lands had become two sides of the same coin.

By the 21st century, some of the old Muslim centers of invention have instead become part of the developing world, with all the ensuing problems such as poverty, economic stagnation, and political instability. Their rich history has been lost, seemingly relegated to the ruins.

The world is changing once again. For every crisis spot, there is now a promising center of innovation in the Muslim world. Immigrant Muslim communities in Europe and the Americas have become meeting places, the intersection of cultures creating not only tensions, but disseminating new ideas and understanding.

The first Muslim golden ages are gone. But new ones are likely being born, even though today's headlines suggest otherwise.

As we look to the future by recovering the past, perhaps the best guiding principle was uttered 900 years ago by the mathematician-poet Omar Khayyám, in his confession of faith:

Both thou and I are born alike
Though some may sink and some may soar
We all are earth and nothing more.

ACKNOWLEDGMENTS

A project of this scope could not have happened without the help of many people.

I would like to thank the National Geographic Society, in particular Kevin Mulroy and Barbara Brownell Grogan, for having the confidence to undertake a difficult work in turbulent times.

I want to thank my editor Karin Kinney for having the time and patience to help me navigate through multiple languages, disputed accounts, and complicated historical paths that led in many directions.

I want to thank my consultant Amin Tejpar in Cairo for sharing his historical and cultural knowledge and his non-traditional perspectives, so that *Lost History* could be more than a conventional retelling of old tales.

I want to thank His Majesty King Abdullah of Jordan for endorsing this book.

I want to thank HRH Prince Alwalid bin Talal Alsaud and the Kingdom Foundation for a grant to help bring the message of this book into television.

My thanks to writers Fahmida Riaz, Susan Hazen-Hammond, Patricia L. Sharpe, Beth Strange, and Elizabeth Trickey-Glassman for reading drafts of the book and suggesting important changes.

I want to thank the many great historians and scholars, Muslims and those of other faiths, who through their many and varied and often conflicting accounts of events of the last 1,400 years, contributed to the tapestry of *Lost History.*

And most of all, I want to thank the many forgotten or ignored heroes and heroines of all faiths now lost to history for having the courage and brilliance to help lay the foundations of modern civilization.

May this book start a conversation that will show how much we all owe to the brilliance of the past ... and so start a process of peace.

BIBLIOGRAPHY

Armstrong, Karen, *Islam: A Short History,* Modern Library, 2002

Babrielle, F. and E.J. Costello, translators, *Arab Historians of the Crusades,* London: Routledge and Kegan Paul, 1984

Barks, Coleman, and John Moyne, A.J. Arberry, Reynold Nicholson, translators, *The Essential Rumi,* Harper San Francisco, 1997

Berggren, J.L., *Episodes in the Mathematics of Medieval Islam,* Springer Verlag, 1986

Beveridge, H., translator, *The Akbamama of Abu L-Fazl,* Baptist Mission Press, Calcutta, 1897-1939

Burton, Sir Richard, translator, *Tales from the Arabian Nights,* David Shumaker, editor, Gramercy Books, New York, 1978

Darke, Hubert, *The Book of Government or Rules for Kings,* London, Routledge & Kegan Paul, 1978

Donsbach, Margaret, "The Scholar and Supernova," Ibn Ridwan quote translated by Bernard Goldstein, *Saudi Aramco World,* July/August 2006, p. 42

Esposito, John L., *The Oxford History of Islam,* Oxford-University Press, 2000

Farmer, H.G., *Historical Facts for the Arabian Musical Influence,* Georg Olms Verlag, Hildesheim, New York, 1970

Gibbon, Edward, *The Decline and Fall of the Roman Empire,* Modern Library, New York, 2003

Gillispie, Charles Coulston (ed.), *Dictionary of Scientific Biography,* New York, Scribner, 1970-1980

Gingerich, Owen, "Islamic Astronomy," *Scientific American,* April 1986 v254

Graves, Robert and Omar Ali-Shah, translators, *The Original Rubaiyyat of Omar Khayaam,* Doubleday & Co., New York, 1968

Grousset, René, *Epic of the Crusades,* New York, Orion Press, 1970

Hamarneh, Sami K., *The Life and Ideas of Al-Kindi,* Hamdard Medicus, 1986

Al-Hasan, Ahmad Y. and Donald R. Hill, *Islamic Technology,* Cambridge University Press, 1986

Hayes, J.R., ed., *The Genius of Arab Civilization, Source of Renaissance,* MIT Press, Cambridge, Mass., 1978

Hill, Donald R., *Islamic Science and Engineering,* Edinburgh University Press, 1993

Hitti, P.K., *History of the Arabs,* Mac Millan St. Martin's Press, 1970

Holmyard, J.E., *The Makers of Chemistry,* Oxford, Clarenden Press, 1931

Horne, Charles F., ed., *The Sacred Books and Early Literature of the East,* Parke, Austin & Lipscomb, 1917

Huff, Toby E., *The Rise of Early Modern Science: Islam, China, and the West,* Cambridge University Press, 1993

Huntington, Samuel P., *The Clash of Civilizations and the Remaking of the World Order*, Simon & Schuster, New York, 1997

Al-Jazari, *The Book of Knowledge of Ingenious Mechanical Devices*, translated by Donald R. Hill, Dordrecht, 1974

King, David, *In Synchrony with the Heavens, Studies in Astronomical Timekeeping and Instrumentation in Medieval Islamic Civilization*, Leiden, Brill 2005; "Astronomical Instruments in the Islamic World," in Selin Helaine *Encyclopedia of the History of Science, Technology and Medicine in Non-Western Cultures*, Dordrecht: Kluwer Academic Publishers, 1997

Levi Provincal, E., *Histoire de l'Espagne Musulmane*, Maison neuve, 1950

Lewis, Bernard, *Middle East: A Brief History of the Last 2,000 Years*, Simon & Schuster, New York, 1997 and *Islam: From the Prophet Muhammad to the Capture of Constantinople*, Vol. 1, 1987, Oxford University Press

Al-Masoudi, Abul Hasan Ali; Paul Lunde and Caroline Stone, translators, *The Book of Golden Meadows*, Keegan Paul, 1989

Menocal, Maria Rosa, *The Ornament of the World: How Muslims, Jews, and Christians Created a Culture of Tolerance in Medieval Spain*, Back Bay Books, 2003

Nasr, Seyyed Hossein, *Islamic Science, An Illustrated Study*, World of Islam Festival Publishing Company Ltd., 1976

Newby, P.H., *Saladin in His Time*, Boston, Faber and Faber, 1983

Ragep, Jamil, "Tusi and Copernicus: The Earth's Motion in Context," *Science in Context 14* (1/2), 2001

Rabadan, Muhammad, from *Islam and the West: The Moriscos: A Cultural and Social History*, Anward G. Gehnje, SUNY Press 1983, p. 163

Rosner, Fred, *Medical Legacy of Moses Maimonides*, Ktav Publishing House, New Jersey, 1998; *The Medical Aphorisms of Moses Maimonides*, Maimonides Research Institute, Israel, 1989; and *Treatises on Poisons, Hemorrhoids and Co-habitation*, Maimonides Institute, Israel, 1984

Sabra, A.I., "Situating Arabic Science: Locality versus Essence," *Isis*, Vol. 87, No. 4 (Dec., 1996) and translator *The Optics of Ibn Al-Haytham*. 2 Vols. Warburg Institute, University of London, 1989

Said, Edward W., *Orientalism*, Vintage, 1979

Saliba, George, "Greek astronomy and the medieval Arabic tradition," *American Scientist*, Research Triangle Park: July/Aug. 2002 Vol. 90, Issue 4, pg. 360; *Al-Biruni, Dictionary of the Middle Ages*, ed. Joseph Strayer, Charles Scribner's Sons, New York, 1980; *Whose Science is Arabic Science in Renaissance Europe?* Columbia University, 1999

Sarton, George, *Introduction to the History of Science*, Williams and Wilkins, Baltimore, 1950-53

Singh, Simon, *The Code Book*, New York, Random House, 1999

Sufi Publishing Company, *Al Ghazali: The Revival of Religious Science,* 1972

Teres, Elias, *Abbas ibn Firnas,* Al-Andalus, 1960

Thompson A., M.A. Rahim, *Islam in Andalus,* Ta Ha Publishers, London, 1996

Turner, Howard R., *Science in Medieval Islam,* University of Texas Press, Austin, 1995

Wiet, Gaston, *Baghdad: Metropolis of the Abbasid Caliphate,* Translated by Seymour Feiler, University of Oklahoma Press, 1971

Wightman, G.B.H., and A.Y. al-Udhari, *Birds Through a Ceiling of Alabaster,* Penguin, 1975

http://www.cyberistan.org

http://198.65.147.194/english/Science/2001/02/article1.shtml

http://www.en.wikipedia.org

http://www.fordham.edu/halsall/sbook.html

http://www-history.mcs.st-andrews.ac.uk/history/

http://www.iiim.org/islamed3.html

http://www.al-islam.org/nahjul/letters/letter53.htm

http://www.islamicity.com/forum/forum_posts.asp?TID=6717&PN=1

http://www.islamset.com/isc/zuhr/main.html

http://www.muslimheritage.com

http://www.muslimphilosophy.com/kindi/index.html

GLOSSARY

Ayat: verse of the Qur'an

Bimaristan: hospital; sometimes also called **maristan**

Caliph: successor of Muhammad

Convivencia: coexistence

Dhimmi: People of the Book: the Jews, Christians, and Muslims

Emir: originally meaning "commander;" it has come to mean governor or ruler

Fuqaha: class of erudite legal scholars

Giaour: infidel, nonbeliever

Hadith: second only to the Qur'an as the sacred literature of Sunni Islam

Ijma: consensus

Imam: prayer leader; among the Shiites, also community leader

Islam: Arabic for "surrender to God"

Jihad: personal struggle to be more righteous; refers to fighting evil and carrying the righteous rule of Islam to the far ends of the Earth

Jumhur: majority

Kaaba: holy shrine in Mecca

Madrassa: school of Islamic studies

Mahdi: the expected messiah of Muslim tradition

Mihna: inquisition, or a questioning of individuals about their true faith

Mihrab: the ornamental wall niche in a mosque that indicates the direction to Mecca

Miraj: Muhammad's ascent through the seven heavens

Mudejar: a Muslim living under a Christian king

Muslim: follower of Islam; in Arabic "one who submits to God"

Quibla: direction of prayer, toward Mecca

Qur'an: sacred scriptures of Islam, consisting of 114 suras, or chapters

Ramadan: the ninth month of the Muslim year, observed by fasting from sunrise to sunset

Shariah: the right path, or guide; the law that comes from divine revelation

Sheik: head of a tribe

Shiite: from Shiat Ali, the party of Ali; the followers believe that Ali (cousin and son-in-law of Muhammad), his descendants, and the imams should lead the Islamic community

Shura: consultation

Sufi: spiritual mystics

Sunnah: word of God

Sunni: majority group of Muslims

Sura: chapter of the Qur'an

Ulema: educated class of Moslem scholars

Ummah: community of Islam

INDEX

Relativity theory 166
Religious coexistence 15–17, 77–78, 263, 278
Renoir, Auguste 248
Reza, Imam 219
Reza Abbasi 235
Richard the Lionheart 271–272
Rimsky-Korsakov, Nikolay 248
Risner, Friedrich 106
Robert of Chester 216
Rockets 173–177, 178
Roderick, King (Spain) 18, 20
Roman Catholicism: control of knowledge 215–216
Rukn al-Din Khurshah 144
al-Rumi, Jalal ad-Din 75, 221, 243–245
Sabians 93–94
Safavids 75
Saladin, Sultan 74, 136, 207, 208, 209, 268–272
Samarkand, Uzbekistan 76, 77, 231–233
Saoud, Rabah 242
Saracens: massacre 266–267
Sarton, George 171
Scheherazade 62, 219–220, 221, 247–249
Sefarad (Jewish homeland) 70, 279
Seljuks 75, 107–108, 111–113
Sephardic Jews 154, 279–280
Seville, Spain 68, 135
Sextants 129
Shah Jahan, Shahbuddin Mohammed 78, 236–239
Shah Mosque, Isfahan, Iran 235
Shahryar, King 247–249
Shahzadi Gauhara Begum 237
Shakespeare, William 248
Shams ad-Din Tabrizi 244–245
Sheikh Lotfollah Mosque, Isfahan, Iran 234
Sherozi, Kavomiddin 232
Shiites: pilgrimages 219; schism with Sunnis 12–13, 17, 35, 44, 52, 56, 99, 110, 275
al-Shirazi 147
Shura (consultation) 13
Sid ibn All 126
Sitt al-Mulk 101, 102
Slavery 119, 255
Smallpox 186
Snakebite 210–211
Sofia, Queen (Spain) 180
Sokollu Pasha, Mehmet 280, 284
Space flights and research 117–119
Spain: invasion by Tariq ibn Ziyad 18–21; Jewish

intellectual communities 136; Muslim rule 69–72; Umayyads 40–41
Spanish Inquisition 71–72
Stars 124, 125, 127–128
Storytelling 59, 246–249
Sufism 162, 243
Suleiman the Magnificent 77, 281–286
Sunnis: centers of learning 74; conflict with Ismailis 112–113; schism with Shiites 12–13, 17, 35, 44, 52, 56, 99, 110, 275; traditionalism 276–277
Supernovae 128
Surgery 198, 200, 203, 206; instruments **202**
Sylvester II, Pope 216
al-Tabari, Ali ibn Sahl Rabban 184–185, 186
Tahir (vizier) 56; family 63
Taifas (city-states) 69–70
Taj Mahal, Agra, India 78, **234,** 237–239
Tamerlane see Timur (Turkic conqueror)
Tariq ibn Ziyad 18–20, **35,** 66
Taxes: collection 264–265; of conquered lands 14, 226; departure 271; record keeping 211, 255; religious 15, 16, 38, 275
Terrorism, war on: treatment of Muslims 252
Thabit, Ibrahim 94
Thabit ibn Qurra 93, 94
Thomas Aquinas, Saint 216, 217
The Thousand and One Nights 62, 219–220, 246–249, 261
Timekeeping 128; *see also* Calendars; Clocks
Timur (Turkic conqueror) 76, 231–232, 248
Timurids 76, 77
Toledo, Spain 131–132, 134
Tours, France 1–5, 21–34
Trigonometry 95, 96, 122, 126, 143, 148
Troubadours 241
Tschaikovsky, Pyotr 248
Tuberculosis 194, 195–196
al-Tusi, Nasir al-Din 123, **134,** 142–143, 145–149
Ulugh Beg 150, 232
Umar I, Caliph 15, 257
'Umar ibn Abi Rabi'ah al-Makhzumi 241
Umayyad Mosque, Damascus, Syria 21, 35–37, **71, 78**

Umayyads: architecture 35–37, **78,** 95, 222, 224–226; conflict with Abbasids 32, 34–35, 39–40, 65, 67, 161, 257, 258; in Cordoba 23, 32, 65–72, 129–130, 155, 223–227, 240; in Damascus 17, 21, 23, 35, 161, 240, 258; enemies 38–39, 69, 226; government administration 38–39, 258, 264; origin 17; religious tolerance 70, 71, 136, 263; science 110, 129–131; similarities to Abbasids 68, 110; in Spain 31, 34, 40–41, 135, 258
UNESCO World Heritage Sites 236
United States: security 251–252
Universe: geocentric structure 122–123
Universities and colleges 60, 73–74, 264
al-Uqlidisi 95
Urban life 182–183
al-Urdi 147
U.S. Congress 251–254
Ustad Ahmad Lahori 238
Uthman, Caliph 15, 257
Vesalius, Andreas 190
Visigoths 18–21
Vision 104, 105
Voltaire 248
al-Walid ibn Yazid, Caliph 21, 36, 62, 241
Washington, D.C. 251–254
Wasit, Iraq: observatory 126
Water clocks 132–133, 173
Water pumps **160,** 173
Water supply 38, 61
Weapons 173–177
Whirling Dervishes 244
Women: physicians 206; political leaders 273–274; rights 10; writers 220
Yahya (brother of Abd al-Rahman I) 39–40, 65
Yakut (historian) 60–62
al-Ya'qubi, Ahmad 57–58
Zahara (wife of Caliph Abd al-Rahman III) 223–224, 227
al-Zahrawi 198–204
al-Zarqali, Abu Ishaq Ibrahim ibn Yahya 131–134
Zero (mathematical concept) 88, 89–90, 91
Zheng He 148
Ziryab (Abu al-Hasan Ali ibn Nafi) 155, 158, 240

تاریخ
ضائع